D1614863

THE GERMAN LANGUAGE TODAY

Modern Languages and Literature

Languages Editor

PROFESSOR R. AUTY
MA, Dr. Phil.

*Professor of Comparative Slavonic Philology
in the University of Oxford*

THE
GERMAN LANGUAGE
TODAY

ITS PATTERNS AND BACKGROUND

W. E. Collinson
Professor Emeritus in the University of Liverpool

HUTCHINSON UNIVERSITY LIBRARY
LONDON

HUTCHINSON & CO (*Publishers*) LTD
178–202 Great Portland Street, London, W.1

London Melbourne Sydney
Auckland Bombay Toronto
Johannesburg New York

First published 1953
Second edition 1962
Third edition 1968

This book has been set in Times, printed in Great Britain
on Smooth Wove paper by William Clowes and Sons, Limited,
London and Beccles, and bound by Wm Brendon, Tiptree, Essex

09 028681 2 (cased)
09 028682 0 (paperback)

CONTENTS

PREFACE TO THE THIRD EDITION

For this revised third edition I have gladly acceded to the suggestion of the editor of the series, Professor Auty, that the space formerly allocated to the historical chapters be reduced to allow for the inclusion of some more modern matter including a section on Eastern Germany. This stressing of the present is more in accord with the title of the book. Accordingly I decided to scrap most of Part II, substituting chapters on the place of German in relation to its neighbours and congeners, its general evolution and unification, its varieties in Austria, Switzerland and elsewhere, the impact of National Socialism, innovations in the Soviet Zone and the influence of contact with the British and Americans. Apart from these drastic changes I have made a number of additions and supplied further practical information. This reexamination of the whole work has served to strengthen my deep gratitude to Dr Marianne Heydorn, whose friendly cooperation helped me so much in launching the first edition. My former colleague, Dr Mina Moore-Rinvoluosi, who has had recent contact with East Germany, kindly supplied me with relevant literature of great value for linguistic developments there. Above all I must not forget another colleague, Dr F. J. Wiener, who typed the new sections and made many useful suggestions. To all these friendly helpers I offer my sincere thanks.

PREFACE TO THE SECOND EDITION

In preparing this edition I have gratefully embodied many suggestions by academic colleagues and several correspondents. In particular I thank Professors F. P. Pickering (Reading) and

R. E. Keller (Manchester), Dr M. O'C. Walshe (Bedford College, London), Dr Max K. Adler, Mr D. Abbott and Mr S. Godman. The justified criticisms by Professors C. T. Carr, in the *Modern Language Review* XLIX, and F. O. Nock, in the *Journal of English and German Philology* LIII, have led me to make a number of corrections and adjustments. Finally I have myself made some additions and clarifications, but not in such a way as to interfere with my chief aim, that of presenting the modes of expression used by my collaborator, Dr Heydorn, whose fine feeling for her native language animates the whole book.

PREFACE TO THE FIRST EDITION

When Professor Jopson asked me to write for his series the volume on the German language, I wondered how I could—within the allotted space—provide a description which would neither be too academic nor merely duplicate existing textbooks. It would be foolish to attempt to compete with Curme, whose German grammar is still unrivalled as a repository of the forms and con- structions of modern Standard German, with an adequate, if unobtrusive background of the history of the language. Its very qualities as an authoritative survey of literary usage in writers from diverse regions make it indispensable to the specialist, but baffling to the layman. The latter needs a book which will tell him concisely what German is and by whom it is spoken and which will show clearly what are its historical and structural relations to English. To achieve the maximum concentration I have attempted to give a straightforward description of the speech of one single educated North German speaker, namely Dr Marianne Heydorn of Hamburg, who joined the German Staff of Liverpool University in 1948. Such a description presents a homogeneous form of German, avoids puzzling the learner by making him choose be- tween alternatives and—by its consistent appeal to the spoken word—brings a certain amount of liveliness into the illustrative examples. In dealing with sounds, forms and constructions I have compared and contrasted the German phenomena with the English. In this task I have received much stimulus from the foreign grammarians of English such as the Dane Jespersen and the Dutch grammarians Zandvoort, Kruisinga, Erades, and Vechtman-Veth. Whatever merits this work may possess are due to Dr Heydorn herself who went through every detail and patiently discussed with me the many subtle problems which are bound to crop up when one makes a close study of spontaneous speech at the everyday level. For her ever ready helpfulness I express my deep gratitude.

Following the nuclear grammar is a brief historical survey of German from the beginning. There are sections dealing with such topics as word-formation, foreign influences, standardization and dialects, followed by specimen texts to illustrate the characteristics of Low German (East Holstein), Swiss German (Bern), Pennsylvania German and Yiddish. In all the later sections my colleague, Dr Fritz Wiener, has given me valuable assistance. For Yiddish I gratefully acknowledge the help of our chief authority on that language, Dr S. Birnbaum of London. My friend Professor R. J. McClean (of Birkbeck College) has earned my gratitude by generously helping me with proof-reading. Finally I am deeply indebted to Professor Jopson, who read the typescript and made many valuable suggestions.

W. E. COLLINSON

INTRODUCTION

Despite two world wars and the shrinkage of her territory Germany has a population of over seventy-five million, of whom somewhat more than a quarter live in the Deutsche Demokratische Republik. Outside Germany there are over four million German speakers in Switzerland, constituting 70% of the total population, and in Austria another seven million. In other continents, particularly North and South America, many Germans have settled, but it is not possible to compute the number who have retained their language. Before the Second World War there were many enclaves and islets of speakers of German dialects scattered throughout the Baltic provinces, Poland, Czechoslovakia, Hungary, Rumania, Yugoslavia, the Ukraine and Russia, extending nearly as far as the Caucasus. In 1941 the USSR dissolved the Volga German Republic centred near Saratov and transferred the Germans—who had been settled there by Catherine the Great in the eighteenth century—to Siberia. Since 1945 many German settlements have been eliminated, in particular from the former territories of Pomerania, West and East Prussia and Silesia, most of which are now under *de facto* Polish rule. With well over eighty-six million speakers of German in Europe alone, German occupies a high place among the world-languages. According to Mario Pei it is sixth in a list led by Mandarin Chinese, English, Hindi (with Urdu), Russian and Spanish in that order and takes precedence—as far as numbers go—over Japanese, Arabic, Portuguese, French and Italian.

The importance of German to the western world is based less on the number of its speakers than the value of its imaginative literature and of its distinguished philosophical, scientific and technical contributions to modern civilization. The names of Luther, Lessing, Goethe and Schiller and of the philosophers Kant, Hegel and Schopenhauer are world-famous and the present generation is much interested in Rilke, Kafka and Brecht. Our language bears the traces of German scientists when we speak of Liebig's extract, Bunsen burners and Röntgen rays and of technicians known from Zeppelins, Messerschmidts and the Volkswagen. Our geologists use a number of words of German appearance, e.g. quartz (Quarz), gneiss, nickel, cobalt, wolfram. However, the influence of English on contemporary German is still more striking, as will appear from Chapter 18.

It does not take long for the student of German to discover that in many ways German is very much like English. That the words we use in everyday speech are often akin to the German may be shown by the following examples in which the German words are grouped together so that the reader may guess the meaning:— *Vater, Mutter, Sohn, Tochter, Bruder, Schwester; Land, Wasser, Feuer; lang, breit, hoch, tief, dick, dünn; haben, machen, gehen, kommen, trinken,* etc. German has a genitive in -*(e)s* for many nouns just like the English possessive (*John's*); a comparative of the adjective in -*er* (*länger*, 'longer', *älter*, 'elder', *besser*, 'better'); a superlative in -*(e)st* (*ältest*, 'eldest'); a declension of the personal pronouns with forms taken from other roots, e.g. *ich*, 'I' /*mich, mir*, 'me', *wir*, 'we', /*uns*, 'us'; regular verbs with a dental consonant in the past tense and part., e.g. *liebte*, 'loved', *geliebt*, '(having) loved', with *ge*—, like *y*—in *ycladde*; verbs with vowel change like *kommen* 'come', *kam*, 'came', *geholfen* cf. *helfen*. It is easy to put together whole sentences in English in which every word has its German counterpart, e.g. 'I saw him yesterday in father's house'/ *ich sah ihn gestern in Vaters Haus*. In the spoken languages, too, especially if North Germany is taken for comparison, there are many likenesses in the stressing and the intonation of the sentence. English is more conservative in keeping such ancient sounds as *w* in *w*ine, *w*ill in which the North Germans pronounce *w* as *v* and the *th* sounds which in German have developed into *d*, e.g. *th*ing/*D*ing, *th*ick/*d*ick, *th*ou/*d*u. On the other hand English has shed most of its grammatical endings where German has kept them and hence English is full of words of one syllable, e.g. 'I shall go there next week with him if I have time', where German has longer words (*ich werde nächste Woche mit ihm dahin gehen, wenn ich Zeit habe*). When we go beyond household words in English or German we find another characteristic difference. The language of English prose literature and of works of a philosophical, legal, scientific or technical character is full of words adopted from Latin, Greek and French. German certainly contains a number of these foreign adoptions (loan-words), but reacts strongly against their predominance, preferring to build up its words by making compounds of its native elements, e.g. 'universe'/ *Weltall*, 'century'/*Jahrhundert* or deriving words from them by means of prefixes and suffixes, e.g. 'progressive'/*fortschrittlich* (*fort—pro*; *Schritt* for Latin *gress*-, and—*lich* for —*ive*). English would be much the poorer without its classical and French elements, but in the language of the feelings it still shows clearly its Teutonic features. It is illuminating to take well-known hymns and count the non-German words. The proportion is very low in the hymns of Watts and Wesley, but higher in Addison. In the Lord's Prayer the only words of French or Latin origin are 'trespasses', 'deliver', 'power' and 'glory' for which German has *Schulden*, 'debts', *erlösen* (cf. 'loosen'), *Macht* (cf. 'might') and *Herrlichkeit* (from *Herr* 'the Lord', a word originally meaning 'older', cf. 'senior', the positive form here being related to the English adjective *hoar* 'grey-haired, old').

In the written language as well as in spoken English syntax and especially word-order are freer and more flexible than in written German. The student of German will notice a certain rigidity in the rules for the placing of the verb and will if he has had a classical training be reminded of some of the features of Latin. This is due partly to the influence of the chancelleries and the humanists of the fifteenth and sixteenth centuries. English has been much influenced by French and has also independently developed certain features which make it appear 'aberrant' from a European point of view.

I

PRONUNCIATION – STRESS – INTONATION –

ORTHOGRAPHY

In German the spelling and pronunciation are linked in a much more regular system than in either French or English. The standard pronunciation as used by announcers on the wireless, and prescribed for teaching in the schools of Germany, is based upon the recommendations of a commission set up in 1898 to regulate the stage pronunciation to be used in serious drama. In the main it follows the usages of careful speakers in the North, where the speakers coming from Low German-speaking regions have striven for a distinct and 'correct' pronunciation of High German. In their everyday talk, however, North Germans show a few deviations from the norm and as some of these are very prevalent they will be noted.

Until 1939 many German newspapers, periodicals and books were printed in the 'Gothic' character (called in German *Fraktur*), and for a time the National Socialists favoured 'Gothic' as being more distinctively German. In 1941, with a view to the propagation of German in occupied countries unused to the Gothic type, newspapers and publishers went over to the 'Roman' (*Antiqua*) type as used by the English, French, etc., but with the addition of a special sign ss for the sound of *s* in *hiss* after a long vowel or at the end of a word. Except for the retention of Gothic type for aesthetic purposes German publishers use Roman type. Some people still use the cursive form of the Gothic character in correspondence and though it is no longer necessary to learn to write it, it is advisable to practise reading it, as also the Gothic book-type.

Vowels

The long vowels *a*, *e*, *i*, *o*, *u*, represented phonetically by (aː) (eː)
(iː) (oː) (uː) are pronounced like the English *ah, eh, ee, oh, oo*, but
with the tongue kept in the same position throughout. In southern
English the speaker tends to add an *i* to (eː) in 'they', a sort of *y*
to (iː) in 'tea', a *u* to (oː) in 'no' and a *w* to (uː) in 'too'. The German
vowels are pure. In pronouncing (oː) in front of a mirror, see that
your lips retain the same position.

The long sounds of the vowels are shown in German writing
in several ways: (1) doubling, e.g. *Aal, Tee, Boot*; (2) addition of
silent *h*, e.g. *Ahn, Lehm, ihn, Lohn, Huhn*; (3) in the case of (iː) by
the spelling *ie*, e.g. *die, Lied*. A single vowel + a single consonant
+ *e* (a weak murmured vowel) is long, e.g. *Atem* (*em* as *om* in
'seldom'), *denen* (*en* as in 'thicken'), *Tode* (*e* as in 'fatter'), *tuten*.
The weak *e* is represented phonetically by (ə).

The vowels *a, o, u* can be 'mutated' and this mutation is shown
in spelling by *ä, ö, ü*. The effect of mutation is to pronounce the
vowels with the front of the tongue instead of the back. Thus the
long *ä* in *mähen* (silent *h* representing lengthening) is in standard
pronunciation (mɛːən), somewhat like the English sound in 'air',
given phonetically as (ɛː), though in the North many pronounce *ä*
like (eː) as in *Tee*. The *ö*-sound (spelt *oe* in *Goethe*) when long is
pronounced with the same part of the tongue as (eː) in *Tee*, but the
lips are closely rounded. The sound is represented phonetically by
(ø) e.g. *töten* (tøːtn), *Goethe* (gøːtə). The *ü*-sound when long is
pronounced like the French sound in *rue*—the tongue is in a
slightly lower position than for (iː) in *die*, the lips are at the same
time very narrowly rounded. The short vowels *e, i* and *u*—short
e is (ɛ), short *i* (ɪ) and short *u* (ʊ)—are like the English vowel in
bet, bit and *foot*. Care is needed with short *a* and short *o*. The short
sound of *a* in *Mann, Matte, Damm* is of the same quality as that of
the long *a* of English 'father'. The southern English sound of *a* in
'man', 'mat', 'dam' is totally different for it is a front vowel somewhat lower than the *e* of *men* and *met*, whereas the German vowel
is pronounced with the back of the tongue more as in northern
English. There is also a marked difference between the *o* of
English 'God' or 'moth' and that of German *Gott, Motte*. The
German sound is higher and nearer the (oː) of *so*, and is accompanied by lip-rounding. In phonetic notation it is (ɔ), e.g., (gɔt)
(mɔtə).

The mutated short vowels *ä*, *ö*, *ü* are pronounced with the front of the tongue. Short *ä* is exactly like short *e*, e.g. *Fälle* like *Felle*, phonetically (*fɛlə*). Short *ö* in *Köln*, *Götter*, *können* is in phonetic notation (œ), e.g., (kœln), (gœtər), (kœnən) and is a short *e* sound as in *bet* pronounced with the lips rounded. Short *ü* in *dünn*, *Glück*, *füllen* is in phonetic notation (ʏ), e.g. (dʏn), (glʏk), (fʏlən) and is the *i* in *bit* pronounced with lips rounded.

In an unstressed syllable *e* is pronounced as a very short pianissimo, murmured vowel given in notation as (ə), e.g. *Grete* (greːtə), *Mode* (moːdə), *Dogge* (dɔgə). In ordinary speech *-el* is pronounced as in English 'idle', i.e. as syllabic *l*, *-en* as in English 'rotten' (rɔtn), *-em* as in English 'seldom' (seldm), cf. G. *Kessel* (kɛsl), 'kettle', *Boden* (boːdn) 'bottom'. This (ə) is a little further forward than the English sound of *a* in 'idea' and adapts itself readily to the articulation of the preceding consonant—thus *b* in *Liebe* (liːbə) is apt to give it the quality of a very short ö (œ).

German has three diphthongs, i.e. combinations of vowels with semi-vowels: (1) one as in English 'my' or 'mine', (but beginning with a vowel nearer to the *a* of 'father'), represented in German spelling by *ei* or *ai*, e.g. *mein*, *Frankfurt-am-Main*, *heil*—in phonetic notation (main), (hail): (2) one somewhat like English *ow* in *how* or *ou* in house, but as in the case of (ai) beginning with a vowel nearer to the *a* of 'father', hence (au), and spelt *au*, e.g., *Haus*, *Maus*, *Laus*; (3) the mutated form of *au*, spelt *äu* if connected with a word containing *au*—otherwise *eu* and pronounced as a diphthong beginning with the (ɔ) of German *Gott* and finishing with the (ɪ) of *bin* or the (ʏ) of *dünn*, e.g., *Heu* is pronounced (hɔɪ) or (hɔʏ), with preference for the latter.

In standard German and in the ordinary speech of the North every word or independent part of a word beginning with a stressed vowel is preceded by a glottal stop, represented in notation as ('), e.g. *alt* ('alt), *beenden* (bə'ɛndn), *eine alte Ulme* ('ainə 'altə 'ʊlmə). This glottal stop is found in the English Cockney pronunciation replacing *t* in *water* or *p* in 'paper'. Note that German never uses a glide—*r* before an initial vowel as many English speakers do in 'India(r) office', 'idea(r) of it'; and *ein Arm* ('ain 'arm) is very different from 'an arm'. When in compounds the components are fully integrated, e.g. *darin*, *herunter*, *beieinander*, there is no glottal stop and many such words have colloquial abbreviations, e.g. *drin*, *runter*, etc. In rapid speech unstressed pronouns like *er*, *es* or verb forms like *ist* drop the glottal stop (which they have when spoken in isolation or slow staccato), e.g. *dasist wahr* 'that's true'; *alser zu uns kam* 'when he came to us'; *dann war[e]s zu spät* 'then it was too late'. Further details in William J. Moulton 'Juncture in Modern Standard German' in *Language XXIII* (1947), p. 212 ff.

Of the consonants the following show certain divergences from English.

(1) Whereas initial *p-* (*Paß* 'passport'), *t-* (*tun* 'do') and *k-* (*kann* 'can') are in North German aspirated as in English, the aspiration is absent in a cluster like *sp-* (*spielen* 'play'), *st-* (*Stadt* 'city'), *sk-* (*Sklave* 'slave') and in final position, e.g. *schlapp* 'slack', *tot* 'dead' and *kuck!* 'look!'. Unaspirated *p, t, k* is also the pronunciation of final *-b, -d, -g*, as in *Leib* 'body' (laip), *Tod* 'death' (pronounced like *tot*) and *Tag* 'day' (taːk). The *k*-pronunciation of final *g* (except in *-ig*) is the 'stage' pronunciation, but in North German *-g* is treated like *-ch* (see below).

(2) After the 'back' vowels, *a, o, u* long or short and the diphthong *au* the consonant *ch* is pronounced as in the Scottish pronunciation of *loch*, in fact the German word *Loch* 'hole' is —apart from the greater degree of lip-rounding—very much like our word. A good example is the interjection *ach!* Other examples of the *ach*-sound are *lachen* 'to laugh', *machen* 'to make', *Buch* (buːx) 'book', *auch* 'also'. After the 'front' vowels *e, ä, ö, ü* long or short and *i, ie*, and the diphthongs *ei, ai, eu* and *äu*, the consonant *ch* has the *ich*-sound which is not found in normal English. Some speakers use it in the English 'human', but perhaps the best way to articulate it is to press the front of the tongue against the lower teeth and while doing so try to pronounce the English *sh* in 'ship'. Another way is to put the tongue in the position for pronouncing *y* in English 'yes', but with the tongue muscles more loose and then unvoicing the *y* by putting an *h* in front. Examples in German are *ich, echt, Nächte, Löcher, Bücher*. The *ich*-sound occurs also after *l, n* and *r*, e.g. *Milch, München, Kirche*. *Ch-* has the *ich*-sound in the diminutive suffix—*chen*, e.g. *Häuschen* (hɔysçən) 'little house', *Frauchen* (frauçən) 'little woman' contrasted with *täuschen* 'to deceive' (tɔyʃən) and *rauchen* (rauxən) 'to smoke', otherwise *ch-* occurs initially only in foreign words in which it is given the *ich*-sound before *e* and *i*, e.g. *Chemie* (çeˈmiː), *China* (çiːna) except in modern French words like *Chef* (ʃef). Before *a* or *o ch-* is pronounced *k*, e.g. in *Charakter* (kaˈraktər), *Chaos, Chor*, also plural *Chöre* (køːrə).

(3) *g-* at the beginning of a syllable has in words of native origin the pronunciation of English *g-* in 'get', 'go' and never that of *g* in 'general', e.g. *gehen* (geːən) 'to go'. Only in some foreign words like French *Genie* is the pronunciation of *g* as in French (ʒe'niː), *Passage* (pa'saːʒə), but *Genius, genial* from Latin with *g* of 'go'.

(4) *h-* is always pronounced in the initial position, e.g. *haben* 'to have', but never when following a vowel, e.g. *gehen* 'to go' (geːən), except in dictating and occasionally in singing.

(5) The consonant *j-* only occurs initially and is equivalent to English *y* though it is spoken with more friction, e.g. *ja* 'yes', *Jahr* 'year'.

(6) The initial cluster *kn-* retains its *k-* in German, so that German *Knie, kneten* are sharply contrasted with English 'knee', 'knead'. There is no vowel between *k* and *n*. *G-* is pronounced in *Gnade*.

(7) In pronouncing *-l* after a vowel care must be taken to use the same tongue-position as in initial *l*, e.g. the *l* in *alt* 'old' with the same position as *l* in *lang* 'long'. English speakers often pronounce post-vocalic *l* with the back of the tongue with *u-*resonance. There is a great difference between English 'elf' and German *elf* 'eleven' and between 'ball' and German *Ball* in both the vowel and the final consonant.

(8) The letter-group *ng* is pronounced in standard German always like the simple *ng* (ŋ) of southern English 'singer' and never with the *ng* of 'finger'. In German *Finger* would rhyme with English 'singer' and not with 'finger'! The cluster *nk* is pronounced as in English, e.g. *danken* 'thank'.

(9) Very characteristic of High German is the 'affricate' *pf* in which the stop for *p* made with both lips is immediately released to form its corresponding continuant (*f*) also formed with both lips. Avoid putting in a vowel between the *p* and *f*. Examples: *Pfeffer* 'pepper', *Pfeife* 'pipe'.

(10) The combination *qu-* is pronounced in the North and in the stage pronunciation as if it were (*kv*), e.g. *Quelle* (kvɛlə).

(11) Though the officially prescribed pronunciation of German *r* is a point-trill of the tongue like the rolled *r* of Scottish speakers, the usual pronunciation of educated speakers is the uvular trill, somewhat like the French *r* in *rue*, but not quite so far back and with more vibration. The weak 'flapped' *r* of southern English 'run', etc., is unknown in German. After a long vowel the German *r*

is often weak or missing, but the trill is heard after a short vowel, e.g. *scharf*, more than after a long vowel, e.g. *Bart*. It is usually heard in the unstressed syllable of *Vater*, *aber*.

(12) Initial *s*- followed by a vowel is always voiced like English *z*-, e.g. *so* (zoː), *sie* (ziː). As in English 'rosy', 'risen', etc., the -*s*- between vowels is also pronounced like *z*, e.g. *sausen* (zauzən), *lesen* (leːzən). Final -*s* is pronounced voiceless like English *s* in 'house', e.g. *Haus*, as are also *ss*[1], e.g. in *lassen* (lasən) and *ss*, e.g. in *fließen* (fliːsən). The initial clusters *sp*- and *st*- are in all parts of Germany except the North pronounced as if *s* were *sch* (ʃ) and this pronunciation, e.g. of *sprechen* (ʃpreçən) and *stehen* (ʃteːon) is also laid down for the stage.

(13) In words of foreign origin *v* is in most cases pronounced at the beginning of a word as in English, e.g. *Vase, Venus, Vergil, Violine, Visum* 'visa', *Valuta* 'currency', *die Vogesen* 'the Vosges', *Venedig* (stress on second *e* which is long) 'Venice'. At the end of a word *v* is pronounced like English *f*, e.g. *Nerv* 'nerve', *aktiv, der Vesuv* 'Vesuvius'. The plural *Nerven* can be pronounced either with *v* or *f*. A few words taken over early from other languages have the pronunciation *f*, e.g. *Vers* 'verse', *Veilchen* 'violet' (but *Viole* with *v*), *Vlame* 'Fleming', *Vlissingen* 'Flushing', *Veit* 'Vitus, Guy'. The native word *Hannover* (with stressed *o*) has *f*, but the derived word with foreign suffix *Hannoveraner* has *v* with the stress on the fourth syllable.

(14) The German *w* is in the North and stage pronunciation like the English *v*, so *Wein* has the same consonants as 'vine'.

(15) Both *x* and *y* occur only in foreign words, *y* being used most frequently as a vowel with the value of *ü*, e.g. *Typ* (tyːp).

(16) The German *z* (as well as *c*- in foreign words) has the value of an 'affricate' (*ts*) where the dental stop *t* is released to articulate the continuant *s*. The sound can occur before *w*, e.g. *zwingen* (tsvɪŋən). The word *zoo* is in English pronounced (zuː) and in German (tsoː). Whereas *z* remains in spelling after a long vowel or diphthong, e.g. *duzen* (duːtsən), *heizen* (haitsən), it is written *tz* after a short vowel, e.g. *Blitz* (blɪts), *Hitze* (hɪtsə).

[1] German printers now use *ss* only between vowels and then only when the first vowel is short, e.g. *lassen, essen*. After a long vowel or diphthong they use *ß*, e.g. *aßen, Soße, fließen, Preußen* as also at the end of a syllable whether the vowel is short or long, e.g. *Paß* (short), *paßte* (short) and before inflectional *t*, e.g. *laßt, mußt*. It is to be noted that the *a* of *Maß, aß, fraß*, the *o* of *groß*, the *u* of *Fuß* and *Gruß*, the *ü* of *Füße* and *Grüße* and the *ö* of *Größe* are to be pronounced long.

Stress

Just as in English words derived with a suffix like *-er*, *-ish*, *-y*, *-ing*, *-ness*, *-hood*, etc. stress the root-syllable, i.e. that which bears the nuclear meaning, so in German it is the root-syllable which is stressed. Compare English 'father', 'fatherly' with German *Vater*, *väterlich* or 'childish' with *kindisch* or 'friendship' with *Freundschaft* or 'friendliness' with *Freundlichkeit*. Similarly both English and German have some unstressed prefixes, e.g. *be-* (pronounced bə in German), *for-* Ger. *ver-* in *be'speak* like German *be'sprechen* or *for'get* like *ver'gessen*, cf. also English 'under'take' and German *unter'nehmen*. These prefixes are the so-called inseparable prefixes. On the other hand adverbial particles like 'out' in English 'go out' or 'up' in 'take up' have stress in both English and German even when in the latter they precede an infinitive and are written together, e.g. English 'go out' and German *'ausgehen (ich gehe 'aus)*, English 'take' up' and German *'aufnehmen (ich nehme 'auf)*.

Compound nouns and adjectives usually have two stresses, a main stress on the first component and a secondary stress on the second, e.g. English 'father,land' and German *'Vater,land*, English 'sun,shine' and German *'Sonnen,schein*.

Foreign words which are nouns or adjectives usually stress the last syllable of the uninflected form, e.g. German *Sol'dat*, *Cel'list*, *Stu'dent*, *dis'kret*, *ele'gant*. Verbs formed with *-ieren* stress the suffix, e.g. *stu'dieren*.

Some place-names stress the final syllable, e.g. *Ber'lin*, *Pa'ris*, *Stett'in* though most have initial stress, e.g. *'Hamburg*, *'Bremen*, *München*, *'Stuttgart*, *'London*, *'Brüssel*. Note *Hannover*, *Ober'ammergau*.

Intonation

North German intonation follows approximately the same principles as English in its use of rising and falling tones, but there is much less 'flicker' of the voice than in southern English. In reading German it is a safe procedure—unless followed too mechanically—to raise the voice towards a comma and drop it towards a full stop. If the reader or speaker gets the main stress accents right in a phrase or sentence and observes the following rules, he should be readily understood.

(1) Falling intonations are characteristic of (a) the statement, e.g. *ich ⁻ glaube nicht, daß es ` wahr ist*, 'I don't believe it's true';

(b) the request, e.g. ⁻*nehmen Sie* `*meinen* (*Bleistift*), 'take my (pencil)'; (c) questions asking for specific information with words like 'who'? 'when'? 'how'?, e.g. `*wann soll ich kommen?* 'when shall I come?'

A more lively utterance is produced by beginning on a rising tone and then dropping suddenly, e.g. *ich* '*protes* `*tiere*, 'I protest', *ver* '*such mal einen* `*andern* (*Plan*), 'well then, try another (plan)', and in exclamations, e.g. '*wie* `*ärgerlich!*, 'what a nuisance!'

(2) Rising intonation is characteristic of a question seeking a decision of 'yes' or 'no', e.g. *ist es* '*schwarz?* 'is it black!' or statements of a hesitant or doubting character, e.g. *nicht daß es so'teuer ist*, 'not that it is so dear', *ich ver'mute*, 'I think so'.

A low-rising tone on the main stress is used in greetings, e.g. ‚*Guten Tag!* as in English 'good morning!', the response being on a falling tone.

(3) An implied contrast or contradiction is conveyed by a snake-like intonation curve consisting of a fall followed by a rise and then a sudden plunge, e.g. *das ist* `*nicht, was*^*ich glaube*, 'it's not what *I* think (though *you* may)'. As Maria Schubiger in 'English Intonation and German Modal Particles' (*Phonetica* XX, p. 65) shows, German often reinforces the contrast with *doch*, e.g. *gestern war dir's doch recht* 'you found it all right yesterday'.

The male voice-register is somewhat lower and speech is both louder and more energetic. Strong stresses and wider tone-intervals give the utterance a more decisive character than that of English.

Some notes on orthography and punctuation

All nouns, including substantivized adjectives, participles and infinitives, are indicated by an initial capital (*die Reise* 'journey', *der Reisende* 'traveller', *der Vielgereiste* 'much-travelled man', *das Reisen* 'travelling'). Unlike English an adjective derived from a proper noun is not capitalized (*die deutsche Sprache* 'the German language'). A noun loses its capital when functioning as a quasi-prefix of a verb (*stattfinden* 'to take place', *gewährleisten* 'to guarantee') and when occurring in a stereotyped group in which the words are written together (*imstande* 'in a position to . . .', but *in der Lage*, *zuhause*).

In regard to the division of words into syllables the conventional rules, as given in Duden's *Rechtschreibung*, do not always conform to the actual pronunciation. The syllable division (*die Silben-trennung*) is made after a long vowel or diphthong (*ra-ten, se-hen, hau-en*), between two consonants (*Hal-le, Damp-fer, Schrek-ken* with *kk* for *ck*) and between the components of a compound (*Haus-tür*).

Punctuation (*die Interpunktion* with *interpungieren* 'to punctuate'; *die Zeichensetzung*) is in the main similar to that of English, but the rules are formulated more precisely and are more strictly observed. The following are important divergences: (1) the use of a full stop (*der Punkt*) to indicate an ordinal number (*den 1. April, Heinrich VI.*); (2) the compulsory use of a comma to mark the boundary between clauses whether main and/or subordinate (*er sagte, er sei krank; er sagte, dass er krank sei; der Mann, der hier wohnt*) and before an introduced infinitival group (*er tat es, um uns zu imponieren* 'he did it in order to impress us'). The semicolon (*das Semikolon, der Strichpunkt*) and colon (*das Kolon, der Doppelpunkt*) are used much as in English as are also the question-mark or query (*das Fragezeichen*) and exclamation mark (*das Ausrufungszeichen,*) except that the latter is still used by some letter-writers in the opening (*Sehr geehrter Herr Doktor!, Sehr verehrte gnädige Frau!*). Quotation marks (*Anführungs-zeichen*) differ in both form and level („Mann" and »Mann«).

Common abbreviations include usw. (=*und so weiter* 'etc.'), u.a. (=*und andere*), d.h. (=*das heisst* 'i.e.'), f (=*folgend*, ff= *folgende* 'following'), S. (=(1) *Seite* 'page' or p. (2) =*sieh* 'see' or q.v.), d.M. (=*dieses Monats* 'inst.'), z.B. (=*zum Beispiel* 'for example' or e.g.), v.H. (=*von Hundert* 'per cent' or %), vgl. (=*vergleiche* 'compare' or cf., cp.), dgl. (=*dergleichen* 'such like'), bzw (=*beziehungsweise* a non-disjunctive 'or'), u.A.w.g. (=*um Antwort wird gebeten* or R.S.V.P.), b.w. (=*bitte wenden* or P.T.O.).

Directions for the printer used in correcting proofs (*Korrektur-zeichen*) are markedly different from English. A fully corrected specimen text is given in Duden's *Rechtschreibung* (1961), pp. 83–87, and in the Brockhaus encyclopaedia.

2

NOUNS AND NOUN GROUPS – GENDER –
NUMBER AND CASE – USE OF THE ARTICLES

Formation of nouns

A large number of nouns inherited from the distant past are simple
forms without affixes today, e.g. *Kind*, 'child', *Arm*, 'arm', *Weg*,
'way', *Volk*, 'people', *Nuß*, 'nut'. Words are in German very often
combined to form compounds. In these the first component is
either the stem form, e.g. *Armband*, 'bracelet' (*Arm + Band*),
Eisenbahn, 'railway' (*Eisen*, 'iron' + *Bahn*, 'course'), or provided
with the genitive -(*e*)*s* or with -(*e*)*n* at the joint between the components, e.g. *Volkslied*, 'folk-song', *Ferienheim*, 'holiday home'.
Many modern compounds have an adjectival or verbal stem as
first component, e.g. *Trockendock*, 'dry dock', *Rollschuh*, 'roller-
skate'. (See section on Word-formation.)

Many nouns are derived from other nouns, adjectives or verbs
by means of suffixes. Thus -*er* is used as in English 'singer' for the
agent or doer, e.g. *Spieler*, 'player', for the inhabitant, say of a
town, e.g. *Berliner*, *Hamburger*, *Kölner*, and for instruments like
Roller, 'scooter', *Sender*, 'transmitter'. Corresponding to English
-*ing* used primarily to designate the action, German has -*ung*, e.g.
Haltung (like 'bearing'), *Windung* (like 'winding'). The commonest
English quality suffix -*ness* is paralleled historically by -*nis* in
German, but this is rare, and the usual equivalent is -*heit*, or -*keit*
(like -*hood* in 'manhood'), e.g. *Neuheit* 'novelty', *Neuigkeit*,
'news'. Like English words in -*ship*, German has -*schaft*,
e.g. *Freundschaft*, 'friendship', and the -*dom* words have as
their parallels words with -*tum*, e.g. *Herzogtum*, 'dukedom,
duchy'.

Gender

German has, unlike French, a neuter gender in addition to masculine and feminine. The gender is shown (i) by the form of the definite article 'the', namely *DER* (masc.), *DIE* (fem.), *DAS* (neuter), e.g. *der Mann, die Frau, das Haus*; (ii) by the form of the pronoun referring to the noun, namely *ER*, 'he' (masc.), *SIE*, 'she' (fem.), *ES*, 'it' (neuter). Although most male beings are masculine and most female beings are feminine, gender is not simply a mark of sex. Non-animate things and abstracts like actions, states or qualities may also be masculine, feminine or neuter. Sense is no guide to gender. Thus 'the arm' is masc., namely *der Arm* and must be referred to by the masculine form for 'he' *er*, *die Hand* must be referred to by 'she', namely *sie*, and only a neuter like *das Haus* or *das Knie* may be referred to by *es*, cf. further *der Löffel* 'the spoon', *die Gabel* 'the fork', *das Messer* 'the knife'.

Some words denoting persons are neuter, e.g. *das Kind* 'child' and *das Weib* 'woman'. As all diminutives in -*chen* and -*lein* are neuter we must say *das Mädchen* for the 'girl' or 'maid', *das Fräulein* for 'the unmarried woman, governess, waitress', etc., *das Männchen* for the male animal and *das Weibchen* for the female animal.

Sometimes the masculine is used for the whole species, e.g. *der Wolf, der Tiger*, but there are some cases where the feminine has the general application, e.g. *die Katze* 'cat', *die Ziege* 'goat'. The words 'horse' and 'pig' are neuter: *das Pferd, das Schwein*.

As in English there are sometimes distinctive words for the male and female, e.g. *der Hengst* 'stallion'/*die Stute* 'mare', *der Bulle*/*die Kuh, der Eber*/*die Sau*, but *das Pferd, das Schwein* generally. The word for 'cat', *die Katze*, has a masculine *der Kater* 'tom-cat', and *die Ziege* 'goat' has *der Ziegenbock* 'billy-goat'.

Most nouns denoting females are derived by means of the suffix -*in*, e.g. *der König* 'king'/*die Königin* 'queen', *der Schauspieler* 'actor'/*die Schauspielerin* 'actress'; *der Fuchs* 'fox'/*die Füchsin* 'vixen', *der Wolf* 'wolf'/*die Wölfin* 'she-wolf'.

Only a few odd masculines are formed by adding the suffix -*erich* to the feminine, e.g. *die Gans* 'goose'/*der Gänserich* 'gander', *die Ente* 'duck'/*der Enterich* 'drake'. This has given rise to a jocular word for 'bridegroom'—instead of *der Bräutigam* people say *der Bräuterich*.

For certain categories of words it is possible to give a few principles regulating their genders.

(1) Nouns formed from the infinitives of verbs are neuter, e.g. *das Leben* 'life', *das Essen* 'meal', *das Sein* 'being', *das Streben* 'striving'.

(2) Abstract nouns formed from adjectives with the suffixes *-e, -heit, -keit* or from nouns with *-schaft* are feminine, e.g. *die Tiefe* 'depth', *die Länge* 'length', *die Güte* 'goodness', *die Einheit* 'unity', *die Fruchtbarkeit* 'fertility', *die Freundschaft* 'friendship'.

(3) Nouns indicating action formed from verbs with the suffix *-ung*, cf. English *-ing* are feminine, e.g. *die Behandlung* 'treatment', *die Regierung* 'government'.

(4) Nouns indicating place or action formed with *-(er)ei* or *-(el)ei* are feminine, e.g. *die Bäckerei* 'bakery', *die Liebelei* 'love-affair'.

(5) Collective words formed with the prefix *Ge-* and usually ending with *-e* are neuter, e.g. *das Gebirge* 'mountains' (*der Berg* 'the mountain'), *das Getriebe* 'gear', etc.

(6) Although the word for 'tree' is masculine (*der Baum*), the tree-names in *-e* are feminine, e.g. *die Eiche* 'oak', *die Ulme* 'elm', *die Buche* 'beech', *die Birke* 'birch', *die Tanne* 'fir', *die Fichte* 'pine', *die Esche* 'ash', *die Eibe* 'yew', *die* Weide 'willow'.

Gender of place names

In Germany the rivers in the West are partly masculine: *der Rhein, der Main, der Neckar* and partly feminine *die Nahe, die Lahn, die Mosel, die Ruhr, die Maas, die Schelde*. The rivers flowing into the North Sea and Baltic are feminine: *die Ems, die Weser, die Elbe, die Oder, die Weichsel*. The Danube (*die Donau*) is feminine. Rivers outside Germany ending in *-e* are feminine, e.g. *die Themse, die Seine, die Loire*—also *die Wolga*. Other large rivers tend to be masculine, e.g. *der Nil, der Kongo, der Sambesi, der Ganges, der Hoang-ho, der Jang-tse-kiang, der Don, der Dnjepr, der Mississippi* —also *der Sankt-Lorenz-Strom* and *der Amazonen-Strom*.

Oceans are masculine, e.g. *der Atlantische Ozean* (*der Atlantik*), *der Stille Ozean* (*der Pazifik*), *der Indische Ozean*. Seas are either (1) neuter with *Meer*, e.g. *das Weisse* (*Schwarze, Rote*) *Meer, das Mittelländische Meer* (*Mittelmeer*), *das Kaspische Meer, das Karibische Meer, das Nord-, Südpolarmeer, das Adriatische Meer*, etc., or (2) feminine with *See*, e.g. *die Nordsee, die Ostsee* 'Baltic', *die Irische See, die Südsee* 'the South Seas'. A channel is masculine, *der Kanal* (*Ärmelkanal* like 'La Manche') 'English Channel', *St Georgskanal*, etc. Gulfs and bays include the masculine *der Golf von Biskaya* (*Guinea*) and *der Bottnische Meerbusen* and the feminine *die Deutsche Bucht* 'Bight of Heligoland'. Islands include the neuter *Sizilien, Sardinien, Zypern, Tasmanien, Island, Neufundland, Neuseeland, Feuerland*, 'Tierra del Fuego' and the plurals *die Balearen, Antillen* 'West Indies' (*Westindien*), *Bahamainseln, Orkneyinseln*, etc. Note the absence of preposition in *die Insel Man*, etc., but *die Straße von Dover* 'the straits of Dover'.

The continents are neuter: *Europa, Asien, Afrika, Australien, Nord Mittel-* and *Südamerika*, but there are the feminine *die Antarktis* and *Antarktika*. The word for 'cape' is neuter, hence *das Kap der Guten Hoffnung* 'Cape of Good Hope', cf. *Kap Hoorn, Kap Finisterre*, etc.

Like *der Berg* most mountain-names are masculine, e.g. *der Harz, der Brocken, der Montblanc, der Ararat, der Mount Everest, der Kilimandscharo, der Aconcagua, der Fudschi-jama*. Owing to the gender of their second component *die Zugspitze* and *die Jungfrau* are feminine and *das Matterhorn* is neuter. Mountain-ranges include *die Alpen, die Karpathen, die Apenninen, die Anden* and the collective singulars *das Uralgebirge, das Felsengebirge* 'the Rockies'.

Names of countries are usually neuter, e.g. *England, Schottland, Irland, Island, Frankreich* 'France', *Deutschland, Rußland, Holland, Spanien, Italien, Norwegen, Schweden, Dänemark, Polen, Jugoslawien, Bulgarien, Indien, Ägypten, Persien, China, Japan*, etc., also regions like *Niedersachsen, Bayern, Rheinland-Westfalen*, etc. There are a few feminines which are always accompanied by the definite article, e.g. *die Schweiz* 'Switzerland', *die Türkei* 'Turkey', *die Tschechoslowakei* 'Czechoslovakia', *die Mandschurei, die Mongolei*. Some modern names are masculine, e.g. *Irak, Iran, Sudan, Kongo, Libanon*, cf. also *der Balkan* 'the Balkans'.

Number

Unlike English, which forms the vast majority of its plurals in *-s*, German has a variety of endings *-e, -er, -(e)n* and in addition, in some cases mutates the vowel, substituting *ä* for *a*, *ö* for *o*, *ü* for *u* and *äu* for *au*. In the German plural there are fewer case-distinctions than in the singular. The dative plural always ends in *-(e)n* and the nominative, accusative and genitive always have the same form. The definite article shows *die* for the nominative and accusative plural of all genders, e.g. *die Männer sind da, ich sehe die Männer*, cf. *die Frauen, die Häuser*. The genitive *der* is the form

28 The German Language Today

for all genders, e.g. (*die Häuser*) *der Männer* (*Frauen*). The dative plural is *den*, e.g. in *den Häusern*.

The following rules, which are by no means exhaustive, may be found useful:

(1) *Masculine nouns*

(a) Strong declension, i.e., those with genitive singular in -(*e*)*s* with several sub-classes according to plural forms.

(i) ⁻e or -*e*. The vowels *a*, *o*, *u* and diphthong *au* usually mutate, e.g. *der Gast/Gäste* 'guests', *Hals/Hälse* 'necks', *Hahn/Hähne* 'cocks', *Knopf/Knöpfe* 'buttons', *Kopf/Köpfe* 'heads', *Fuchs/Füchse* 'foxes', *Fuß/Füße* 'feet', *Gruß/Grüße* 'greetings, kind regards', *Baum/Bäume* 'trees', also the non-mutating *der Fisch/e* 'fishes', *Brief/e* 'letters', *Dieb/e* 'thieves', *Freund/e* 'friends', *Feind/e* 'enemies', *König/e* 'kings'.

There are a few instances where the vowels *a*, *u* and *au* do not mutate, e.g. *der Arm/e* 'arms' (of body), *Halm/e* 'stalks', *Grad/e* 'degrees', *Huf/e* 'hooves', *Ruf/e* 'calls', *Schuh/e* 'shoes', *Hund/e* 'dogs', *Punkt/e* 'points', *Laut/e* 'sounds'.

(ii) If the noun ends in -*el*, -*en*, -*er* no ending is added, but *a*, *o*, *u* usually mutate, e.g. *der Engel/-* 'angels', *Lehrer/-* 'teachers', *der Vogel/Vögel* 'birds', *Apfel/Äpfel* 'apples', *Vater/Väter* 'fathers', *Bruder/Brüder* 'brothers' and by analogy the feminine *die Mutter/Mütter* 'mothers', *die Tochter/Töchter* 'daughters', but *die Schwester/n* 'sisters', *der Garten/Gärten* 'gardens', *der Ofen/Öfen* 'stoves'.

A few nouns like *der Knochen/-* 'bones' and *Kuchen* 'cakes' do not mutate.

(iii) ⁻er, i.e. mutated vowel and ending -*er*. This is really a neuter mode of declension, but a few masculines follow it, e.g. *der Gott/Götter* 'gods', *Mann/Männer* 'men', *Wald/Wälder* 'woods', *Wurm/Würmer* 'worms'.

(iv) -(*e*)*n* in spite of genitive singular -*s*, e.g. *der Dorn/en* 'thorns', *der Mast/en* 'masts', *Schmerz/en* 'pains', *Strahl/en* 'rays', *Nachbar/n* 'neighbours', *Bauer/n* 'farmers', *Vetter/n* 'cousins', *Muskel/n* 'muscles'.

(b) Weak declension with gen. sing. in -(*e*)*n* and all cases singular and plural (except the nominative singular) in -(*e*)*n*. All masculines in -*e* except *der Käse* 'cheese' are declined weak, e.g. *der Affe/n* 'monkeys', *Hase/n* 'hares', *Löwe/n* 'lions', *Rabe/n* 'ravens'; *der Bote/n* 'messengers', *Neffe/n* 'nephews'; *der Deutsche/n* 'Germans', *Franzose/n* 'Frenchmen', *Däne/n* 'Danes', *Schwede/n* 'Swedes', *Russe/n* 'Russians', *Preuße/n* 'Prussians', *Schotte/n* 'Scots'. N.B. *der Wille* 'will' has genitive *Willens* and *der Friede/n* 'peace' has *Friedens*.

Weak masculines without *-e* in the nominative singular are usually nouns designating persons and in a few instances animals, e.g. the titles *der Fürst/en* 'princes', *Prinz/en* 'princes' (of blood-royal), *Graf/en* 'earls, counts', *Herr/en* 'gentlemen, masters'; also *der Mensch/en* 'human beings', *der Held/en* 'heroes', *Narr/en* 'fools' (also *Tor/en*); *der Student/en* 'students', *Präsident/en*, *Soldat/en*, *Philosoph/en*, *Geograph/en* 'geographers', (cf. *Photografen, Geologen, Theologen, Philologen, Artisten*); the animals *der Bär/en* 'bears', *Elefant/en* 'elephants'.

(2) *Neuter nouns*

All neuters take *-(e)s* in the genitive singular. They form their plurals as follows:

(a) ⸚*er* (if the vowel is *a*, *o*, *u*, *au*), otherwise simply *-er*, e.g. *das Kalb/Kälber* 'calves', *das Lamm/Lämmer* 'lambs', *das Land/Länder* 'lands', *das Dach/Dächer* 'roofs', *das Glas/Gläser* 'glasses', *das Dorf/Dörfer* 'villages', *das Loch/Löcher* 'holes', *das Buch/Bücher* 'books', *das Huhn/Hühner* 'chickens', *das Haus/Häuser* 'houses'; *das Feld/Felder* 'fields', *das Nest/Nester* 'nests', *das Kind/Kinder* 'children', *das Ei/Eier* 'eggs'.

(b) *-e* without mutation, e.g. *das Jahr/e* 'years', *Haar/e* 'hair(s)', *Schaf/e* 'sheep', *Schiff/e* 'ships', *Boot/e* 'boats', *Pferd/e* 'horses', *Schwein/e* 'pigs', *Werk/e* 'works', *Spiel/e* 'games', *Heft/e* 'exercise books', *Beil/e* 'choppers'.

(c) After *-el*, *-en*, *-er*, there is no ending, e.g. *Rätsel* 'riddles', *Zeichen* 'signs', *Kissen* 'cushions', *Laken* 'sheets', *Zimmer* 'rooms', *Ufer* 'shores'. Diminutives in *-chen* and *-lein* also remain unchanged, e.g. *Mädchen* 'girls, maids', *Fräulein*, etc.

(d) A few words have plural in *-(e)n*, e.g. *das Auge/n* 'eyes', *Ende/n* 'ends', *Ohr/en* 'ears', *Bett/en* 'beds', *Hemd/en* 'shirts', *Insekt/en* 'insects'. The word *das Herz* 'heart' which has a gen. sing. *Herzens* and dat. sing. *Herzen* forms its plural *Herzen*.

(3) *Feminine nouns*

There are only two classes (a) with mutated vowel and *-e* to form plural and (b) with *-(e)n*.

(a) ⸚*e*, e.g. *die Axt/Äxte* 'axes', *Bank/Bänke* 'benches', *Gans/*

Gänse 'geese', *Stadt/Städte* (often with long *ä*) 'towns, cities', *Wand/Wände* 'partitions, walls', *Macht/Mächte* 'powers', *Kraft/ Kräfte* 'forces', *Nacht/Nächte* 'nights'; *Frucht/Früchte* 'fruits', *Nuss/Nüsse* 'nuts', *Wurst/Würste* 'sausages', *Kunst/Künste* 'arts'; *Braut/Bräute* 'fiancées', *Faust/Fäuste* 'fists', *Maus/Mäuse* 'mice', *Laus/Läuse* 'lice'.

(b) -*(e)n.*

All feminines with -*e* in the nominative singular take -*n* throughout the plural and the vast majority of feminines ending in a consonant take -*en*, e.g. *die Blume/n* 'flowers', *Knospe/n* 'buds', *Beere/n* 'berries', *Birne/n* 'pears', *Kirsche/n* 'cherries', *Pflaume/n* 'plums'; *die Eiche/n* 'oaks', *Buche/n* 'beeches', etc.; *die Fliege/n* 'flies', *Mücke/n* 'gnats', *Biene/n* 'bees', *Lerche/n* 'larks', *Schwalbe/n* 'swallows'; *die Kirche/n* 'churches', *Schule/n* 'schools', *Straße/n* 'streets'; *die Farbe/n* 'colours', *Stimme/n* 'voices'. Without -*e* in singular: *die Tat/en* 'deeds', *Uhr/en* 'watches, clocks', *Zahl/en* 'numbers', *Zeit/en* 'times'; all feminines in -*ung* like *die Hoffnung/ en* 'hopes', -*schaft* like *die Wissenschaft/en* 'science', -*heit* like *die Einheit/en* 'units', -*keit* like *die Flüssigkeit/en* 'fluid' and -*in* like *die Freundin/nen* 'woman friend'.

Plural -*s*

In colloquial speech there is a plural—formed as in English in -*s*—used especially with words designating persons, e.g. *Jungens*, 'boys' (really a double plural), *Mädels* 'girls', *Kerls* 'fellows' *Bräutigams* 'fiancés, bridegrooms', *Fräuleins* and many foreign words like *Kinos, Restaurants, Autos*. Also family names may take -*s*, e.g. *Müllers haben Besuch*, 'the Millers have visitors'.

Plural substitutes

Some German nouns do not take the ordinary plural endings, but in the plural are replaced by either compounds or by affix-derived nouns. To the first type belong *Atem* 'breath'/*Atemzüge*; the use of -*fälle* to form the plurals of *Glück* 'luck', *Unglück* 'misfortune' and *Tod* 'death', namely *Glücksfälle* 'pieces of good fortune', *Unglücksfälle* 'misfortunes, accidents', and *Todesfälle*; 'murders' are *Mordtaten* or *Morde*; der *Schmuck* is collective for 'ornament', so the plural has to be *Schmucksachen*. To the second type belong *das Bestreben/ Bestrebungen* 'efforts', *der Segen/ Segnungen* 'blessings', *der Trost* 'consolation'/*Tröstungen* 'consolations', *die Furcht/Befürchtungen* 'fears', *der Verzug* 'delay'/

Verzögerungen 'delays'; *der Betrug/Betrügereien* 'deceptions', *der Raub/Räubereien* 'robberies', *der Verrat* 'treason'/*Verrätereien* 'acts of treachery', *der Zank* 'quarrel'/*Zänkereien* 'quarrels'; *das Erbe* 'inheritance'/*Erbschaften* 'inheritances', cf. *Liebschaften* 'love affairs'; *der Streit* 'dispute'/*Streitigkeiten* 'disputes'.[1]

English plural corresponding to German singular and vice versa

The plant-names 'oats' and 'hops' are *der Hafer* and *der Hopfen* respectively. There are several words indicating an amount like *der Erlös* 'proceeds', *der Lohn* 'wages', *der Gewinn* 'winnings', *der Schadenersatz* 'damages', *der Rückstand* 'arrears'. There are the card-terms *Herz* 'hearts', *Karo* 'diamonds', *Treff* 'clubs', *Pik* 'spades', *ist Trumpf*: 'hearts, etc., are trumps'. There are collective terms like *das Feuerwerk* 'fireworks', *die Gasanstalt* 'gas-works', *die Kaserne* 'barracks', *die Treppe* 'stairs', *das Uhrwerk* 'the works, mechanism', *das schottische Hochland* 'the Highlands of Scotland', *Westindien* 'the West Indies', *das Mittelalter* 'the Middle Ages'. Some names of diseases and disorders are plural in English but singular in German, e.g. *der Ziegenpeter* 'mumps' (but *die Masern* 'measles' is plural in German). In English 'means' is used for an expedient, but German says *das einzige Mittel* 'the sole means' and *ein Mittel* 'a remedy, a device'.

On the other hand where English uses a word like 'hair' collectively German can say either *das Haar* or *die Haare*. On the whole German prefers the plural *Kenntnisse* for 'knowledge' about a subject, plural *Fortschritte* for 'progress' and *Geschäfte* for the 'business' transacted in contrast with *das Geschäft* for the firm and its premises.

Use of Leute 'people'

The word *Leute* is used for a vague number of people, e.g. *viele Leute* 'many people', whereas for an exact number a phrase like *zwei Menschen* or *zwei Personen* would be more appropriate. For the singular use of 'a people' the word *ein Volk* (*das Volk*) is available (*Völker* 'peoples').

Compound words with *-mann* having some occupational meaning take *-leute* in the plural, e.g. *Geschäftsmann/-leute* 'business men', *Kaufmann/-leute* 'merchants, tradesmen', *See-*

---

[1] As law terms the plural of *Betrug* is *Betrugsfälle*, that of *Raub* is *Raubüberfälle* and of *Hochverrat* there is a new plural *Hochverrate*. In an indictment the plural is implied by the use of *mehrfach* 'multiple' with the singular, e.g. *wegen mehrfachen* (*Betrugs, Raubs, Verrats*).

mann/-leute 'sailors', *Hauptmann/-leute* 'captains (army)'. A distinction is made between *Ehemänner* 'husbands' and the common gender *Eheleute* 'married people'. The plural of *Staatsmann* is *Staatsmänner* 'statesmen' and *Schneemänner* is used for 'snowmen'.

Nouns of material

Nouns of material like *Tee, Kaffee, Milch* may form a plural to indicate various kinds, e.g. *Teesorten* '(various blends of) teas', though there are such plurals as *Gesundheittees* 'tisanes' and *Tanztees* 'tea-dances'. In ordering more than one portion one may say, e.g. *zweimal Eiskaffee* 'two iced coffees'.

Use of singular in expressions of measurement

German goes further than English in using the singular of the noun of measurement, cf. 'two foot six'. With a masculine or neuter noun followed by the expression of that which is measured (or weighed or counted) the singular is the rule, e.g. *zwei Glas Bier, vier Pfund Tee* 'four pounds of tea'—also *sechs Fuß hoch* 'six feet high'; *zwei Mann hoch* 'two deep'; *ein Führer mit zehn Mann* 'a leader with ten men'; *drei Eßlöffel voll Zucker* 'three tablespoonfuls of sugar'. Feminine words have the plural, e.g. *zwei Tassen Tee*; *hundert Tonnen Ladung* 'a hundred tons of cargo'; *zwei Rollen Garn* 'two reels of cotton'.

Case

In the noun English has only two cases, a common case, e.g. *the man* and a genitive or 'possessive' case (mainly for animates), e.g. *the man's*. The English pronoun, however, has a nominative case (*I, he, she, we, they, who*) and a general oblique case (*me, him, her, us, them, whom*) used for the direct object, e.g. *he saw me* and the indirect object, e.g. *he gave me the book*.

German has four cases in both noun and pronoun, namely the nominative (*who*-case), the accusative (direct object or *whom*-case), the genitive like the English noun case in -'s (*whose*) and the dative (or indirect object case). It is only in the masculine singular in the articles, nouns and pronouns that there is any difference between the nominative and accusative (*DER/DEN, EIN/EINEN, KEIN/KEINEN* 'no', *ER/IHN*), e.g. *der Mann ist hier, er ist hier/ich sehe den Mann, ich sehe ihn*. In the masculine nouns it is only one set of words, mainly names of persons like *der Prinz, der*

Fürst, der Graf, der Bote 'messenger' and of animals like *der Bär* 'bear', *der Affe* 'monkey' which take a specific accusative ending, namely *-(e)n*, e.g. *ich sehe den Prinzen, den Boten, den Bären, den Affen*. In all other masculine words as well as in feminines and neuters the nominative and accusative have the same form. Thus in the above sentences the word *Mann* did not change, but the accusative case was shown by *DEN*. Examples of the coalescence of nominative and accusative in the feminines are *die Frau ist hier, eine Frau ist hier, sie ist hier/ich sehe die Frau, ich sehe eine Frau, ich sehe sie*. Neuter examples are *das Kind ist hier, ein Kind ist hier, es ist hier/ich sehe das Kind, ich sehe ein Kind, ich sehe es*.

The genitive case corresponds to the English form in *'s* ('John's, the man's') and to a phrase with 'of' ('the end of the day'). In German the genitive is shown by the form of the definite article (masc. and neuter *DES*, fem. *DER*, cf. *EINES/EINER, KEINES/KEINER*). Since the feminine noun never changes in the singular, the article is the only way of indicating the case. All neuters have a genitive singular in *-s* or *-es*, e.g. from *das Haus* we form a genitive in [*der Herr*] *des Hauses* '[the master] of the house'. Except for those masculine words like *der Prinz, der Bär* already mentioned which form their oblique cases with *-(e)n*, all masculines, like the neuters, have *-s* or *-es* in the genitive, e.g. [*der Sohn*] *des Königs* '[the son] of the king, the king's [son]'. The genitive usually follows the noun it qualifies, except in the everyday language where personal nouns like 'father's' may go first and have no article, e.g. *Vaters Haus, Onkels Haus, Schwiegervaters Haus* 'father-in-law's house' and—by analogy—even in feminines which strictly speaking have no specific genitive form, e.g. *Mutters Haus, Tantes Haus, Kusine Elly's Haus*. Germans do not say *Bruders* or *Schwesters Haus*, but *das Haus meines Bruders* (*meiner Schwester*).

A few prepositions are constructed with the genitive, e.g. *kraft des Gesetzes* 'by virtue of the law (*das Gesetz*)', *jenseits des Ozeans* 'beyond the ocean (der Ozean)', *diesseits des Flusses* 'on this side of the river (*der Fluss*)', *infolge des Unfalls* 'in consequence of the accident'.

The dative case in the singular is indicated by the special form of the articles for the masculine and neuter *dem, einem, keinem* and for the feminine *der, einer, keiner*. The only specific dative ending of the noun in the singular is *-e* which is often added to short especially monosyllabic masculine and neuter 'strong'

2

stems, i.e. those with genitive in -(e)s, e.g. *dem Mann(e)*, *dem Buch(e)*. The 'weak' or -(e)n stem masculines show the general oblique ending -(e)n, e.g. *dem Boten* '(to) the messenger', *dem Bären* '(to) the bear'. As stated above feminines have no case-endings in the singular.

The dative case is used in German chiefly to indicate (1) the indirect object of a verb of giving something to someone or taking something from someone, e.g. *ich gebe dem Mann das Buch*, *ich gebe ihm das Buch*, *ich gebe der Frau Geld* 'I give the woman money, I give money to the woman'; (2) the sole object of certain verbs such as those of serving or obeying or the like (see below), e.g. *der Schüler gehorcht dem Lehrer (der Lehrerin)* 'the pupil obeys the teacher'; (3) the complement of certain prepositions like *mit* 'with', *zu* 'to', *von* 'of, from, by', etc., (see below), e.g. *mit dem Hammer* (from *der Hammer*), *mit dem Messer* (from *das Messer*) 'with the knife', *zu der Universität* 'to the University (building)' (*die Universität*), *von der Stadt* 'from the town' (*die Stadt*). Details of all these constructions are given under the chapters on the verb and the preposition.

Definite and indefinite articles

As shown above the definite article has three genders *der*, *die*, *das*. For the indefinite article 'a' or 'an' the forms are *EIN* (masc.), *EINE* (fem.) and *EIN* (neuter), e.g. *ein Mann*, *eine Frau*, *ein Haus*, cf. also the negative article for 'no' or 'not any', *KEIN Mann*, *KEINE Frau*, *KEIN Haus*. The only difference between the masculine and neuter of *ein* and *kein* is the case-distinction which the masculine makes between the case of the subject (*ein*) and the direct object (*einen*), the neuter *ein* and *kein* remaining unchanged.

There are certain divergences as between the English and German uses of the articles which may be summarized as follows:

(1) Definite article in German, no article in English:

(a) Universality or generality: *der Mensch* 'man', *die Menschen*, *die Leute* 'people'; *die Menschheit* 'humanity'; *die Ereignisse* 'events'; *die Natur* 'nature'; *die Vorsehung* 'Providence'; *der Himmel* 'heaven'; *die Hölle* 'hell'; *das Paradies* 'paradise'; *das Fegefeuer* 'purgatory'; *das Leben* 'life', *der Tod* 'death'; *die Zeit* 'time'; *die Ewigkeit* 'eternity'; *das Schicksal* 'fate'; *das Glück* 'fortune'; *die Geschichte* 'history'; *das Altertum* 'antiquity';

die Wissenschaft 'science', 'scholarship'; *die Kunst* 'art'; *der Ackerbau* 'agriculture'; *die Sitte* 'custom, etc.'

(b) Parts of the day, meals, periods, etc., e.g. *der Tag* 'day'; *die Nacht* 'night' (but *Tag und Nacht* 'day and night'); *das Frühstück* 'breakfast', *das Mittagessen* 'lunch', *der Kaffee* (cf. 'tea'), *das Abendessen* 'supper'; *das Semester* 'term'; *die Pause* 'break'. However, German—unlike English—omits the article in *Anfang Juli* 'at the beginning of July', *Mitte August* 'in the middle of August', *Ende September*, etc.

(c) Where in English we say 'school has begun', 'church is over', 'prison is hard', 'hospital' or 'bed is the place for him', or 'go to town', German must use respectively *die Schule, die Kirche, das Gefängnis, das Krankenhaus, das Bett, die Stadt*.

(d) For 'Parliament' and 'Congress' German must always say *das Parlament* and *der Kongreß*.

(e) For 'Nurse' and 'Cook'—sometimes used in English without article—German says *die Schwester*, (*das Fräulein*), *die Köchin*.

(2) Definite article in German, but indefinite in English. English says 'so and so much a pound' in the distributive sense, but German says, e.g. *zwei Mark das Pfund, fünfzig Pfennig das Stück* 'apiece, each'.

(3) In cases where English uses 'a pair of -s', the simple indefinite article is used in German, e.g. *eine Zange* 'a pair of tongs', *eine Brille* 'a pair of spectacles', *eine Schere* 'a pair of scissors', *eine Hose* 'a pair of trousers', *ein Blasebalg* 'a pair of bellows'.

(4) In a few cases English has to use a phrase with 'a' or 'an', where German has the simple indefinite article, e.g. *ein Glück* 'a piece (or stroke) of luck', *eine Nachricht* 'an item of news' or—as in French—*eine heftige Grippe* 'a severe bout of flu'.

(5) In a descriptive group with 'of' English omits the article where German requires an indefinite article, e.g. *der Posten eines Kurators* 'the post of curator', *der Rang eines Majors* 'the rank of major', the phrase in German being in the genitive case.

(6) Where English uses the indefinite article of a person's nationality, rank or profession German omits the article altogether, e.g. *er ist Engländer*[1] (*Franzose, Deutscher, Russe*); *sie ist Engländerin* (*Französin, Deutsche, Russin*); *der Mann war Offizier* (*Boxer, Fußballspieler*); *die Frau ist Schneiderin* 'a dressmaker'; *er*

---

[1] Note that German does not employ the adjective as English does in 'she is French', etc., but the noun. Of religion it is permissible to say either *er ist katholisch* (*protestantisch, evangelisch*) or *er ist Katholik, Protestant*, etc.

ist ein Kunstfreund 'a connoisseur of art', *ein Musikfreund* 'fond of music', *jugendlicher Liebhaber* 'young lover (in a play)'; (*er ist*) *Bierbrauer* 'a brewer'/*ein Biertrinker*, (*er ist*) *Schauspieler* 'an actor'/*ein Schauspieler* (in behaviour). If the noun has an adjective the article must be used, e.g. *er ist ein guter (starker) Esser* 'he is a good (big) eater', *ein starker Trinker* 'a heavy drinker', *ein schwacher Esser* 'a poor eater', etc.

3

THE ADJECTIVE – STRONG AND WEAK

DECLENSION – GRADING – COMPARISON

Adjectives

Adjectives are either (1) simple, e.g. *gut/schlecht, gross/klein, lang/kurz, dick/dünn, alt/jung,* etc., or (2) derived by means of suffixes of which the commonest are *-ig,* e.g. *grasig* 'grassy', *felsig* 'rocky'; *-lich* in *sportlich* 'sporting' and *-bar* e.g. *tragbar* 'portable', *heizbar* 'heatable', etc., or (3) compounds, which sometimes have as first component a noun indicating the object compared, e.g. *grasgrün* 'grass-green', *schneeweiß* 'snow-white', *hundemüde* 'dog-tired', or the object placed in relation with a quality, e.g. *feuerfest* 'fire-proof'. (For further details see chapter on Word-formation.)

Adjectives forming the complement of verbs of being, becoming or continuing have no case, gender or number ending, e.g. *der Mann is alt, er wird alt* 'he is getting old'.

Strong and weak declension

(1) When the adjective is used before a noun without any article or demonstrative (*this, that*), or indefinite (*any*), preceding it, it takes the endings of the definite article. This is the so-called 'strong' declension of the adjective, but a better term would be 'pronominal'. Thus the masculine word for 'wine' preceded by the adjective 'good', namely 'good wine' has the following declension.

Nominative: *GutER Wein* (*ist teuer*) 'good wine (is dear)',

Accusative: (*er trinkt*) *GutEN Wein* '(he drinks) good wine',

Dative: (*mit*) *GutEM Wein* '(with) good wine',

when the endings are like *DER, DEN, DEM.* The genitive, however, has *-EN,* e.g. (*ein Glas*) *guten Weines.*

Feminine: Nominative *warmE Milch* 'hot milk'.

Accusative (*er trinkt*): *warmE Milch* '(he drinks) hot milk'.

Genitive (*ein Glas*): *warmER Milch* '(a glass) of hot milk'.

Dative (*mit*): *warmER Milch* '(with) hot milk'.

Cf. *DIE, DIE, DER* (gen.), *DER* (dat.).

Neuter: *kaltES Wasser* 'cold water'.

(*er trinkt*): *kaltES Wasser* '(he drinks) cold water'.

(*ein Glas*): *kaltEN Wassers*, cf. masculine above.[1]

(*mit*): *kaltEM Wasser* '(with) cold water'.

(2) If the adjective is preceded by the indefinite article (*EIN, KEIN*) or the possessive adjectives, namely *MEIN* 'my', *DEIN* 'thy, your (fam.)', *SEIN* 'his, its', *IHR* 'her, its'; *UNSER* 'our', *EUER* 'your (familiar plural)', *IHR* (with capital I) 'your (polite singular or plural)', *IHR* 'their', it takes the same endings as in (1) in the nominative and accusative singular,

e.g. (masc.) *ein gutER Mann* (nom.)

einEN gutEN Mann (acc.)

(fem.) *eine gutE Frau* (nom. and acc.)

(neuter) *ein gutES Haus* (nom. and acc.).

In all other cases, both singular and plural, the adjective takes the ending *-EN*, e.g. *meinEM gutEN Mann* (dat.), *meinER gutEN Frau* (gen. or dat.) *in meinEM altEN Haus* (dat.) etc.

(3) If the adjective is preceded by the definite article or by the demonstratives (*DIESER* 'this', *JENER* 'that') or *JEDER* 'each', it is declined 'weak' i.e. with the ending *-e* in the nom. sing. masc., nom. and acc. sing. fem. and nom. and acc. sing. neuter, all the other cases having—as in (2)—the ending *-EN*. Thus *DER gutE Mann, DIE gutE Frau, DAS gutE Haus*; in *DEM gutEN Haus, von DER gutEN Frau*, etc.

In the nominative and accusative plural *alle* 'all' takes the weak or *-en* form, e.g. *alle guten Männer*. Adjectives for indefinite numbers like 'some', 'many', 'several', 'few' have the strong form of the adjective, e.g. *einige gute Männer* 'some good men', *viele gute Männer* 'many . . .', *mehrere gute Männer* 'several . . .', *etliche gute Männer* 'some few . . .', *wenige gute Männer* 'few . . .'.

When the adjective in English is used independently it is pro-

---

[1] In literary German the *-EN* genitive without the article appears in a number of set phrases, e.g. *trockenen Fußes* 'dry shod', *allen Ernstes* 'in all seriousness', *wachen Auges* 'with watchful eye'.

vided with the supporting word 'one', e.g. 'a good one', 'the good one', 'good ones'. In German the inflexion of the adjective enables it to be used independently without further support, e.g. 'a good one' referring to a masculine word like *der Hut* is *ein guter*, 'the good one' is *der gute*, plural *gute, die guten*. The masculine and feminine when not referring back to a particular noun imply a person, e.g. *der Kluge* 'the clever man', *der Reisende* 'the traveller', *ein Reisender* 'a traveller'/*die Reisenden* (pl.), *Reisende* (pl.); *der Beamte* 'the official', *ein Beamter*/*die Beamten, Beamte*. When the neuter definite article is used with the weak form of the isolated adjective, the meaning is usually that of the universal abstract, e.g. *das Gute, das Wahre, das Schöne* 'the good, the true, the beautiful'. Sometimes, however, this use has as its equivalent in English 'the (adjective) thing' e.g. *das Dumme (an der Sache)* 'the stupid thing (about the business)'. The adjective is not inflected in some foreign colour-names like *rosa* 'pink', *lila, beige* and in *groß A, römisch Eins*, etc.

The adjective may have its application modified by particles or phrases like *ganz [gut]* 'quite [good]', *sehr [gut]* 'very [good]' and the superlative forms *höchst, äußerst* and the like treated below under comparison. The English 'fairly' indicating a satisfactory, though relatively low grade is in German *ziemlich* with some stress, e.g. *ich kenne ihn 'ziemlich gut* 'I know him 'fairly well'. If *ziemlich* is unstressed, it conveys the sense of English 'rather', i.e. a higher degree than expected, e.g. *ich bin ziemlich 'müde* 'I'm rather 'tired', cf. *es geht ihm etwas 'besser* 'he's rather (somewhat) better', *ich bin ein bißchen müde* 'rather (just a bit) tired', *verhältnismäßig groß für sein Alter* 'rather (relatively) big for his age'. The still higher degree in the medium scale expressed by 'pretty' may be rendered in various ways, e.g. *die Aussichten waren reichlich düster* 'the prospects were pretty grim', *so ziemlich dasselbe* 'pretty much the same', *eine ziemlich gute Vorstellung* 'a pretty shrewd idea', *eine ziemliche Gemeinheit* 'a pretty mean trick'. The equivalent of 'practically' is either *praktisch* or *so gut wie* 'as good as', e.g. *so gut wie fertig* 'practically finished'. The approximation to a goal is indicated in English by 'nearly' or 'almost' and in German by *beinahe* or *fast*, e.g. *fast unmöglich* 'almost impossible'. The English 'scarcely' or 'hardly' is rendered by *kaum*, e.g. *kaum möglich* 'hardly possible'. The word 'barely' is usually accompanied by a numerical expression or a verb, e.g. *knapp zwei hundert* 'barely two hundred'.

There is a class of compound adjectives in which the first component serves to intensify the meaning of the second, cf. in English 'pitch-dark'. In spoken North German the following are prevalent today; *pechschwarz* 'pitch-black', *stocksteif* 'as stiff as a poker', *stocktaub* 'stone-deaf', *jammerschade* 'a thousand pities', *hundeelend* 'like nothing on earth', *hundemüde* 'dog tired', *erzdumm* 'awfully stupid', *splitternackt* 'stripped to the skin', *sperrangelweit* 'wide open', *funkelnagelneu* 'brand new'. There are also substantives like *die Bärenkälte* 'freezing cold', *einen Bärenhunger haben* 'to be ravenous' (also *Wolfshunger*), *Hundewetter* 'filthy weather', etc.

Compounds with *blut-*, e.g. *blutarm*, *blutjung* and *blutwenig*, or with *kreuz-*, have rather gone out of fashion in speech. The modern spoken language has a great variety of intensifiers, of which the following are typical, but by no means exhaustive: *völlig* [*blind*] 'completely [blind]', *furchtbar* [*klein*] 'awfully [small]', *entsetzlich* [*unhöflich*] 'abominably [rude]', *scheußlich* or *gräßlich* [*kalt*] 'atrociously [cold]', *wahnsinnig* (*unglaublich*) [*reich*] 'incredibly [rich]', *ungeheuer* (*namenlos*) [*billig*] 'extremely [cheap]—cf. *spottbillig* 'dirt cheap' now out of vogue—*masslos* [*dumm*] 'enormously [stupid]', *riesig* [*nett*] 'extremely nice', *hundertprozentig* [*sicher*] '100 per cent [sure]', *außerordentlich* (*ungewöhnlich*) [*groß*] 'extraordinarily (uncommonly) [big]', *ordentlich* [*erschrocken*] 'properly [frightened]'.

A peculiar type of qualifier is the English 'nice and ...' e.g. in '[keep] nice and warm' of which the German equivalent is [*halte dich*] *schön warm*, cf. *sei schön ruhig* 'be nice and quiet' (when talking to a child). In some parts of Germany *hübsch* and *fein* are used in such phrases, but not in current speech in Hamburg.

Not only adjectives, but also substantives can be intensified, e.g. *eine Affenschande* 'a crying shame', *eine Affenhitze* (*Bärenhitze*) 'infernal (tropical) heat', *ich habe einen Wolfshunger*, cf. 'I am as hungry as a hunter'.

With words like *alt* 'old', *jung* 'young', temporal expressions and numerals adverbs implying a relation to a goal or limit are often combined, e.g. *schon* [*zwei Jahre*] *alt* 'already [two years] old', *noch jung* 'still young', *erst zwei Jahre alt* 'only two years old' (i.e. *noch nicht drei* 'not yet three').

Comparison

Like English German forms a comparative degree in *-er* and a superlative degree in *-est*. Monosyllabic adjectives like *alt* 'old', *jung* 'young', *groß* 'big', *lang* 'long', *kurz* 'short' mutate the vowel, e.g. in *älter* (cf. English elder), *jünger, größer, länger, kürzer* and superlative *der, die, das älteste, jüngste, größte* (not *größeste!*), *längste, kürzeste*. There are, however, some which do not mutate, e.g. *froher* 'gladder', *stolzer* 'prouder', *voller* 'fuller', *schlauer* 'more astute'. The adjective *hoch* 'high' has comparative *höher*, but superlative [*der*] *höchste*, cf. *nah* 'near', *näher*, but [*der*] *nächste*. German uses the endings *-er* and *-est* even after a word of several syllables where English uses 'more' and 'most', e.g. *eleganter* 'more elegant', *entschiedener* 'more decided', etc. However, *meist* is often used before a past participle, e.g. *das meist gelesene Buch* 'the most read book'.

The superlative of the adjective has two principal forms, one with the definite article, e.g. *er ist der älteste von uns allen* 'he is the oldest of us all', *eine der bedeutendsten Erfindungen aller Zeiten* 'one of the most significant inventions of all time,' and one with *am -sten* when there is a specific comparison, e.g. *dieser Berg ist hoch, der Berg da ist höher und der da drüben ist am höchsten*, '[the] highest'. The latter form is also used adverbially, e.g. *er arbeitet am fleißigsten* 'he works hardest', and in a comparison between different grades of quality in the same object, e.g. *hier ist das Wasser am tiefsten* 'here the water is [at its] deepest'.

When the comparison is made between *two* adjectives the comparative of the first is expressed by *mehr* 'more' (or *weniger* 'less'), e.g. *mehr lang als breit* 'more long than broad', *weniger hoch als breit* 'less high than broad'.

The superlative 'least' + adjective is always indicated by *am wenigsten*, e.g. *von allen ist er am wenigsten fleißig* 'he is the least hard-working of all'.

Some adjectives and adverbs form their comparatives and superlatives from other stems, e.g. *gut, wohl* 'well'/*besser*/*best, am besten*; *viel* 'much'/*mehr* 'more'/*meist*,[1] *am meisten* 'most'; *wenig* 'little'/*weniger*, *minder* 'less'/*mindest*, etc., 'least'; *bald* 'soon'/*eher* 'sooner'/*baldigst* 'as soon as possible'; *gern* 'gladly, willingly'/*lieber* 'rather, preferably'/*am liebsten* 'most gladly'. (Note that the comparative of *ungern* is rendered by *weniger gern* 'less willingly'.)

Occasionally the comparative form in *-er* is used as an

[1] Note *die meiste Zeit* 'most of the time', *die meisten Studenten* 'most students'.

extenuating form, e.g. *ein älterer Herr* 'an elderly gentleman' where *älter* implies 'not so young'. In advertisements *besser*, e.g. *bessere* [*Apotheken*] implies 'superior [chemists shops]'. A phrase like *ein längerer Aufenthalt* 'a longish stay' is literary rather than colloquial. The adverbial *öfters* is frequent in speech for the simple *oft*, and has a rival in the more official *des öfteren* 'pretty often'. English often uses a positive adjective for the German comparative, e.g. *bei näherem Zusehen* 'on close(r) inspection', *die neuere Literatur* 'modern literature', *das Nähere* 'details', etc.

The comparative can be reinforced as in English by such particles as *etwas* [*älter*] 'somewhat [older']', *viel* [*besser*] 'much [better]', *weit* [*höher*] 'far [higher]', *noch* [*größer*] 'still [bigger]', *bedeutend* [*schwerer*] 'considerably [heavier]', *unendlich viel* [*reicher*] 'infinitely [richer]', *unvergleichlich* [*besser*] 'incomparably [better]', *noch viel* [*klüger*] 'ever so much [cleverer]'. The English phrase 'all the —er' is rendered by *um so* [*besser*] or *desto* [*besser*].

For the superlative used 'absolutely', i.e. without any manifest comparison the literary expression is sometimes *aufs* + superlative, e.g. *aufs beste, aufs schönste, das Problem hat uns aufs stärkste beschäftigt* 'we have been most intensely pre-occupied with that problem'. In the spoken language the normal expression for 'in the best way' is *auf die beste Weise* or *so gut* [*man*] *kann*. In many cases the uninflected form of the superlative is used, e.g. *baldigst* 'as soon as possible', *meist* (*meistens*) 'mostly', *möglichst* [*schnell*] 'as [quickly] as possible, *ein möglichst großes Stück* 'as big a piece as possible'. More idiomatic are *noch längst kein Grund* 'very far from being a reason', *gefälligst* 'if you please' (insistently) in *willst du das wohl gefälligst lassen?* 'will you please stop that?' and the expression of highest degree like *höchst erfreut* 'highly delighted', *äußerst unangenehm* 'extremely unpleasant'. Other examples are *das bestrenommierte Geschäft* 'the business with the best reputation', *die schlechtest bezahlten Arbeiten* 'the most poorly paid jobs', *die meist gelesenen Bücher* 'the most read books', *die wenigst häufigen Fälle* 'the least frequent (most infrequent) cases', *die mindest kräftigen Einschläge* 'the least vigorous strains'. In some cases like *die dichtest bevölkerte Gegend* 'the most densely populated region', the spoken form is preferably *am dichtesten*. To be noted are the modern compounds *der Höchstpreis* 'maximum price' and *der Mindestlohn* 'minimum wage', also phrases like *die denkbar schwerste Aufgabe* 'the hardest task imaginable'.

In some cases—as with the ordinal numerals—(e.g. *zweitens*

'secondly', etc.)—a suffix *-ens* is added to the superlative, e.g. *frühestens* [*um drei*] 'at earliest', *spätestens* 'at latest', *höchstens* [*zwei Kilometer*] 'at most', *'danke bestens*[1] 'thanks very much'. Note the subtle distinction between the superlatives for '(at) least' in the sentences *zum mindesten hatte ich ja erwartet, daß wenigstens Hans mitkommen würde* 'at the very least I had expected that Hans at least would join us' and *am wenigsten hatte ich erwartet, daß* . . . 'least of all had I expected . . .'. Often *wenigstens* and *mindestens* are near synonyms.

The superlatives of local expressions like 'upper' prefix *zu-*, e.g. *die Hemden kommen zuoberst und die Strümpfe zu unterst* 'the shirts come on top (cf. uppermost) and the stockings at the bottom (cf. undermost)'. There is also the phrase *ich bin zutiefst erstaunt* (*deprimiert*) 'I am most deeply surprised (depressed)'. Where, however, the literary language would use *zuvorderst* for 'right in front', speech prefers *ganz vorne*, cf. *ganz hinten* 'right behind' and often uses a phrase with *am weitesten*, e.g. *am weitesten* [*nach*] *oben* 'furthest up', cf. the comparative *weiter hinein* 'further in'. With 'left' and 'right' it is possible to use *mehr* and *am meisten*, e.g. *mehr links* 'more to the left', *am meisten links* 'furthest to the left', but it is also possible to say *weiter* [*nach*] *links* and *am weitesten nach links*.

Adjective-adverbs

The uninflected adjective is used in an adverbial function like English *-ly*, e.g. *schwer verwundet* 'severely wounded', *eng verbunden* 'closely connected', etc. Inversely some German independent adverbs form adjectives in *-ig*, e.g. *heutig* 'today's', *dortig* (*dort* 'there').

Adverbs as predicates

As in English—though less frequently—German uses adverbs as the predicate complement of the verb 'to be', e.g. *das Gas ist an* (=*brennt*) 'the gas is on', *er war früh auf* 'he was up early', *es ist aus mit der Verlobung* 'the engagement is off', *das Theater ist aus* 'the play is over', *die Zeit ist um* 'the time is up', *er ist sehr herunter* 'he is feeling pretty down'.

---

[1] Note *bestenfalls, im günstigsten Falle* 'at best' and *auf der Höhe* 'at [one's] best'.

4

THE PERSONAL PRONOUNS – POSSESSIVES –

INTERROGATIVES – DEMONSTRATIVES

Personal pronouns

The first person singular, i.e. the actual speaker is *ich*, which is written with a small *i* in contrast with English. The first person plural is *wir* 'we' which as in English may imply either 'I and you' or 'I and he, she or they'. As in English editors of newspapers and rulers in their proclamations use *wir* with singular reference. Sometimes it is used condescendingly to an individual, e.g. *na, wie geht's uns heute, Fräulein B?* 'well, how are we today, Miss B.?'

The second person singular and plural comprises several words. The most useful pronoun for foreigners while still on a formal footing with Germans is the polite *Sie* always written with a capital letter and like English 'you' standing for both singular and plural. It is incidentally the easiest to use for its verb always has the ending *-en*. The pronoun *du* which has its verb in the *-(e)st* form is in origin the same as English 'thou' and like the latter is used in the Bible and in prayers, e.g. *Unser Vater, der du bist im Himmel* 'our Father, who art in Heaven' and *du sollst nicht stehlen* 'thou shalt not steal'. Unlike, however, modern English 'thou', the German *du* is also used as the familiar and intimate pronoun. It is used by adults when talking to children say under fifteen, also by children talking to relatives and by near-relatives among themselves, by friends male or female who have agreed to be on a more intimate footing and by both young and old in talking to animals. In schools the teacher uses *du* until the children at the age of fifteen or sixteen pass into the upper grade. In letter-writing *Du* and its cases and the possessive *Dein* begin with a capital letter. The plural of *du* is *ihr* which always refers to more than one. Its verbal ending is -(e)t, e.g. *ihr singt*. It is used in military commands, e.g. *rührt euch* 'stand at ease'.

The third person singular is in three genders: *er* 'he, it (of masculine nouns)', *sie* 'she, it (of feminine nouns)' and *es* 'it'. The word *es* may refer to a neuter noun like *Mädchen* or *Fräulein* which designates females, but if the pronoun is not in the immediate neighbourhood of the noun 'it' is often replaced by 'she' (*sie*). As in English 'it' is used as grammatical subject of so-called impersonal verbs, e.g. of climatic conditions like *es regnet* 'it is raining', *es friert* 'it is freezing', etc. As in English, too, *es* is frequently used as an anticipatory subject in the equivalents of such phrases as 'it is necessary (to do so)'. German *es ist nötig . . .* or 'it occurs to me that . . .' *es fällt mir ein, daß . . .* German often uses *es* where English prefers the personal subject 'I' 'you', etc. *es tut mir leid*, e.g. 'it causes me regret' 'I am sorry', *es gefällt mir* 'it pleases me', 'I like it'; *es gelingt mir*—lit. 'it prospers to me', 'I succeed in it', *es wundert mich*—lit. 'it marvels me, I wonder at it'. Sometimes when the subject designated by *es* is vague and unspecifiable it is rendered in English by 'there', e.g. *es klopft* 'there is a knock at the door'; *es klingelt* 'there is a ring at the bell'. The English 'there is'/'there are' is rendered by *es gibt* with singular or plural noun following or by *es ist* + singular and *es sind* + plural. The difference between *es gibt* and *es ist/sind* lies in the contrast between generality and particularity. Thus we should say for 'there is retribution (much misery) in life' *es gibt eine Vergeltung (viel Elend) im Leben*; 'what news is there?' *was gibt's Neues?*; 'what is there for (dinner) today?' *was gibt's heute?*; 'there are such people', *es gibt solche Menschen*; 'there are lions in Africa but not in Europe' *es gibt Löwen in Afrika, aber nicht in Europa*. On the other hand, 'there are white elephants in this menagerie' *es sind weiße Elefanten in dieser Menagerie* or 'there have been a lot of people here' *es sind viele hier gewesen*. Occasionally 'there is' + abstract is rendered in German by *es besteht* (lit. 'there exists'), e.g. *es besteht die Möglichkeit* 'there is a possibility'. As the object of certain verbs *es* corresponds to the English *so*, e.g. *er hofft es* 'he hopes so', *er glaubt es* 'he thinks so, believes so', *er sagt es* 'he says so', *er tut es* 'he does so'. The German *ich weiß es* corresponds to the English 'I know' (with object omitted). The *es* is not always compulsory in German, e.g. *ich glaube, ich glaube es* 'I believe so'.

The third person plural *sie* 'they' has no gender distinctions. In this respect it is unlike the Romance languages, e.g. Fr. *ils/elles*.

There is an indefinite personal pronoun *man* 'one' which often corresponds to English 'we', 'you', 'they', 'people' or the use of the passive, e.g. *man sagt* 'they say' 'it is said'.

The accusative case in the singular is indicated by the forms *mich* 'me', *dich* 'you' (familiar), *ihn* 'him', (*sie* 'her' and *es* 'it' as the nominative). In the plural the forms are *uns* 'us', *euch* 'you' (familiar plural), *Sie* 'you' (polite singular and plural), *sie* 'them'. There is also a reflexive pronoun *sich* without distinction of gender or number for 'himself', 'herself', 'itself', and 'themselves'. The indefinite *man* has accusative *einen*, dative *einem* and reflexive *sich*.

The accusative of the pronouns is used just as in nouns (1) as direct object of a verb, e.g. *er lobt mich* 'he praises me', *ich lobe ihn* 'I praise him'; (2) after certain prepositions, e.g. *durch mich* 'through me', *ohne Sie* 'without you'. The reflexive accusative *sich* is exemplified by *er lobt sich* 'he praises himself', *sie lobt sich* 'she praises herself', *sie loben sich* 'they praise themselves'. In the other persons the reflexive is indicated by the accusatives *mich*, *dich*, *uns*, *euch*, and the originally third person *sich* for the polite form 'yourself, yourselves'. Examples: *ich wasche mich* 'I wash myself', *wir waschen uns* 'we wash ourselves', *Sie waschen sich* 'you wash yourself and *sie waschen sich* 'they wash themselves'. Many verbs in German are reflexive in cases where English uses the simple verb, e.g. *ich freue mich* 'I rejoice', *ich beeile mich* 'I hurry'.

The personal pronouns can be reinforced in English by 'myself', 'yourself' etc. and in German by the simple uninflected *selbst* or *selber*. As in English, these words may either follow directly upon the pronoun, e.g. *ich selbst* 'I myself' or come after the verb *ich kam selbst* 'I came myself'. Where English uses 'myself' etc. as mere reflexives, e.g. 'I wash myself' German uses the simple pronouns *mich* etc., unless there is special emphasis, e.g. *ich werfe es mir selbst vor* 'I reproach myself (i.e. not anyone else)'. If *selbst* precedes the pronoun (or other part of speech) it bears like the French *même* the meaning of 'even', e.g. *selbst ich* 'even I'.

The accusative (and dative) case of the plural personal pronouns, namely *uns*, *euch* and *sich* can be used in a 'reciprocal' sense like 'each other' or 'one another', e.g. *wir duellieren uns*, *sie duellieren sich* 'we (they) fight a duel (with each other)';

sie sehen sich jeden Tag 'they see each other every day' (with the same form as *sie sehen sich im Spiegel* 'they see themselves in the looking-glass'); *sie begegneten sich* (dative) 'they met (each other)'. The more specific expression of reciprocity is *einander* which could have been used, e.g. in the last sentence. It is used in close connexion with a preposition, e.g. *sie gerieten aneinander* (*sie gerieten einander in die Haare*) 'they came to blows'; *sie standen nebeneinander* 'they were standing next to each other'. In the genitive *ein* and *ander* are declined separately e.g. *sie schworen, einer des andern Tod zu rächen* 'they swore to avenge each other's death'.

The genitive of the pronouns is rare in the spoken language. The forms are *meiner* 'of me', *deiner* 'of thee', *seiner* 'of him' *ihrer* 'of her', *unser* 'of us', *euer* 'of you' (fam. pl.), *Ihrer* 'of you' (polite sing. and plural), *ihrer* 'of them'. The genitive of *es* is supplied by the demonstrative *dessen* lit. 'of that'.

The ancient genitive *es* survives only in a few fixed phrases, e.g. *ich bin es satt* 'I am sick of it', *ich bin es müde* 'I am tired of it' and *ich bin es zufrieden* 'I am satisfied with it'. In literature there occur instances of the genitive with certain verbs, e.g. *ich gedenke seiner* 'I am mindful of him' and *er gedenkt meiner* 'he is mindful of me', *ich schäme mich dessen* 'I am ashamed of it'.

The dative has in the singular the forms *mir, dir, ihm*, '[to] him', *ihr* '[to] her', *uns* '[to] us', *euch* '[to] you' (fam.), *Ihnen* '[to] you' (polite sing. and pl.), *ihnen* '[to] them'. The reflexive *sich*—originally an accusative form like *mich, dich*, etc.—is used also as a dative in the sense of '[to] himself, herself, itself, yourself' (polite), 'yourselves' (polite), 'themselves'. The dative of *es* is the demonstrative *dem*. The dative of *man* is supplied by *einem*. As in the noun so in the pronoun the dative case is used (1) as the object of certain verbs like 'serve', 'obey', e.g. *ich diene ihm* 'I am of service to him', *er gehorcht mir* 'he obeys me' (cf. French *servir à* and *obéir à*), (2) as the indirect object of verbs meaning 'giving' or 'taking' and the like, e.g. *ich gebe es ihm* 'I give it to him', *ich sage es ihr* 'I say it to her', *ich nehme es Ihnen* 'I take it from you'. With a noun as direct object the indirect object precedes, e.g. *ich gebe ihm das Buch* 'I give him the book'; (3) after certain prepositions, e.g. *mit mir* 'with me', *zu dir* 'to you' (familiar), *neben ihm* 'beside him', *unter uns* '(between us (ourselves)' *zwischen ihnen* 'between them', *ich komme zu mir* 'I come to myself', *er kommt zu sich* 'he comes to himself'.

Possessive adjectives and pronouns

The possessive adjectives meaning 'my', 'your', 'his', 'our', etc., are declined like *ein* or *kein* when they stand before a noun or noun-group. They are *mein* 'my', *dein* 'thy, your' (fam.), *sein* 'his', *ihr* 'her'; *unser* 'our', *euer* 'your' (plur. fam.), *Ihr* 'your' (polite sg. and pl.), *ihr* 'their'. Examples are *mein Vater, meine Mutter, mein Haus, unser Vater, ihre Mutter*. Note that the masculine when used as an adjective with the noun never takes the ending *-er*, thus *mein* not *meiner*. The *-er* of *unser, euer* is not a nominative ending but part of the possessive stem like *-r* in 'our', 'your'. The possessive form for 'its' is usually *dessen* if it refers to a masculine noun and *deren* if to a feminine noun. *Deren* can also be used for 'their' referring to inanimate objects. The possessive 'one's' is the same as 'his', namely *sein*, but only when referring back to a previously expressed *man*. If 'one's' is the subject German uses *jemandes*.

When used independently or non-attributively the possessives have in English the specific forms 'mine', 'hers', 'ours', 'yours', 'theirs', the forms 'his' and 'its' remaining unchanged. German has three ways of indicating the independent possessive: (1) the use of inflected *meiner/meine/meines* pl. *meine*, cf. *unserer/unsere/unseres* pl. *unsere*; (2) *der meine/die meine/das meine//die meinen*, etc.; (3) *der meinige/die meinige/das meinige//die meinigen*, etc., cf. *der unsrige*, etc. In the spoken language the most prevalent forms are those cited in (1), e.g. *sein Bleistift ist länger als meiner* 'his pencil is longer than mine', *Ihre Ohren sind nicht so groß als meine* 'your ears are not as big as mine'. Where English indicates the fact of possession by 'it is mine', etc., spoken German prefers *es gehört mir* 'it belongs to me'.

The possessive adjectives can be reinforced in English by 'own' and in German by *eigen*, e.g. *mein eigenes Haus* 'my own house'. Unlike English German can use *eigen* alone, e.g. *auf eigene Faust* 'on one's own', *in eigener Sache* 'on one's own behalf', *wir haben nichts Eigenes* 'we have nothing of our own'.

Interrogatives

The question WHO? is asked by *wer* in German for both genders and (as a predicate) for both numbers, e.g. *wer ist da?* 'who is there?', *wer seid ihr?* 'who are you' (pl.)?. German can use *wer* like the English 'who' in such phrases as 'who are the Schmidts anyhow?' i.e. *wer 'sind die Schmidts denn schon?*

The accusative WHO(M)? is in German *wen?* and is either the direct object of the verb, e.g. *wen sehen Sie?* 'who[m] can you see?' or the object of certain prepositions. In English we can say both 'who are you thinking of?' or 'of whom are you thinking?', but in German the preposition must precede, e.g. *an wen denken Sie?*

The genitive WHOSE? is in German *wessen?*, e.g. *wessen Haus?* 'whose house?'. If we say 'whose is that house?' or 'whose house is that?' it is more usual in North German to say *wem gehört [das Haus]?* i.e. 'to whom does this house belong?'.

The dative (TO) WHOM? is in German *wem?* and is used as the indirect object, e.g. *wem geben Sie das Buch?* 'who are you giving the book to?' or 'to whom are you giving the book?' or after certain prepositions, e.g. *mit wem sprechen Sie?* 'who are you talking to (conversing with)?', *von wem sprechen Sie?* 'who are you talking about?'

The neuter interrogative equivalent to English WHAT? is in German *was?*, which is both singular and plural and remains the same in both nominative and accusative, e.g. *was ist das?* 'what is that?', *was kostet das?* 'what does that cost?', *was bedeutet das Wort?* 'what does the word mean?', *was sind die Vorteile und Nachteile ...?* 'what are the advantages and disadvantages ...?', *was ist sein Vater?* '(of) what (profession) is his father?'. With a preposition German often employs a compound form of the same type as English 'wherewith', 'whereto', etc. the German equivalent *womit*, *wozu* belonging to the spoken as well as the written language. Occasionally, however, especially in the colloquial a preposition may be followed by *was*, e.g. *um was bittet er?* 'what is he asking for?', *für was hält er sich?* 'what does he think he is?', *auf was ist er aus?* 'what is he up to?'. Examples of WO-compounds are: *wozu dient es?* 'what is it used for?' (lit. whereto does it serve?), *worüber sprechen Sie?* 'what are you talking about?', *woran erkannt man ihn?* 'what does one recognize him by?', *womit kann ich dienen?* often used in a shop for 'what can I do for you?'.

The German *was für* has become stereotyped in the sense 'of what kind of ...?' 'what sort of ...?' or simply 'what ...?' Thus *was für ein Mann?* (nominative, not accusative!) 'what sort of man?', *was für einen Mann sehen sie?*, *was für Leute?* 'what sort of people?', *was für welche?* 'what kinds?'. The phrase *was für?* can be used with a preposition, e.g. *in was für einer Stadt?* (the preposition taking its appropriate case) 'in what sort of town?'.

The German stem *welch-* is declined like a strong adjective,
i.e. with the endings of the definite article: nom. *welcher/welche/
welches*; masc. acc. *welchen*; masc. and neuter gen. *welches* and
fem. sing. *welcher*; masc. and neuter dative *welchem* and fem.
welcher; plural (all genders) nom. acc. *welche*, gen. *welcher*, dat.
welchen. Occasionally the uninflected form *welch* occurs either for
the neuter *welches* in the question *welch ist* ...? 'which is ...?'
and in exclamations for 'what a ...', but *welches Glück!* is the
usual form for 'what luck!' (note *wie schade!* for 'what a pity!').
The German forms *welcher* etc. correspond to (1) 'which' in a
question asking for a selection to be made within a limited set and
(2) 'what' asking for a description or characterization. Occasionally
was für is equivalent, but with a slightly different nuance, e.g.
welchen Sport treiben Sie? 'which of the various sports do you go
in for?' *was für Sport treiben Sie?* 'what sort of sports ...?' The
following phrases with *welch-* are of practical utility: *welche
Marke?* 'what brand (make)?', *welche [Kragen] nummer?* 'what
size [collar]?', *welcher Unterschied besteht zwischen A und B?*
'what difference is there between A and B?', *welche Art von Film?*
'what kind (type) of film?', *welche Wirkung?* 'what effect?',
welchen Zweck hat ...?, 'what is the purpose (point) of ...?',
welcher Prozentsatz? 'what percentage?', *welcher Nationalität ist
er?* (gen. case) 'of what nationality is he?'. There are many instances
of prepositions with *welche*—e.g. *in welcher Höhe (Tiefe)?* 'at
what height (depth)?', *bei (unter) welchem Druck?* 'at what
pressure?', *durch welche Mittel?* 'by what means?', *in (unter)
welchem Winkel?* 'at what angle?', *auf Grund welcher Para-
graphen?* 'on the ground of what sections?', *bis zu welchem Grade?*
'to what degree (extent)?', *in welchem Maß?* 'in what measure?',
durch welchen Zufall? 'by what chance?', *aus welchen drei Haupt-
teilen besteht es?* 'of what three main parts does it consist?', *aus
welchem Holz ist es gemacht?* 'what wood is it made of?', *von
welchem Bahnsteig?* 'from what platform?'.

If the response is to be an adjective or description English has
recourse to the question 'what is ... like?'. German usually
has the word for 'how', namely *wie?*, cf. Fr. 'comment?'. Thus
wie ist die Feder? 'what is the pen like?' (i.e. is it blunt, or smooth,
etc.?). Otherwise *wie?* corresponds to 'how', and is synonymous
with the phrase *auf welche Weise?* 'in what way?', e.g. *wie heizt
man die Wohnung?* 'how is the flat heated?' (lit. 'how does one
heat ...?'), *wie unterscheidet man* ...? 'how does one distinguish

...?', *wie spricht er deutsch?* 'how does he speak German?'. As in English 'how', the German *wie* can stand before an adjective or adverb to ask a quantitative question, like 'how much (many)?', 'how big?', etc. The following is a selection of useful German phrases: *wieviel [Geld]?* 'how much [money]?', *wie viele?* 'how many?', *wieviel Leute?* 'how many people?', *wieviel Geschwister haben Sie?* 'how many brothers and sisters have you?', *wieviel Verspätung hat der Zug?* 'how much is the train overdue?', (*Verspätung* 'lateness, delay'); *wie gross?* 'how big?', *wie alt?* 'how old?', *wie hoch?* 'how high?', *wie tief?* 'how deep (low)?', *wie lange?* (for) how long (a time)?', *wie lang?* 'how long?' (of dimension), *wie oft?* 'how often?', also *inwiefern?* 'how far, to what extent?'.

Sometimes *wie?* is rendered in English by 'what?', e.g. *wie, bitte?* (lit. 'how please?') 'what did you say?', *wie ist Ihr Name?* or *wie heißen Sie?* 'what is your name? or 'what are you called?'. The compound word *wieso?* often implies 'what (or how) do you mean?'.

The question WHERE? in the sense of 'at what place?' is given in German by *wo?*, e.g. *wo wohnen Sie?* 'where do you live?', *wo sind Sie geboren?* 'where were you born?'. German, like English, has such synonyms as *an welchem Orte?* 'at what place?', *in welcher Gegend (Stadt)?* 'in what region (city)?, etc. In ordinary speech English uses 'where?' for the goal as well, the fuller form being 'where ... to?', e.g. 'where are you going (to)?'. In such cases German must indicate the direction by using *hin* with *wo* either combining them into *wohin?* or separating them, e.g. *wo gehen Sie hin?* or *wohin gehen Sie?* 'where are you going to?', *wo (kommen Sie) her?* or *woher (kommen Sie)?* 'whence' or 'where ... from'. Different degrees of precision of the where-question are made by saying: *wo genau ...?* 'where exactly ...?' and *wo ungefähr ...?* 'whereabouts (where roughly)?'.

The interrogative of time corresponding to the more specific *zu welcher Zeit?* 'at what time?' or *in welcher Periode?* is *wann?*, 'when', e.g. *wann kommt er?* 'when is he coming?'. To indicate the limit of time conveyed in English by 'till' or 'by' the expression *bis wann?* may be used, e.g. *bis wann bleibt er?* 'till when is he staying?', *bis wann bekomme ich es?* 'by what time can I have it?' (answer: *bis Freitag* 'by Friday'), cf. *seit wann wohnt er hier?* 'since when has he been living here?'.

The word WHY? in English and its equivalent *warum?* in

German is both retrospective to the cause and prospective to the purpose. The more specific phrase for cause is *aus welchem Grunde?* 'for what reason?' and for purpose is *zu welchem Zwecke?* 'for what purpose?'. Examples of *warum* in both functions are: *warum sagen Sie das?* 'why do you say that?' and *warum (wozu) kommt er morgen?* 'why is he coming tomorrow?' 'what is he ... for?'.

Demonstratives

Like English, German has two main demonstratives, one for 'that' and one for 'this'. In the spoken language the usual form for 'that' is the definite article *der/die/das//* pl. *die* strongly stressed and with *der* pronounced with the full long *e* vowel. It frequently stands for the English 'this' as well, e.g. in pointing *ist das ein Buch?* 'is this (that) a book?', *was ist das?* 'what is this (that)'?, *das ist Johanns Buch* 'this is John's book'. Note that the singular *das* is sometimes used with a plural verb, e.g. *das sind Bücher* 'these (those) are books'. For the sake of explicit contrast with the remoter subject German uses *dieser/diese/dieses* 'this'//*diese* 'these' and can contract the neuter form to *dies*, e.g. *sind dies Ihre oder meine Schuhe?* 'are these shoes yours or mine?', *dies Buch gehört Johann* 'this book is John's'. In a narrative passage English often uses 'this' in reference to what has just passed as though retaining the impression whereas German prefers *das*, e.g. '. . . the official said there were not enough stamps on the letter. *This* caused some delay'.

With a preposition the words for 'this' and 'that' in German are often replaced by 'here' and 'there', cf. the English 'herewith', 'therein' etc., but with normal everyday employment and not simply in legal style, e.g. *hierin (darin) hat er Recht* 'he is right about this (that)'.

Literary German has the word *jener/jene/jenes//jene* which corresponds to the spoken *der*, etc., but is not in North German speech a normal equivalent of English 'that'. It is, however, usual in such phrases as *wir sprachen von diesem und jenem* 'we talked about this or that', *er fragte mich dieses und jenes* (or *dies und das*) 'he asked me this and that', *so dies und das und jenes* 'this, that and the other thing'. As in English the demonstrative can be used with emotive force, *dies* having a nuance of that which is close enough to be in the news or even obsessive and *das* perhaps a tendency to keep something at a distance, e.g. *was soll dieser Krach hier?*

'what's all this noise about?', *was bedeutet alles dies Gerede über die Schließung der Universität?* 'what's all this talk about closing the University?', *was hat es eigentlich auf sich mit dieser neuen Theorie von Einstein?* 'what is all this new theory of Einstein's about?', and with *das: warum das?* 'why that?'; *was bedeutet das alles, was ich über Sie höre?* 'what's all this I hear about you?'.

Applying the demonstrative to quality English has the adjective 'such' and German either *ein solcher/eine solche/ein solches//solche* or *solch ein*, etc., or especially in speech in the singular *so ein* (often *so'n*), *so eine* (often *so'ne*), e.g. *so'n Mann, so'ne Frau, solche Kinder; solche Gemeinheit!* or *so'ne Gemeinheit!* 'how beastly!', *mit einem solchen Menschen spreche ich nicht.* In some contexts *so ein* with less stress on *so* and more on the following noun does not imply 'such', but 'a kind of', e.g. *ich habe so eine Ahnung, dass er kommt* 'I have a kind of inkling that he is coming'. There is also an adjective *derartig* derived from *der Art* 'of that kind', e.g. *nichts derartiges* 'nothing of the kind'. For 'such a thing' German uses *so etwas.*

In application to the manner of doing something 'like this' or 'like that', German is usually content with the word *so*, e.g. *so macht man es* 'it is done in that way' or 'that's how it is done'. The German *so* also applies to the 'nature' of something, e.g. *so ist das Leben* 'life is like that', *so sind die Menschen* 'that's how people are'.

The demonstratives of place in English are 'here' and 'there' with corresponding German expressions *hier, da* and the rather more emphatic or remoter *dort.* Where in older English 'hither' and 'thither' were used to indicate the direction of an action German has *hierher/hierhin* and *dahin* or *dorthin*, e.g. *er zeigte hierhin und dorthin* 'he pointed this way and that', *kommen Sie hierher* (or simply *her*) 'come here', *geben Sie es her* or *her damit* 'hand it over!'. For 'yonder' German uses the equivalent of 'over there' *drüben.*

In English the demonstrative adverbs of time are 'then' (at that time) and 'now' (at this time). The etymological equivalent of 'then' in German is *dann*, but *dann* does not refer to a definite point of time, but is used (1) for a subsequent occurrence, e.g.— *und ging dann weg* 'and then went away' and (2) for an implicit condition, e.g. *auch dann* 'even if (we did, etc.), 'even in that case'. For the indication of time in a remoter past, e.g. in a narrative of former times German uses either *damals* or *zu der Zeit* or especially in speech *da*, which is also used in such phrases as *von da an* 'from then on', 'from that time henceforward' and with the suffix *-hin* (stressed) of direction: *bis dahin* 'till then'. From its use for 'hence' the German *her* can indicate 'ago', e.g. *das ist schon lange her* 'that is quite a long time ago'. German has two words for 'now', one merely temporal *jetzt* and the other *nun* with a nuance of influence from the past. The word *jetzt* may imply a time shortly before or shortly after the actual present, e.g. *er verließ mich eben jetzt* 'he left me just now', *er wird jezt gleich kommen* 'he'll be here any moment now'. The word *jetzt* is appropriate in such time-contexts as *jetzt oder nie* 'now or never', *zwischen jetzt und Weihnachten* 'between now and Christmas', *von jetzt an* 'from now on'. With its indication of a resultant state or occurrence *nun* is used in such phrases as *das ist nun schon dein sechster Fehler* 'that is already your sixth mistake', *nun wissen wir ja* 'well, now we know', *was wird nun kommen?* 'what will happen now?'.

The most useful word to refer to cause or effect is in German *so* which, as shown already, is primarily an adverb of manner ('in this, that way'). In English, too, the word 'so' or the phrase 'and so' is often a weaker synonym of 'therefore'. German uses *so*, e.g. *so war alles vergebens* 'so (and so, thus) everything was in vain'. To indicate a consequence or inference there is *also*, e.g. *also können wir erst morgen abreisen* 'so (thus, this being so) we cannot leave till tomorrow'. The more precise words for 'therefore' are *daher*, cf. English 'hence' and *darum*, equivalent to the phrase *aus 'dem Grunde* 'for that reason'.

5

OTHER PRONOMINAL WORDS AND
SUBSTITUTES – NUMERALS

Indefinites

There is no fundamental distinction in German as there is in English between 'some' and 'any' where 'some' applies to a particular, though unspecified item and 'any' indicates 'this, that or another' item generally and unspecifically, but in an affirmative statement German distinguishes 'any' by using the equivalent of 'every' e.g. *jeder kann das sagen* 'anyone can say that'. In a question the matter is often settled in German by leaving out the some/any word, e.g. 'have you some bread there?' is *haben Sie Brot da?* and 'have you some strawberries?' is *haben Sie Erdbeeren?*, 'is there any hope?' *ist noch Hoffnung vorhanden?*. With a negative 'not' German usually coalesces 'not any' into *kein* 'no', 'not anyone' into *keiner/keine* and 'not anything' into *nichts* 'nothing'. In the German counterpart for 'will you have any more?' *wollen Sie noch mehr haben?* the word *noch* 'yet, still' goes some way towards indicating 'any'. The 'some' in '(I should see) some lawyer (about it)' would be *einen Rechtsanwalt*, cf. '(I do not see why we should not look up) some book' *ein Buch*. To bring out the English nuance of 'any' with an imperative, e.g. 'draw any two cards' German might say *ziehen Sie zwei Karten* 'which you like,' adding *nach Belieben*, lit. 'according to discretion'. Sometimes 'any' may be rendered by *eventuell* (in officialese *etwaig*), e.g. *eventuelle Wünsche (Beschwerden) sind an den Fremdenführer zu richten* 'any wishes (complaints) are to be addressed to the guide'. In cases where English uses 'any' with a comparative German simply omits any such word, e.g. 'I can't bear it any longer' *ich kann es nicht länger ertragen*; 'I can't go any farther' *ich kann nicht weiter gehen*; 'was he any better?' *ging es ihm besser?* The English phrase 'not any too . . .' could be rendered by, e.g. *er kam keine Minute zu früh* 'he didn't come any too soon', *es geht mir keineswegs gut (nichts weniger als gut)* 'I don't feel any too grand'.

To the English 'something' corresponds the German *etwas*, but this word when used for measuring a quantity is often like 'some', e.g. *etwas Brot* 'some bread' and when used with an adjective is the equivalent of 'somewhat' or 'rather', e.g. *etwas geizig* 'somewhat miserly'. When in English 'something' is used in the pregnant sense of 'something worth while', German, too, uses *etwas*, e.g. *das ist jedenfalls etwas* 'that is something anyhow', *damit wäre jedenfalls etwas gewonnen* 'that would mean something achieved anyhow', *es ist schon etwas in dem, was er sagt* 'there is something in what he says'. With certain verbs both 'something' and *etwas* have more specific implications, e.g. *nehmen Sie etwas für Ihre Erkältung* 'take something (i.e. a remedy) for your cold', *lesen Sie uns etwas vor* 'read us something', *spielen (singen) Sie uns etwas vor* 'play (sing) us something', *Sie hat etwas auf dem Herzen* 'she has something on her mind', *er ist etwas im Zoll* 'he is something in the customs'. For 'he is something of a poet' in reference to skill, German says *er ist so'n halber Dichter*, cf. 'he is something of a doctor', *er ist so etwas wie ein Doktor*. In a question like *haben Sie etwas von ihm gehört?* we say 'anything' in 'have you heard anything of him?', but one may say *irgend etwas*, cf. also *ohne etwas zu unternehmen* 'without undertaking anything'. Where English indicates a vaguer particular by 'some . . . or other', 'someone (somebody) . . . or other', etc., German places the indeclinable *irgend* in front, e.g. *irgend ein Buch* 'some book or other', *irgend einmal* 'sometime or other'. The word *irgend* is also used to form the indefinite adverbs, e.g. *irgendwie* 'somehow, anyhow'; *irgendwo* 'some-, anywhere'; *irgendwohin* 'to some or any place'; *irgendwann* 'sometime, at any time'. The word 'some time' can be rendered by either (1) *irgendwann*, e.g. *sie kommt irgendwann im Laufe des Tages* 'she'll be coming some time in the course of the day' or simply (2) *[ein]mal*, e.g. *kann ich Sie mal sprechen?* 'can I have a word with you sometime', cf. *ich möchte Sie gelegentlich einmal sprechen*. On the other hand 'sometimes' (on several unspecified occasions) is *manchmal*. Sometimes 'any' may be rendered by *irgend welch*—e.g. *in jeglichem Dorf von irgend welcher Bedeutung* 'in every village of any importance'. A disparaging 'anyway' is

indicated by particles in *was sind Schmidts denn überhaupt?*
'What are the Schmidts anyhow (anyway)?'

The usual word for 'somebody' in German is *jemand* which
can take the accusative ending (*jemanden*), the genitive (*jemandes*)
and dative (*jemandem*) or in the accusative and dative remain
uninflected, e.g. *ich habe jemand (jemanden) gesehen*. In English
'somebody' is occasionally used in speaking with a particular
intonation to a child or to a friend in a half-teasing manner,
e.g. 'someone (i.e. your fiancé) was asking after you' *ein gewisser
Jemand hat nach dir gefragt*; 'I seem to remember someone talking
quite differently' *ich habe jemanden aber früher ganz anders reden
hören*; 'someone promised me to be good' *ein gewisser Jemand hatte
mir versprochen, artig zu sein*. Then there is the use of 'somebody'
indicating a particular, but unnamed person competent to advise,
etc., e.g. 'I shall have to see someone about this matter'; German
would say *mit jemand offiziellem*—(colloquially *offizielles* with
retained neuter nominative—accusative in spite of *mit*) or *mit
einem Fachmann* ('expert', 'professional') or, simply, *mit jemand,
der es versteht* ('who understands it'), but it is quite possible to say
ich muß jemanden holen, der es repariert 'I must get somebody in to
repair it' or *ich muß jemanden zu Rate ziehen* 'I must consult
someone'. If 'somebody' is used in the sense of someone important, e.g. in 'he thinks himself somebody' German says *er hält sich
für wunderwas* (which is also the equivalent of 'he thinks something
of himself').

The phrases 'something or other' '(or) something' are used in
English, if we cannot take the trouble to give the precise details.
Thus we might say 'Llan-something or other' in which case
German would usually say *Llan und so weiter*, lit. 'and so on', cf.
'eighteen hundred and something' *achtzehn hundert so und so viel*,
'at five something' *um fünf Uhr so und so viel*; 'Mr. something or
other' *Herr so und so* (cf. English 'so and so'), *Herr, wie heißt er
doch?* or *Herr, wie war doch sein Name?* 'Mr. what's his name?',
'some General Smith or other' *irgend ein General Schmidt oder so*.
If 'or something' refers to a whole sentence German uses the
equivalent of 'or something similar', e.g. *er hat sich den Arm
gebrochen oder so was* (=*etwas*) *ähnliches* 'he has broken his
arm or something', cf. *also ein Antrag so ungefähr dieser Art*
'some such offer'. As to the colloquial English 'that's something
like' German would have to paraphrase with some such phrase as
das laß' ich mir gefallen ('I can put up with that') or *das ist wirklich*

mein Fall ('my case') or *das lohnt sich wenigstens* ('that is at least worth while').

Totality

German does not distinguish so clearly as English between (1) the separate item of a limited total regarded as an individual or as an item for distribution or correlation (EACH) and (2) the items regarded as adding up to or tending towards the totality (EVERY), i.e. the singular of ALL. The word *jeder/jede/jedes* usually stands for both 'each' and 'every'. Even *ein jeder* and *jeder einzelne* (*einzeln* 'single') can be translated by 'each' or 'every' according to the context. Examples of *jeder*, etc. are: *ich habe jeden Grund* 'I have every reason', *das sagt doch nun ein jeder heutzutage* 'why, everyone says so nowadays', *jeder Student hat ein Zimmer* 'every student has a room'/*jeder Student hat sein eigenes Zimmer* 'each student has his own room'; *er sprach ein paar Minuten mit jedem von uns* (*einem jeden von uns, jedem einzelnen*) 'he had a few minutes' talk with each of us'; *jeder einzelne wurde genau untersucht* or *der Reihe nach wurde jeder [beim Hereinkommen] untersucht* 'each man (everyone) was thoroughly searched [as he came in]'; *jeder von ihnen ist ein ehrlicher Mann* 'everyone of them is an honest man'; *er kommt jede Woche her* 'he comes here every week'; *jeder von uns bekam ein Päckchen Zigaretten* 'each of us was given a packet of cigarettes'. Occasionally the German *jeder* is translated by *all* where the English word is almost a vague collective or a process rather than a single act, e.g. *über jeden Zweifel erhaben* 'beyond all doubt'; *er haßte jede Einmischung* 'he hated all (any) interference'. If strongly stressed 'every' is rendered by *jeglich*, e.g. *es ist jegliches Anzeichen vorhanden, daß . . .* 'there is every indication that . . .' (but *diese Regierung hat jeglichen Anspruch verloren . . .* 'this government has lost whatever claim it had . . .'). The distributive 'each' is often rendered by *pro Stück*, *das Stück*, e.g. *diese Äpfel kosten einen Groschen das Stück* and sometimes by *je* or *à*, e.g. *die zwei Pferde werden je auf 1000 M geschätzt* 'the two horses are valued at 1000 mks. each', *ich sende sie Ihnen à (zu je) drei Stück in einer Kiste verpackt* 'I am sending them to you packed in boxes each containing three', *Sie erhielten jeder* (or *je*) *M 500* 'each one received 500 mks.', also expressed by *jeder von ihnen erhielt . . .*'. A combination of *je* and *pro* is found in *wir bekamen je ein Ei pro Woche* 'we were each allotted one egg a week'. In some cases two renderings are possible, e.g. *je* 25 *Schüler bilden eine Klasse* 'each class is made up of 25 scholars' or 'every 25 scholars form a class'.

The border-line case where *jeder* would in English be rendered by 'any', e.g. in 'anyone could do that' is discussed in the section on the indefinites.

In a phrase indicating successive groups in a series 'every' has as its equivalent *alle* with noun in the plural, e.g. *alle paar Tage* 'every few days', *alle zwei Tage* 'every two days', *alle vierundzwanzig Stunden* 'every 24 hours', but *jeder* with an ordinal number and singular noun, e.g. *jeder zweite Tag* 'every other day'. The collective 'everything' is in German either the neuter *alles* or *das ganze* 'the whole', e.g. *alles hat seine zwei Seiten* 'there are two sides to everything'. This neuter form also corresponds to English 'all' in such phrases as *das ist alles, was ich wünsche* 'that is all I desire'; *das war noch nicht alles* 'that was not all' (*noch* 'yet'), *alles Deutsche* 'everything (all things) German'. Sometimes 'everyone' is interchangeable with 'all' and if so, German prefers the plural *alle*, e.g. *ich habe es allen gesagt* 'I have told everyone (them all)', *ich sah seine Freunde, denen ich allen geschrieben habe* 'I saw his friends to everyone of whom (to all of whom) I have written'.

Where 'all' is used with a singular noun the usual equivalent in German is *ganz* either indeclinable or declined with the definite article *der/die/das ganze* or possessive, but in some cases *all* is used, e.g. *all sein Geld* 'all his money', *sein ganzes Geld* 'the whole of his money', *ganz Deutschland* (cf. *in ganz Deutschland*) 'all Germany', *das ganze Deutschland* (and as the article is obligatory with a feminine, always *die ganze Schweiz*) 'the whole of Germany (Switzerland)', *der ganze Tag* 'all day', *all das Gold* or *das ganze Gold* 'all the gold', *bei all der Pracht* 'with all the splendour'. The last two examples together with *all sein Geld* show a use parallel to the English 'all the . . .', 'all his . . .' with a singular noun, and in such cases the *all* in German is not declined. However, with a plural it is possible to say either *all die Studenten* or *alle Studenten* (without article), *all diese Bücher* or *alle diese Bücher*. The inflected form *alle* would be used in *alle unsere Studenten*. The inflected form would be normal also when there is no determinative word between 'all' and the noun, e.g. *alle Mathematik, die ich konnte* 'all the mathematics I knew', *alle Freude* 'all the joy'. In '(he had lost) all interest (in . . .)' the equivalents would be *alles*

Interesse, jedes Interesse or *sein ganzes Interesse*. Though 'each of us' would be translated into German by *jeder von uns*, 'all of us' is *wir alle*, 'all of you' *Sie alle*, etc. The plural *alle* can follow the verb, e.g. *sie waren alle mit Schmutz bedeckt* 'they were all (i.e. all of them were) covered with mud' with which may be contrasted *sie waren ganz mit Schmutz bedeckt* 'they were all (completely) covered with mud'.

German has an idiom with *alle* used as the predicate in the sense of 'all gone', e.g. *das Brot ist alle* 'the bread is all used up', *meine Geduld ist alle* 'my patience is exhausted'.

Occasionally the English 'all' has a strong negative implication excluding everything else and hence resembling 'sheer' or 'nothing but'. This in German is usually *lauter*, e.g. [*das sind*] *lauter Lügen* 'all lies', *sie ist lauter Leben* 'she is all animation'.

Negative pronominals

The negative corresponding to a noun is NOTHING, Ger. *nichts*. It can be combined with a neuter strong adjective, e.g. *nichts Gutes* 'nothing good' or with a prepositional phrase, e.g. *nichts von Bedeutung* 'nothing of importance'. Exclusion of all save the item or items mentioned is conveyed by *nichts anderes* 'nothing further, no other' or *sonst nichts* 'nothing else'. In German *nichts weniger als*, lit. 'nothing less than' implies a high degree of the opposite quality, e.g. *er ist nichts weniger als dumm* 'anything but stupid, [in fact very clever]'. On the other hand the English use of 'nothing short of [a miracle]' is expressed in German positively: *geradezu* [*ein Wunder*] where *geradezu* is like English 'downright'. To express 'nothing like so'+adjective there is a phrase with *lange nicht* or *bei weitem nicht*, e.g. *lange nicht so klug* 'nothing like so clever'. The word *nichts* can be reinforced by various grading adverbs, e.g. *gar nichts* 'nothing at all', *absolut nichts*, *ganz und gar nichts* 'absolutely nothing at all', *überhaupt nichts* 'nothing whatever'. To express 'not for anything [on earth]' German can say *nicht um alles* [*in der Welt*] or *um keinen Preis*.

All of the above intensives can be used with the adjectival form *kein* 'no' (and its independent forms *keiner/keine/keines// keine*) and with the adverbial *nicht* 'not'.

The negative adverb of place is *nirgends* or *nirgendwo* 'nowhere', with the *hin* ending to indicate direction, *nirgendwohin* [to go] 'nowhere', lit. 'nowhither'. The negative time-expression is *nie* 'never' or *niemals* which is rather more emphatic. German uses *nie* in the phrase *fast nie*, lit. 'almost never', where in English 'hardly ever' is more usual.

There are no specific simple negatives for cause any more than there are in English, so it is necessary to use the phrase *aus keinem Grunde* 'for no reason'. Corresponding to 'by no means' German has *auf keine Weise* 'in no way' or *keineswegs*.

Substitutes for numerals

Some words indicate sets of items and measured quantities in a vaguer way than the cardinal numbers. Thus a relatively small number is indicated in English by 'some' or if not more than say four or five by 'several'. German has for 'some' *einige*, e.g. *einige Bücher sind wertlos* 'some books are worthless', and for 'some few' *einige wenige*. Sometimes as in English the word *einige* is contrasted with *andere* 'others'. Where the word 'some' is deliberately used to convey vagueness or mere approximation German can use *einige*, e.g. *einige zwanzig Tage* 'some twenty days', *ein Dorf von einigen hundert Häuschen* 'a village of some hundred cottages', but there are other modes of indication such as *es waren so an die zwanzig*, cf. 'somewhere about twenty' or *etwa siebzig Kilometer entfernt* 'at a distance of some seventy kilometres'. Occasionally *einig-* is used in the singular, e.g. *ich habe einige Erfahrung* 'I have some experience' or *einiges weiß ich* 'I do know something about it (i.e. some details)'.

A phrase which is very frequent in spoken German for 'a few' is *ein paar*, often pronounced *'n paar*. It remains undeclined, e.g. *ein paar Soldaten* 'a few soldiers', *vor ein paar Tagen* 'a few days ago', *während ein paar Monate* 'during a few months'. Without the indefinite article *paar* is used with other determinatives, e.g. *in den paar Tagen* 'in the few days', *die paar neuen Mitglieder* 'the few new members', *diese paar Worte* 'these few words'. It is to be noted that *ein Paar* with a capital and often with more stress on *ein* means a pair, e.g. *ein Paar Schuhe* 'a pair of shoes'.

The specific word for 'several' is *mehrere* which takes the strong form of the adjective after it, e.g. *mehrere wichtige Dinge* 'several important things'. Rising in the scale from *mehrere* 'several' German provides *manche* for 'quite a number, a fair number, quite a few'. In the neuter singular *manches* is used in such phrases as *ich habe Ihnen manches zu erzählen* 'I have quite a lot (or various things) to tell you', *es hat manches Gute* 'it has some good points'.

The strongly declined singular, e.g. *mancher General, manche Blume*, or the uninflected *manch* with the indefinite article, e.g. *manch eine Blume* is literary and resembles in use the English 'many a'. The forms of *manch* always indicate a number and not a measured quantity. The plural *manche* is followed by the adjective in the strong form, e.g. *manche alte Leute*.

Another synonym of 'some few' is *etliche* which is used in speech in the Rhineland, but is not prevalent in spoken North German, except in some regions where it indicates a relatively large quantity, e.g. *wir werden noch etliche Kilometer zurücklegen müssen* 'we shall have to cover quite a few more miles', *das hat etliches gekostet* 'that has cost quite a bit'. For the contrasted pair 'few/many (a lot of)', German has *wenig(e)/viel* and for 'little/much (a lot of)' *wenig/viel*. It is permissible to say either *wenig* or *wenige Bücher* and *viel* or *viele Bücher* (cf. *wie viel* or *wie viele Leute?*, but when the noun is missing there is a distinction between *wieviel?* 'how much?' and *wie viele?* 'how many?'). Apart from the strong neuter forms *weniges* and *vieles*, e.g. *ich habe vieles* (cf. *manches*) *erlebt* 'I have had a great deal of experience', the words *wenig* and *viel* used independently remain uninflected in the singular, e.g. *mit wenig Mühe* 'with little trouble', *mit viel Vergnügen* 'with much pleasure', but *vielen Dank*. If, however, the words *wenig* and *viel* follow the definite article they are declined weak like any ordinary adjective, e.g. *das wenige, was ich habe* 'the little that I have'; *die viele Milch, die wir brauchen* 'the lots of milk we need' or *die vielen Bücher* 'the number of books'. When *viel* and *vieles* are used alone there is a shade of difference between them, as shown by *ich habe vieles gesehen* which implies 'I have seen many different things' and *ich habe viel gesehen* in which *viel* is a collective singular for 'a lot' or 'a great deal'.

Just as in spoken English 'little' and 'few' contain an implicit negation in their meaning of 'not much', 'not many', so in German *wenig* and *wenige* are synonymous with *nicht viel* and *nicht viele* respectively. If the implication is positive English uses 'a little' and 'a few' and German *ein wenig* (*Brot*) and *ein paar* (*Bücher*). For *ein wenig* a synonym much used in speech is *ein* (or *'n*) *bißchen*, cf. English 'a bit', e.g. *ein* [*klein*] *bißchen* [*Geduld*] 'a little bit [of patience]', *kein bißchen* 'not a bit', and *das bißchen* [*Geld*] 'the bit [of money] . . .'. The use of *bißchen* is paralleled at the upper end of the scale by *eine* (*'ne*) *Menge*, also *'ne Masse, ein* (or *'n*)

Haufen for 'a lot, a heap', etc., e.g. *eine Menge Leute* 'a crowd of people', *eine Masse Arbeit* 'lots of work', *ein Haufen Geld* 'a lot of money'.

Pronominals in a group of two

English distinguishes much more clearly than German the members of a group of two from those of a plurality generally. Thus we say 'any(one) of the three', but 'either of the two', 'every one (or each) of the three', but only 'each of the two' and 'all of the three', but 'both (of the two)'. The negative forms are 'none (not one) of the three', but 'neither of the two'. We no longer use the specific form 'whether (of the two)?', but use 'which' of any plurality. Of these specific forms German has only *beide* 'both', which can be reinforced as *alle beide*. English and German differ in the position of *beide* in a noun-phrase, e.g. *seine beiden Hände* 'both his hands', *diese beiden Punkte* 'both these points', *die beiden Schwestern* (or *beide Schwestern*) 'both (the) sisters'. In some cases *von beiden* is equivalent to 'of the two', e.g. *welches von beiden?* 'which of the two?', *einer von beiden* 'either of the two', *keiner von beiden* 'neither of the two'. Corresponding to 'both of us', German can say either *jeder von uns* or *wir beide*. As with English 'both', the word *beide* can in a sentence either precede the subject or follow the verb, e.g. *beide Eltern sind wohl* or *die Eltern sind beide wohl* 'both parents are well' or 'the parents are both well' (cf. the varying positions of *selbst* 'self', in the section on identity). *Beide* is normally 'strong' but the North German spoken language uses the weak form *beiden* in the phrase *welche beiden* 'which ... both ...' 'both of which'. Sometimes English uses 'either' in place of 'each' or 'both', but German prefers *beide*, e.g. *in beiden Fällen* 'in either case', *auf beiden Seiten der Strasse waren Bäume* 'there were trees on either side (both sides) of the street', and the strong neuter in *beides ist richtig* 'either is correct'. As in English the phrase synonymous with 'both the boys' is 'the two boys', so in German *beide Jungens*, *die beiden Jungens* or *die zwei Jungens*.

The correlatives 'either ... or ...' and 'neither ... nor ...' are discussed in the section on co-ordinate sentences, cf. also 'I have not seen him either'.

Numeral expressions

From the grammarian's point of view the chief interest of numbers is the mode of their formation. Like English, German has specific cardinals (*eins, zwei, drei, vier, fünf, sechs, sieben, acht, neun, zehn, elf, zwölf*) up to and including twelve and then forms the 'teens (*dreizehn* to *neunzehn*), beginning the decades with twenty (*zwanzig, dreißig, vierzig, fünfzig, sechzig, siebzig, achtzig, neunzig*). The contracted forms *sechzig, siebzig* are paralleled in the teens: *sechzehn, siebzehn*. The intermediate numbers are formed like the old-fashioned English 'one and twenty', etc. and 'one' is *ein* (*und zwanzig*) and not *eins*—it is likewise indeclinable within the group. The word '(a) hundred' is *hundert* or with contrastive 'one' *ein Hundert* with plural *Hunderte* 'hundreds' as against *zwei hundert*, etc. The numbers following the hundred are usually added without any 'and', e.g. *hundert eins, zweihundert fünf und dreißig, neunhundert neun und neunzig*. The word for 'thousand' is *tausend* or *ein Tausend*, pl. *Tausende*. In dates German, like English, usually employs the 'teens, e.g. *neunzehn hundert zwei und fünfzig*, but 1066 is *tausend sechs und sechzig*. The phrase 'in 1952' is rendered either without preposition or with the full form *im Jahre* (abbreviated *i. J.*) 1952. A 'million' is in German a substantive *eine Million*, pl. *Millionen—tausend Millionen—eine Milliarde*. The number 'zero' is *null* (noun: *die Null*, pl. *Nullen*) which has to be used, unlike English, in a decimal expression of a number less than one, e.g. 0,5 (*nullkommafünf*) for .5 and 0,01 (*nullkommanulleins*) for .01, cf. also *Normalnull* for 'sea-level' (*Meeresniveau*), *in Null komma nichts* 'in a jiffy' and *er ist eine Null* 'he is a mere cipher'. The blanket-numeral 'umpteen' has a partial parallel in *-zig*, e.g. *zigmal*.

Cardinals are often used as in English as alternatives to ordinal numbers to designate chapters (*Kapitel I* or *eins*), pages (*Seite* 10), bus or tram routes (*Linie 1*, cf. *mit der Eins fahren*, i.e. no. 1 tram), cards (*die Pik sechs* 'six of spades'). The starter says *Eins, zwei, drei, los!* 'one, two, three, off!'. For the one on dice there is the feminine *Eins* with plural *Einsen*. Idioms with cardinals include: *mir ist alles eins* 'it is all one to me', *er bestand* [*die Prüfung*] *mit eins* 'he got a first'; *ich ließ es mir nicht azweimal sagen* 'I did not need telling twice'; *er kann nicht bis drei zählen* cf. 'he doesn't know how many beans make five'; *unter vier Augen* 'tête à tête', *auf allen Vieren* 'on all fours'; *wir wollen fünf gerade sein lassen* 'we'll stretch a point'; *Siebensachen* 'goods and chattels'; *eine böse Sieben* 'a termagant'; *jetzt schlägt's dreizehn* 'that's torn it'. Adjectives with preposed numerals often have the suffix *-ig*, e.g. *einäugig* 'one-eyed', *zweischneidig* 'two-edged', *dreischichtiges*

Holz 'three-ply wood', *eine vierstellige Zahl* 'four figures'. Note that cardinals indicate clock-time, e.g. *Ein Uhr* or *eins, zwei Uhr zehn*, etc., and that 'half past' is indicated by *halb* followed by the next hour, e.g. *halb sechs* 'half-past five'.

In military parlance and in telephoning it is customary to use *zwo* for *zwei* (and *zwote* for '2nd') to avoid confusion between *zwei* and *drei*. This usage is spreading to ordinary speech. It is possible to inflect *zwei* and *drei* in the genitive and dative, e.g. *das Haus zweier (von zwei) Familien*; *zu zweien*, but the usage is literary rather than colloquial.

The figures used for cardinals are used as full nouns by the addition of the suffix *-er*, e.g. *zwei Fünfer* 'two fives', cf. phrases like *in den zwanziger Jahren* (of both age and date), *er kommt in die Vierziger (geht auf die Vierziger zu)* 'he is getting on for forty'. In rowing the forms *Vierer* and *Achter* are used for a 'four' and 'eight' oared boat respectively.

The ordinals are adjectives—here given in the weak masc. nom. sing.—formed with *-t-* up to 19 and with *-st-* for the decades, hundreds and thousands, e.g. *der erste, zweite (zwote), dritte, vierte*, etc., to *neunzehnte*, then *zwanzigste, hundertste, tausendste*, etc. In a date like *den 5. Mai* the full stop shows that the number is to be read as an ordinal *den fünften Mai*. This applies also to titles, e.g. *Heinrich IV.—Heinrich der Vierte*. In an address the house-number and flat are often written, e.g. *Hochstraße* 34ᴵᴵᴵ read *vier und dreißig dritte (Etage)*, cf. 34ᵖ for *Parterre* 'ground-floor', and *hp*, i.e. *Hochparterre* 'mezzanine'. Idiomatic ordinal phrases include 'first thing' *in aller Herrgotts frühe* and 'last thing' *als letztes*.

Fractions like one-third or three-quarters are formed with a suffix *-tel* (up to nineteenth), *-stel* (twentieth onwards) developed out of an unstressed *Teil* 'part', e.g. *viertel (ein Viertel, das Viertel)* 'quarter', *dreiviertel* 'three-quarters', *fünf achtel* 'five-eighths'. The word for 'half' is *halb* (noun *die Hälfte*, pl. *Hälften*), 'one and a half' is *eineinhalb* or *anderthalb*, 'two and a half' is *zweieinhalb*, 'two and three-quarters' *zwei dreiviertel*, etc. In giving clock-time *halb* in front of the cardinal indicates the half past the hour preceding, e.g. *halb zehn* 'half past nine'. It can also be used as a declined adjective, e.g. *ein halber Mensch* 'half a man' and in such phrases as *halb so viel* 'half as much'. For 'halfway' German has *halbwegs*, but for 'half way up' says *in halber Höhe*. Besides the loan *fifty fifty* there is the colloquial *halbpart* or *halbe halbe machen*.

3

The usual way of expressing in words a 'power' (*die Potenz*) like 5^2, 10^3, etc., is *fünf hoch zwei, zehn hoch drei*, but 'squared' can be given by *im Quadrat* and the other expressions with a phrase like *zur dritten* (*Potenz*) 'to the third'.

The multiplicatives are formed with *-mal*, e.g. *zweimal* 'twice', *zweihundertmal* 'two hundred times' (*zweimalzwei ist vier*, etc.). With an ordinal *Mal* is used as a noun for 'time, occasion', e.g. *das zweite Mal, zum dritten Male* 'for the third time', *als ich ihn zum ersten Mal sah* 'the first time I saw him'.

The variatives (Curme's term) are formed with *-lei*, e.g. *zweierlei* 'of two kinds', cf. *allerlei* (*allerhand*) 'of all kinds', *vielerlei* 'of many kinds'.

The equivalent of English '-fold' is *-fach*, e.g. *dreifach* 'three-fold', 'triple', etc.

Distributive expressions are formed in several different ways. Thus 'two by two' is *zwei und zwei, zu zweien* or *je zwei*. For 'apiece', 'each', German can use either (*zwei Mark*) *pro Stück*, *das Stück* or (*sie kosten*) *je* (*zwei Mark*).

As Germans employ the metric system a few rough equivalences may be useful. For weight: an ounce is about 28 grammes (*Gramm*), a pound nearly half a kilogram (*Kilogramm*), a stone a little over 6 kg, a hundredweight about 51 kg and a ton 1016 kg. For length: an inch is nearly $2\frac{1}{2}$ centimetres (cm = *Zentimeter*), a foot roughly a third of a metre (*Meter*), a yard about $\frac{9}{10}$ m (1 m = $3\frac{1}{3}$ ft) and a mile rather more than $1\frac{1}{2}$ km (*Kilometer* = $\frac{3}{5}$ mile). In the square measure an acre is just under half a hectare (*Hektar*), a square mile is 259 hectares and a German *Morgen* is about $2\frac{1}{4}$ acres. For measuring capacity a pint is just over half a litre (*Liter* = $1\frac{3}{4}$ pints), so a quart is a little over a litre and a gallon about $4\frac{1}{2}$ l. The Germans measure temperature by the Centigrade scale, which they call *Celsius* after a Swedish astronomer. The formula of conversion is F > C: subtract 32 and multiply by $\frac{5}{9}$, C > F: multiply by $\frac{9}{5}$ and add 32.

6

THE VERB (PART I)

CONJUGATION OF SIMPLE AND COMPOUND TENSES –
MOODS – FORMATION OF PASSIVE – PREFIXED VERBS

Forms of simple and compound tenses

German grammarians distinguish, as we do, between (1) active
and passive voice 'I love'/'am loved', (2) indicative, subjunctive
and imperative mood 'I am'/'if I be (were)' 'be ...!' and (3)
present, preterite (or past—often called in German *das Imperfekt*),
future, conditional, perfect 'I am', 'I was', 'I shall be', 'I should be'
—perfect tenses: 'I have been', pluperfect 'I had been', future
perfect 'I shall have been', conditional perfect 'I should have been'.
Though these terms are not always used consistently by grammarians, they are so familiar that it is better to make use of them.

The conjugation of the verb in German is in principle parallel
to that in English, though English has lost some of the personal
endings and word-forms which German has retained. Both
languages have but two simple tenses—a present and a preterite.
All the others are formed by auxiliary verbs. In contrast with
French, both English and German have an analytic future and
conditional—all three languages form their perfect tenses with
auxiliaries + past participle. English has two innovations which
are shared by neither French nor German, namely the provision
of a complete series of 'progressive' tenses, e.g. 'I am singing, was
singing', etc., and a form with 'do', e.g. 'I do like', 'Do you like?',
etc.

Present tenses

In all verbs except 'I am' and modal auxiliaries like 'I can', the

first person singular of the present tense both indicative and subjunctive ends in -*e* and verbs like *handeln* 'to act' with -*eln* and
zittern 'to tremble' with -*ern* drop the *e* and form *ich handle*. In
the first person no distinction is made between the two moods,
e.g. *ich liebe* 'I love', *ich komme* 'I come'. The exceptions to the
regular forms in -*e* are *ich bin* 'I am'/subj. *ich sei*; *ich darf* 'I may'/
subjunctive *ich dürfe*; *ich kann* 'I can'/*ich könne*; *ich mag* 'I like'/
ich möge; *ich muß* 'I must'/*ich müsse*; *ich soll* 'I am to'/*ich solle*;
ich will 'I will, want to'/*ich wolle*.

The second person singular of all tenses of all verbs has, as in
English, the ending -*st*, before which *e* is inserted (1) if the verb
stem ends in a dental consonant (*t, d, s, ss, z* but not *n*), e.g. *rett-en*
'to save', *du rettest* 'thou savest'; *reden* 'to speak', *du redest*;
rasen 'to rage', *du rasest* (in speech *du rast*); *reizen* 'to stir up',
du reiz[e]st—but they only require -*e*- after them when the vowel
of the verb root is unchanged, otherwise *lesen* 'to read', *du liest*,
also *du weißt* 'thou knowest'; (2) to mark the difference between
present indicative and present subjunctive, e.g. *du kommst* 'thou
comest'/subj. *du kommest*; *du liebst*/*du liebest*.

The third person singular of the present indicative of all verbs
except *wissen* and the modal auxiliaries ends in -(*e*)*t*, the vowel *e*
being inserted after a *t, tt, n* or *d*, e.g. *er liebt, singt*; *bittet, redet*,
but *er weiß* 'he knows', *er darf, kann, mag, muß, soll, will*. Some
strong verbs mutate the vowel of the root, e.g. *er fährt* 'he goes
(in a vehicle)' or have *i* instead of short *e* and *ie* instead of long
e, e.g. *er gibt* 'he gives', *er bricht* 'he breaks'; *er stiehlt* 'he steals',
the infinitives being *geben, brechen, stehlen* respectively.

In the present subjunctive all verbs except 'to be' have -*e* in
the third person singular, e.g. *er liebe, singe, bitte, rede, handle*
like the first person. The present subjunctive of *sein* 'to be' is *sei*.

In the plural the first and third person (also the polite second
person) take -(*e*)*n* in both indicative and subjunctive, e.g. *wir,
sie, Sie lieben* (*singen, dürfen, kommen*, etc.). The only exceptions
are the verb 'are' with *wir, sie, Sie sind*. Verbs in -*eln*, -*ern* and
tun 'do' omit -*e*-, e.g. *wir handeln, wandern, tun*. The present
subjunctive corresponding to *sind* is *seien*.

The familiar second person plural indicative ends in -*t* (with
-*et* after a *t, tt, n* or *d*), e.g. *ihr liebt*, (*singt, kommt, handelt,
zeichnet*, etc.); *rettet, redet, ratet*, the only exception being *ihr
seid* 'you are'. The present subjunctive form is shown by the insertion of -*e*- before *t* in all cases, e.g. *ihr liebet* (*singet*), also *seiet*.

The imperative

The second person singular and plural have distinctive forms: weak verb: sing.—*e setze, lege, sage*/pl.—*t setzt, legt, sagt*, strong verb: sing.—*komm, fahr, tu*/pl.—*t kommt, fahrt, tut.* Verbs which substitute *i* or *ie* for *e* in the second or third person singular present indicative like *treten/er tritt* have the vowel *i* in the imperative singular, e.g. *brich, sprich, stich, gib, nimm, wirf, iß, friß*, etc., but *e* in the plural *brecht, sprecht, stecht, gebt, nehmt, werft, eßt, freßt; lies/lest, stiehl/stehlt, sieh/seht, befiehl/befehlt.* N.B. *erschrick nicht* 'don't be frightened'/*erschrecke ihn nicht* 'don't frighten him'.

In literary language the missing persons are replaced by the present subjunctive forms, e.g. *er gehe* 'let him go', *gehen wir* 'let us go', *alle stehen auf* 'let all stand up'. In North German speech one frequent substitute is—especially for the first person plural—the imperative of *lassen*, i.e. *laß uns* [*gehen*] 'let us go' (fam.), *laßt uns* [*gehen*] (fam. plural), *lassen Sie uns* [*gehen*] (polite). Another substitute is *wir wollen*, e.g. *wir wollen heute schwimmen gehen* 'let's go for a swim today'. See pp. 94 and 100.

If the English imperative contains a warning with or without an implied threat, German sometimes uses a *daß*- clause with the verb at the end, e.g. *daß du dich nur ('ja) nicht erkältest!* 'now don't go and catch cold!' or *daß du dich 'ja warm hältst!* 'mind you keep warm!'

Classes of strong verbs

Verbs showing internal vowel change in forming their preterite tense and past participle fall into classes according to the specific variation of vowel. In some classes the *-e-* of the present stem is replaced by *i* or *ie* in the second and third person singular of the present indicative and stems in *a, o, au* normally mutate in those persons of the present indicative.

Class 1:

   (a) *ei/i/i.* Type *greifen* 'to seize' *ich greife/ich griff/ich habe gegriffen.*

      Verbs in *ei*+voiceless consonant (*f, ch, ss, t*): *pfeifen* 'to whistle', *gleichen* 'to resemble', *beißen* 'to bite', *reißen* 'to tear', *reiten* 'to ride' together with two verbs in *d* showing an ancient consonantal change as well: *leiden* 'to suffer', *schneiden* 'to cut' which have *litt/gelitten* and *schnitt/geschnitten* respectively.

(b) *ei/ie/ie*. Type *bleiben* 'to remain' *ich bleibe/ich blieb/ich bin geblieben*. Verbs in *ei* + voiced consonant or without any following consonant: *reiben* 'to rub', *schreiben* 'to write', *steigen* 'to ascend', *schweigen* 'to be silent', *leihen* 'to lend', *verzeihen* 'to pardon', *schreien* 'to shout'.

Class 2:

(a) *ie/o/o*. Type *schießen* 'to shoot', *ich schieße/ich schoß/ich habe geschossen*. The only other verbs are *schließen* 'to close', *fließen* 'to flow'.

(b) *ie/ō/ō*. Type *bieten* 'to offer', *ich biete/ich bot/ich habe geboten*.

Verbs in *ie* + voiced consonant (*g, r*) or *h* and vowel, e.g. *biegen* 'to bend', *fliegen* 'to fly', *wiegen* 'to weigh'; *frieren* 'to freeze', *verlieren* 'to lose'; *fliehen* 'to flee'. To this class belong two verbs which formerly had *ie*, but now have *ü*; *lügen* 'to lie'/*log/gelogen* and *betrügen* 'to deceive'/*betrog/betrogen*. cf. also *schwören* 'to swear'/ *schwor/geschworen* and *heben* 'to lift'/*hob/gehoben*.

Class 3:

(a) *i/a/u*. Type *finden* 'to find', *ich/finde/ich fand/ich habe gefunden*.

Verbs in *i* + *nd, ng, nk*, e.g. *binden* 'to tie, bind'; *singen* 'to sing', *springen* 'to jump', *dringen* 'to press, urge', *zwingen* 'to compel'; *sinken* 'to sink', *trinken* 'to drink'.

(b) *i/a/o*. Type *schwimmen* 'to swim', *ich schwimme/ich schwamm/ich habe geschwommen*.

Verbs in -*mm* and -*nn*-, e.g. *beginnen* 'to begin', *gewinnen* 'to gain, win', *sinnen* 'to meditate'. Also *kommen* 'to come'/ *ich kam/ich bin gekommen* (originally Class 3c).

(c) *e/a/o*. Type *helfen* 'to help', *ich helfe/du hilfst/er hilft, ich half/ich habe geholfen*.

Verbs with *l* or *r* + consonant, e.g. *werfen* 'to throw', *verderben* 'to spoil', *verbergen* 'to hide', *sterben* 'to die'. Some verbs have the *r* in front of the vowel, namely *brechen* 'to break' and *sprechen* 'to speak' with *du brichst, er bricht* and *du sprichst, er spricht*—these have their preterite with a long *a* in *brach, sprach* but the past participles *gebrochen* and *gesprochen* are short. cf. *treffen* 'to strike'/*trifft/traf/ getroffen*. To this class now belong the verbs with long vowel in present, *nehmen* 'to take' (*du nimmst, er nimmt/ nahm/genommen*) and *befehlen* 'to order' and *stehlen* 'to steal', both of which have *ie*, namely *du befiehlst, er befiehlt/ befahl/befohlen*, cf. *du stiehlst, er stiehlt/stahl/gestohlen.*

Class 4:

e/a/e. Type *geben* 'to give', *ich gebe/du gibst, er gibt*, long despite spelling/*ich gab/ich habe gegeben.*

Apart from *geben* and *treten* 'to step' verbs with long *e* in the infinitive replace *e* by *ie* in the second and third person singular present indicative, e.g. *ich sehe* 'I see'/ *du siehst, er sieht/sah/gesehen, geschehen* 'to happen', *es geschieht/es geschah/es ist geschehen*, and *ich lese* 'I read'/ *du liest, er liest/las/gelesen.* Other verbs of the class are *essen* 'to eat' (*ißt/aß/gegessen*), *fressen* 'to eat' (of an animal), like *essen, messen* 'to measure' (*mißt/maß//gemessen*), *vergessen* 'to forget' (*vergißt/vergaß/vergessen*). Two verbs have *i* in the present: *bitten* 'to ask' (cf. E. 'ran') with *ich bat, ich habe gebeten*, a verb which must not be confused with *bieten/bot/geboten* 'offer' or the weak *beten/betete/gebetet* 'pray'; *sitzen* 'to sit'/*ich saß/ich habe gesessen*, a verb of which the causative is the weak verb *setzen/setzte/gesetzt* 'set, put'. Finally there is the verb *liegen* 'to lie, be lying down'/*ich lag* 'I lay'/*ich habe gelegen* 'I have lain, been lying down', a verb of which the causative is the weak verb *legen/legte/gelegt* 'lay, put'. The verb *liegen* 'to lie (down)' must not be confused with *lügen/log/gelogen* 'tell a lie', cf. Class 2*b* above.

Class 5:

a/u/a. Type *fahren* 'to go, travel', *ich fahre/du fährst/ er fährt, ich fuhr/ich bin gefahren.*

These verbs with the exception of *schaffen* mutate the vowel *a* in second and third person sing. pres. indic. All have *a* in the infinitive, e.g. *graben* 'to dig' (*gräbst, gräbt/ grub/gegraben*), *laden* 'to load', *tragen* 'to carry, wear', *schlagen* 'to hit, beat', *waschen* 'to wash' (*wäschst, wäscht*), *wachsen* 'to grow' (*wächst, wächst*; the *u* of *wusch* is long).

Class 6:

a/ie/a. Type *schlafen* 'to sleep', *ich schlafe/du schläfst, er schläft/ich schlief/ich habe geschlafen.*

All verbs in this class have preterite in *ie* except *fangen* 'to catch', and *hangen* 'to be hanging', which have *fing*, *hing*, with short *i* vowel. There are present stems with *a* like *schlafen, blasen* 'to blow' (*bläst/blies/geblasen*), *raten* 'to advise' (*rätst, rät/riet/geraten*), *fallen* 'to fall' (*fällst, fällt/ fiel/gefallen*), *halten* 'to hold' (*hältst, hält/hielt, gehalten*), *lassen* 'to let, leave' (*läßt/ließ/gelassen*). Also verbs with other vowels, e.g. *ich heiße* 'I am called' (*hieß/geheißen*), *ich laufe* 'I run' (*läufst, läuft/lief/gelaufen*), *ich stoße* 'I push, thrust' (*stößt/stieß/gestoßen*), *ich rufe* 'I call' (*rufst, ruft/rief/gerufen*).

Compound forms

Before the compound forms of the verb for the future, conditional, perfect and passive are set forth the conjugational forms of the auxiliary verbs *sein* 'to be', *haben* 'to have', and *werden* 'to become' are here given.

	Present Indicative	Present Subjunctive	Preterite Indicative	Preterite Subjunctive
ich	*bin* *habe* *werde*	*sei* *habe* *werde*	*war* *hatte* *wurde*	*wäre* *hätte* *würde*
du	*bist* *hast* *wirst*	*seiest* *habest* *werdest*	*warst* *hattest* *wurdest*	*wärest* *hättest* *würdest*
er	*ist* *hat* *wird*	*sei* *habe* *werde*	*war* *hatte* *wurde*	*wäre* *hätte* *würde*
wir, pol. *Sie, sie*	*sind* *haben* *werden*	*seien* *haben* *werden*	*waren* *hatten* *wurden*	*wären* *hätten* *würden*
ihr	*seid* *habt* *werdet*	*seiet* *habet* *werdet*	*wart* *hattet* *wurdet*	*wäret* *hättet* *würdet*

The future is formed in German by the use of the forms of *werden* followed by the infinitive. In the principal clause the infinitive comes at the end, all objects direct and indirect and all circumstantial words and phrases being fitted between the form of *werden* and its infinitive, e.g. *ich werde morgen kommen* 'I shall come tomorrow', *ich werde ihm morgen das Buch geben* 'I shall give him the book tomorrow.'

The conditional

The conditional is formed by the preterite subjunctive of *werden*, namely *ich würde/wir würden*, etc. It can sometimes be replaced by the preterite subjunctive of the verb it governs, e.g. *ich würde kommen—ich käme*; *ich würde haben—ich hätte*, etc.

Corresponding to the English 'should'/'would' forms, German uses *würde (-st,-; -n, -t, -n)*. This form occurs more frequently in the main clause than in a subordinate clause, where the simple past subjunctive is usually preferred e.g. *ich würde es kaufen, wenn ich Geld genug hätte* 'I should buy it if I had enough money' where the implication is negative, i.e., 'I shall not in the circumstances . . .' and *wenn Sie in Not geraten sollten, würde ich Sie gern unterstützen* 'if you should be in distress (at any time), I would gladly support you' where a contingency is indicated. In spite of purists there is some excuse for using *würde* in the subordinate clause if there is no distinction between subjunctive and indicative (*liebte, sagte*) or the subjunctive form is anomalous (*begönne, stürbe*).

The form (*ich*) *würde* (*kommen, es tun*) is even in the main clause frequently replaced by the more condensed simple past subjunctive, e.g. *ich käme* 'I should come', *ich täte es* 'I should do so'.

In an indirect statement *würde* represents a 'shifted' future, e.g. *er sagte, er würde uns besuchen* 'he said he would visit us', where the direct statement would run *ich werde Sie besuchen*; *ich nehme an, Sie würden Barzahlung vorziehen* 'I expect you would prefer cash'.

The perfect tenses

In English the perfect tenses are formed with the verb *have*. They are four in number:

(1) I have seen (it)/I have come;
(2) I had seen (it)/I had come;
(3) I shall have seen (it)/I shall have come;
    (will)   (will)
(4) I should have seen (it)/I should have come.
  (would)   (would)

In German the perfect tenses are formed with *haben* in the case of all verbs with an object, including reflexives, and of some intransitives, but *sein* is used to form the perfect of most intransi-

tives (see below). The perfect tenses in German corresponding to
the English examples given are:

(1)   *ich habe (es) gesehen/ich bin gekommen.*
(2)   *ich hatte (es) gesehen/ich war gekommen.*
(3)   *ich werde (es) gesehen haben/ich werde gekommen sein.*
(4)   *ich würde (es) gesehen haben/ich würde gekommen sein.*
     =*ich hätte (es) gesehen*   =*ich wäre gekommen.*

Haben forms the perfect of (a) all verbs with an accusative
object: *ich habe den Brief gelesen* 'I have read the letter'; (b)
verbs with the accusative of the reflexive (-self) pronoun: *ich habe
mich gewaschen* 'I have washed myself'. Note the difference from
French: *je me suis lavé*; (c) verbs without any object (intransitive
verbs) if they express an occurrence lasting over a certain time or
being repeated: *ich habe [lange] gewartet* 'been waiting', *gezögert*
'hesitating', *gestanden* 'been standing', *gelegen* 'been lying down',
gesessen 'been sitting', *geschwiegen* 'kept silent', *geweint* 'been
crying', *gelebt* 'lived, been alive', *geatmet* 'breathed'; *es hat lange
gedauert* 'lasted, taken'; *er hat [hier] gewohnt* 'lived', 'been living'
or 'staying'. *Sein* forms the perfect of (a) *sein* 'to be': *ich bin [hier]
gewesen* 'I have been [here]'; (b) *werden* 'to become': *ich bin
[alt] geworden* 'I have become [old]'; (c) *bleiben* 'to remain':
ich bin [hier] geblieben 'I have remained [here]'; (d) verbs indicating
a change of state, e.g. *er ist gestorben* 'has died' (*vergangen*
'passed', *verschwunden* 'disappeared'), *ich bin gefallen* 'I have
fallen' (*gesunken* 'sunk', *gestürzt* 'crashed'), *er ist gewachsen*
'he has grown', *er ist gekommen* 'he has come', *er ist gegangen*
'he has gone', *es ist geschehen* 'it has happened', *es ist mir gelungen*,
lit. 'it has prospered me', i.e. 'I have succeeded', *die Tasse ist
gesprungen* 'the cup has (is) cracked', *das Eisen ist gerostet* 'the
iron has rusted', *der Schnee ist geschmolzen* 'the snow has melted',
der Teich ist zugefroren 'the pond has frozen over'.

   Some verbs of motion like *schwimmen, rudern, reiten* take
haben for action over a period of time or repetition, e.g. *ich habe
viel geschwommen*, but *sein* if there is mention of some goal, i.e.,
a change of place, e.g. *ich bin über den See geschwommen* 'I have
swum across the lake'.

   Durative verbs like *sitzen* 'to be sitting', *liegen* 'to be lying',
stehen 'to be standing' take *haben*, e.g. *wir haben lange gesessen*
(*gelegen, gestanden*). The verbs marking the beginning of the
period of sitting or lying like 'to sit down', 'to lie down', are in

German reflexive, e.g. *ich habe mich gesetzt (gelegt)*, cf. Fr. *s'asseoir, se coucher.*

The passive

The passive of action is in German indicated by the use of forms of *werden* with the past participle. Thus corresponding to the active *ich lobe ihn* 'I praise (am praising) him', *ich lobte ihn* 'I praised him', *ich werde ihn loben* 'I shall praise him' are the passive forms *er wird [von mir] gelobt* 'he is [being] praised [by me]', *er wurde gelobt* 'he was praised', *er wird gelobt werden* 'he will be praised'. To the perfect tenses *ich habe ihn gelobt* and *ich hatte ihn gelobt* correspond the perfect passive in which the passive-forming phrase consists of a form of the verb *sein* + past participle of main verb + *worden* (instead of *geworden*), e.g. *er ist gelobt worden* 'he has been praised' and *er war gelobt worden* 'he had been praised'.

The so-called actional passive thus formed with the auxiliary *werden* is used when the main verb indicates an occurrence either actual or habitual, e.g. *die Tür wird jetzt geschlossen* 'the door is now being closed' (sometimes *wird* + past participle is a sufficient indication of a future event 'the door will be closed'); *die Tür wird jeden Abend um sechs Uhr geschlossen* 'the door is closed (gets closed) every evening at six o'clock'. If no agent is mentioned, the test is to see whether the passive phrase can become active by using *man* 'one', e.g. *man schließt die Tür.*

Unlike English there is an impersonal passive in German, e.g. *Oben wird getanzt* 'there is dancing on upstairs', *um Eins wird gegessen* 'dinner is at 1 p.m.'

If the English phrase 'am', 'is', 'was', etc. + past participle indicates a state and not an occurrence, German like English uses forms of the verb *sein*, e.g. *die Tür ist geschlossen* 'the door is closed, i.e. not open', just like *die Tür ist angelehnt* 'ajar' or *offen* 'open', *ich war erschöpft* 'I was exhausted' just like *ich war müde* 'I was tired'.

The passive is used more frequently in English than in German. Various equivalents of such English constructions as 'he was heard to say', 'known to be', etc., are discussed with the modal auxiliaries.

Verbs with prefixes

Like English, German has a large number of verbs formed with prefixes, e.g. *be-* (*besprechen* formed like 'bespeak'), *ver-* (*vergessen* like 'forget'). These prefixes together with *emp-* or *ent-* (*entkommen* 'escape'), *er-* (*erreichen* 'reach'), *ge-* (*gerinnen* 'coagulate'), *miß-* (*mißfallen* 'displease'), *wider-* (*widerstehen*, cf. 'withstand'), *zer-* (*zerhacken* 'chop to pieces'), *hinter-* (*hinterlassen* 'bequeath') are inseparable and unstressed. They omit the *ge-* of the past participle, e.g. *besprochen, vergessen, erreicht, widerstanden, zerhackt.* English has some examples of the prefixes like 'under' and 'over' which are inseparable in verbs like 'undertake' and 'overtake', but used as separate particles in 'go under' and 'take over'. In German *unter-, über-, um-* and *durch-* are used as unstressed inseparable prefixes with some verbs, e.g. *unternehmen* 'to undertake'/*unternahm*/ *unternommen*; *übersetzen* 'to translate'/*übersetzte*/*übersetzt*; *durchdringen* 'to permeate'/*durchdrang*/*durchdrungen.* When these three prefixes are stressed they belong to the class of separable prefixes which show a certain resemblance to the looser English groups like 'take over', 'go under', 'put through', etc., e.g. *ich kriege ihn unter* 'I get him down', *ich setze ihn über* 'I ferry him across', *ich reise durch* 'I travel right through', cf. further *die Milch läuft über* 'the milk is spilling over'/*es überläuft mich kalt* 'my blood runs cold'. Separable *um-* indicates a downward motion in *ich falle um* 'I fall over' (*ich falle hin* 'I fall down') and a transfer in *ich steige um* 'I change (trains)'. When inseparable it indicates 'all round' as in *umgeben* 'to surround', *umarmen* 'to embrace'. Note *ich gehe mit ihm um* 'I associate (go about) with him', but *ich umgehe das Hindernis* 'I dodge the obstacle'.

There are a number of detachable prefixes in German of which the chief are *ab* 'off', (*ich fahre ab* 'I start'), *an* 'on' (*ich ziehe es an* 'I put it on'), *auf* 'up, open, on' (*ich mache es auf* 'I open it'), *aus* 'out' (*ich gehe aus* 'I go out'), *bei* 'by, at' (*ich stehe ihm bei* 'I stand by him'), *ein* 'in' (*ich dringe ein* 'I penetrate'), *fort* 'away' (*ich gehe fort* 'I go away'), *hin* 'down' (*ich falle hin* 'I fall down'), *mit* 'with' (*ich teile es mit* 'I communicate it'), *nach* 'after' (*ich laufe ihm nach* 'I run after him'), *vor* 'before, in front' (*ich ziehe es vor* 'I prefer it'), *weg* 'away' (*ich nehme es weg* 'I take it away'), *zu* 'to, shut' (*ich mache es zu* 'I close it'), *zurück* (*ich komme zurück* 'I come back') and *zusammen* 'together' (*ich bringe sie zusammen* 'I bring them together'). Among the compound separable prefixes are those formed with unstressed *hin-* indicating direction away from the speaker and with unstressed *her-* indicating direction towards the speaker, e.g.

  ich gehe hinauf 'I go up'/*er kommt herauf*;
  ich gehe hinaus 'I go out'/*er kommt heraus*;
  ich gehe hinein 'I go in'/*er kommt herein*;

  ich gehe $\begin{cases} hinab \\ hinunter \end{cases}$ 'I go down'/*er kommt* $\begin{cases} herab \\ herunter \end{cases}$

In North German speech *heraus* ('*raus*) and *herunter* ('*runter*) are often used instead of the *hin*-forms for direction from the speaker.

Unlike English the stressed separable particles go to the very end of the main clause, e.g. 'I am going out this evening', *ich gehe heute abend aus*. In the infinitive they precede their verb and are written together with it, e.g., *ich werde heute abend ausgehen*. The present participle too, has *ausgehend*. In the past participle *ge-* is inserted between the prefix and the verb, e.g. *ich bin heute abend ausgegangen* and if the infinitive has *zu* this is also inserted, e.g. *ich habe die Absicht, heute abend auszugehen*.

In the subordinate clause the finite, i.e., personally conjugated verb follows the separable prefix as it itself occupies the end-position, e.g., *wenn ich heute abend ausgehe* 'if I go out this evening'; *da ich heute abend ausgegangen bin* 'as I have gone out this evening'; *da ich heute abend ausgehen will* 'as I want to go out this evening'.

7

THE VERB (PART II)

USE OF TENSES AND MOODS

Present

The present tense is in German the basic tense, for it indicates not only present and universal time, but also in certain contexts and situations the future and even the past.

In relation to present time the present refers to an action in progress, e.g. *ich schreibe* 'I am writing' or a state lasting through the present, e.g. *er sitzt drüben* 'he is sitting over there'. The nuance of the English progressive form with *-ing* can be brought out by a phrase like *ich bin am* (*beim*) *Schreiben* or *ich bin mit Schreiben beschäftigt* 'busy writing', cf. *der Arzt ist dabei, seinen Blutdruck zu messen* 'the doctor is taking his blood-pressure'. Occasionally a particle like *gerade* 'just (now)' or *jetzt* or *noch* 'still' or *immerhin* 'always' or *schon* 'already' with the simple verb gives the impression of a progressive action, e.g. *seine neue Stelle gefällt ihm schon* 'he is liking his new job', *der Junge findet sich noch ein bißchen schwer zurecht* 'the boy is not finding things easy', *will er uns nur ärgern?* 'is he being tiresome?', *was sagt man denn in Amerika zu dieser Krise?* 'what are they saying in America about this crisis?'.

The present is also used for an habitually repeated action, e.g. *ich wohne im Winter in der Stadt* 'in winter I live in town'. Hence also the present describes a characteristic, e.g. *er schreibt schön* 'he writes beautifully'.

Further, the present is used for a general truth, e.g. a philosophical, scientific or any objective statement as in *zweimal zwei ist vier* 'twice two are four', *das Wasser siedet bei* 100° *C* (=

hundert Grad Celsius) 'water boils at 100° C, *der Rhein entspringt in der Schweiz* 'the Rhine rises in Switzerland', etc.

In relation to past events the so-called 'historical present' is used for dramatic effect, e.g. *er kommt plötzlich herangeritten. Was tut er?* . . . 'suddenly he comes riding up. What does he do? . . .'.

As in English the present is used when appealing to a past pronouncement, e.g. *Goethe sagt* . . . 'Goethe says . . .' or *Goethe meint* 'is of opinion . . .', cf. *ich höre, daß* 'I have heard that . . .'

The present is very often used to indicate future time (1) when the verb is in a subordinate clause introduced by a temporal conjunction like *wenn* 'when', *bis* 'until', or *bevor* 'before', e.g. *warten Sie, bis ich da bin* 'wait till I am there'; *ich will ihn sprechen, bevor er nach Hause geht* 'I want to see (speak to) him, before he goes home', and (2) when the context makes it clear whether by temporal specification or not that the future is meant, e.g. *wir fahren morgen* 'we are travelling tomorrow', *wann kommt er?* 'when is he coming?', *Sie finden einige Angaben im Reallexikon* 'you will (can) find some data in the encyclopaedia'.

The present is used for a peremptory request as in speaking to children, e.g. *du kommst sofort mit* 'you'll come (you're coming) along with me at once'.

The present tense is further used as it is in French for an action beginning in the past and lasting through the actual present, e.g. French *nous demeurons ici depuis* . . ., German, *wir wohnen hier seit* . . . In such cases English has recourse to the perfect, sometimes the progressive perfect, e.g. 'we have been living here for several years' or 'we have known him a long time'. The following are some typical cases of the German present: *wie lange wohnen Sie schon hier?* 'how long have you been living here? (*schon* 'already'); *wohnen Sie hier schon lange?* 'have you been living here long?'; *ich suche Sie überall* 'I have been looking for you everywhere'; *wir kennen uns seit vielen Jahren* 'we have known each other for many years'. A touch of vividness is added to the German by the use of *nun schon*, lit. 'now already', e.g. *unser Mädchen geht nun schon seit sechs Monaten mit diesem jungen Mann* 'our maid has been going about with this young man for six months now'; *der spricht nun schon seit zehn Minuten* 'the man has been speaking for the last ten minutes'.

N.B. When the English perfect is negated, German also uses a perfect tense, e.g. *wir haben uns schon seit Jahren nicht* (*mehr*) *gesehen* 'we have not seen each other for years'.

The present is used in German also for the English perfect in such phrases as 'I have come to pay my bill', where English refers more to the completion of an action previously started, e.g. *ich komme um die Miete* 'I've come about the rent'. On the other hand 'I forget what his name is' is rendered *ich habe vergessen, wie er heißt.*

Preterite

The simple past tense (*das Präteritum, die Vergangenheit, das Imperfekt*) is used in German as in English to indicate past events in narrative, e.g. *ich kam, sah, siegte* 'I came, I saw, I conquered'. Its range covers progressive action, e.g. *er rauchte eine Zigarre, als ich hereinkam* 'he was smoking a cigar, when I came in', also a constant, regular or habitual occurrence in the past, e.g. *er hinkte* 'he used to limp', *er ging jeden Abend spazieren* 'he went for a walk every evening' (more explicitly *er war gewohnt, jeden Abend spazierenzugehen* 'he used to go for a walk . . .' and in a more literary setting *er pflegte jeden Abend spazierenzugehen* like 'he would go . . .'.

In the musings of inner speech (*erlebte Rede*) the preterite may even refer to future time. Duden's grammar quotes from Hermann Hesse 'Mein Gott, wie bald, dann *sah* ich sie nicht mehr.' 'I should not see her.'

Future tense

The future tense formed with *werden* is used in a principle clause to indicate intention or simple future event, e.g. *ich werde ihn morgen besuchen* 'I shall visit him tomorrow', *es wird morgen regnen* 'it will rain tomorrow'.

As in English the future is usually replaced in dependent clauses by the present (see above).

The future progressive in English sometimes indicates a prior arrangement or understanding which can be hinted at in German by means of a modal particle, e.g. *ich kann Sie morgen in Hamburg absetzen, da ich doch nach Lübeck fahre* 'I can drop you at Hamburg tomorrow, as I shall be driving to Lübeck'. Usually, however, the simple future in German must suffice, e.g. *was wirst du morgen um diese Zeit tun?* 'What shall you be doing tomorrow at this time?'.

The future often indicates a surmise or probability, e.g. *er wird wohl da sein* 'I expect he is there', *er wird sechzig sein* 'he will probably be sixty'. The future is also used in a lively interrogative sentence, expressing surprise, e.g. *glücklich? meinst du, ich werde glücklich sein?* 'happy? how do you expect me to be happy?'.

The future can be used as an imperative in giving advice or in admonishing, e.g. *du wirst morgen mitgehen* 'I want you to go along with us tomorrow' or in interrogative form when speaking to a child: *wirst du still sein?* 'now, keep quiet'. It is a shade less peremptory than the use of the present *du bleibst hier!* 'you (jolly well) stay here!'.

The English construction 'I am (was) going to . . .' (cf. French *je vais* with infinitive) has no exact analogue in German, which—to indicate the future—uses *werden* or the simple present. The various nuances of the English phrase can be rendered: (1) imminence of action: *ich wollte gerade aufstehen* 'I was just going to get up', (2) intention: *ich habe die Absicht (ich denke daran) nächsten Sommer in Deutschland zu reisen* 'I am going to travel in Germany next summer', (3) unfulfilled apprehension: *er fühlte, daß er hinfallen würde* 'he felt he was going to fall', (4) strong determination not to submit: *ich lasse mich nicht um meinen Anteil betrügen* 'I'm not going to be cheated of my share'.

Perfect

In North German the perfect is used much as in English, though it is sometimes difficult to render the difference between the simple perfect 'I have done' and progressive perfect 'I have been doing'.

The German perfect may indicate a past event the effects of which last into the present—this may be called the 'resultative perfect', e.g. *wo habe ich die Brille hingelegt?* 'where have I put my spectacles?' (present result: 'I can't find them'); *was haben Sie getan?* 'what have you done?'; *ich habe einen neuen Wagen gekauft* 'I have bought a new car' (and now have it); *Sie werden naß—Sie haben Ihren Mantel nicht ordentlich zugeknöpft* 'you'll get wet—you haven't done up your coat properly'; *ich habe es überall gesucht, aber kann es nicht finden* 'I've looked everywhere, but can't find it'.

Another use of the perfect is with a time indication like 'always', 'frequently', 'at various times', 'ever (at any time)', 'rarely', 'never', e.g. *sind Sie jemals in Italien gewesen?* (also *waren Sie jemals in Italien?*) 'have you ever been to Italy? (were you ever in Italy?)'; *ich habe ihn noch nie in meinem Leben gesehen* 'I've never seen him in my life'; *er ist in vielen Filmen (auf vielen Bühnen) aufgetreten* 'he has appeared in many films (in many plays)', *ich bin ihm immer sorgfältig aus dem Weg gegangen* 'I have always studiously gone out of his way'.

This use of the perfect is closely connected with the 'perfect of experience' used in reminiscences, e.g. *ich habe oft stundenlang am Wasser gesessen und zugesehen, wie die Wellen sich brachen* 'I have often sat for hours at the water's edge watching the waves as they broke' or *Menschen sind schon über Nacht grau geworden* 'men have turned grey in a night'.

In a dependent clause the perfect often has as in English the force of a future perfect, e.g. *ich muß warten, bis ich genug gespart habe* 'I must wait, till I have saved enough'; *wenn Sie die Strümpfe fertig gestopft haben*, 'when you have finished darning the stockings'; *wenn wir nach Osnabrück kommen, sind wir drei Stunden unterwegs gewesen* 'when we get to Osnabrück, we shall have been travelling for three hours' (lit. 'have been on the way').

Sometimes English uses the progressive perfect with a note of annoyance or reproach. In such cases the shade of meaning can at a pinch be brought out in German by modal particles, e.g. *haben Sie etwa mit ihm über den Brief gesprochen?* 'have you been talking to him about the letter?'; *wer hat denn überhaupt heute morgen hier die Adressen geschrieben?* 'who has been writing the addresses here this morning?'; *Sie haben schon wieder die Kartoffeln zu stark gesalzen* 'you've been putting too much salt in the potatoes once again'; *die blauen Flecke in deinem Gesicht zeigen, daß du dich schon wieder mal geprügelt hast* 'the bruises on your face show that you have been fighting again'.

The perfect is also used in German like an English imperative 'have this done' etc., in such cases as a firm request to young people *zum Frühstück hast du aber dein Gesicht gewaschen* 'have your face washed by breakfast time!'.

Pluperfect

In English the pluperfect indicates a past beyond the past, e.g. 'I had already finished the letter, when he came in', or 'we had been living there five years when he joined us' and in such cases German also uses the pluperfect with *hatte* or *war*+past participle. Here are some typical examples: *ich hatte gehofft den 8.30 (acht Uhr dreissig) Zug zu erwischen, aber er war schon weg* 'I had hoped to catch the 8.30 train, but it had already left'; *wir hatten schon fünf Jahre in Kiel gewohnt, als er dorthin zuzog* 'we had been living in Kiel for five years, when he moved there'.

The pluperfect is used in a dependent clause as in English for a 'future in the past', e.g. *ich wartete, bis ich genug gespart hatte* 'I waited till I had saved enough'.

Future Perfect

In German this tense is no more frequent than it is in English. In both languages it indicates the completion of an act at or before a certain time in the future, e.g. *bis morgen werde ich alles verkauft haben* 'by tomorrow I shall have sold everything'. In a dependent clause the perfect is enough, e.g. *warten Sie, bis ich den Brief geschrieben habe* 'wait till I have written the letter', cf. *bis Sie fertig sind, hat der Tee gut gezogen* 'by the time you are ready, the tea will be well brewed'.

Use of the passive substitutes

In English it is possible to say instead of 'soldiers were billeted on them' the active 'they had soldiers billeted on them', cf. German *sie bekamen Soldaten einquartiert* (*bekommen* 'to get'), *ich bekomme das Geld ausgezahlt* (*einen Platz zugewiesen*) 'I have the money paid out (a place allotted)'; similarly *ich möchte dieses Buch eingebunden haben* 'I should like to have this book bound', *wir müssen heute nachmittag das Fenster eingesetzt haben* 'we must have the window put in this afternoon'. It will be noted that there is sometimes an underlying notion of cause about the use of *haben* and it is in the above cases possible to substitute an infinitive with *lassen* (see below). Thus instead of saying *ich möchte das Bild eingerahmt haben* 'I should like to have the picture framed' German can say *ich möchte das Bild einrahmen lassen*. With *haben* the view-point is that of completion, with *lassen* that of initiation. The use of *lassen* is very prevalent where English uses 'have', as shown by the following examples: *ich lasse mir die Haare schneiden* (*einen neuen Anzug machen, ein Haus bauen*) 'have my hair cut (a new suit made, a house built)'.

In colloquial North German there is a curious use of the verb *gehören* 'to belong' with a past participle in the sense of 'ought to be' in such sentences as *er gehört schon längst versetzt* 'he ought to have been transferred long ago', *du gehörst ins Gefängnis gesteckt* 'you ought to be put in prison'. The standard equivalent is the use of a tense of *sollen* or *müssen* of which the applications are discussed in detail below, so that the sentences would run *er hätte schon längst versetzt werden sollen (müssen)* and *du solltest ins Gefängnis gesteckt werden.*

The subjunctive mood

The German subjunctive has two simple tenses, a present and a past. In main clauses the present is used chiefly to indicate (1) a wish, e.g. *Es lebe (lange lebe) die Königin!* 'Long live the Queen!', (2) a hypothesis, e.g. *ABC sei ein gleichschenkliges Dreieck* 'let ABC be an isosceles triangle', especially as a substitute for the missing persons of the imperative, e.g. *ein Punkt P werde durch eine Kraft K nacht rechts gezogen* 'let a point P be pulled to the right by a force K'; *es sei vorläufig nur kurz bemerkt, daß . . .* 'let us note briefly that'; *man nehme eine Zahl . . .* 'take a number . . .'; (3) acquiescence, e.g. *dem sei, wie es wolle* 'be that as it may' (cf. *wie dem auch sei* 'however that may be'). In subordinate clauses the present subjunctive is much less prevalent in North German speech than in the south and in exalted literary style, but it is heard especially in indirect speech and in an 'as if' comparison (see below). Otherwise it tends to give way to the indicative.

In a main clause the chief use of the past subjunctive is to indicate a wish that something may happen which so far has not done so, e.g. *käme er doch!* (=*wenn er doch käme!*) 'if only he would come!'; *wäre er nur hier!* 'if only he were here!'

8

THE VERB (PART III)

THE MODAL AUXILIARIES – INFINITIVE –
PRESENT AND PAST PARTICIPLES

There are certain verbs like 'can/could', 'may/might', 'must', 'shall/should', 'will/would' and 'let' which in both English and German take a following simple infinitive. The application of the German equivalent *können, mögen, sollen, müssen, wollen* and *lassen* agrees in some respects and differs in others when compared with the English verbs. Also, German has a verb *dürfen* 'to be allowed' for which English has no single modal verb corresponding. The indicative forms in German are:

INFINITIVE	PRESENT	PRETERITE
können 'to be able to'	*ich kann/wir können* *du kannst/ ihr könnt* *er kann/sie können*	*konnte/n*, etc.
dürfen 'to be allowed to'	*ich darf/wir dürfen* *du darfst/ihr dürft* *er darf/sie dürfen*	*durfte/n*, etc.
mögen 'to like to'	*ich mag/wir mögen* *du magst/ihr mögt* *er mag/sie mögen*	*mochte/n*, etc.
sollen 'to be expected to'	*ich soll/wir sollen* *du sollst/ihr sollt* *er soll/sie sollen*	*sollte/n*, etc.
müssen 'to be obliged to'	*ich muß/wir müssen* *du mußt/ihr müßt* *er muß/sie müssen*	*mußte/n*, etc.
wollen 'to want to'	*ich will/wir wollen* *du willst/ihr wollt* *er will/sie wollen*	*wollte/n*, etc.
lassen 'to let', 'to cause'	*ich lasse/wir lassen* *du läßt/ihr laßt* *er läßt/sie lassen*	*ließ/en*, etc.

The specific subjunctive forms are (1) for the present tense: *ich(er) könne, du könnest*; *ich(er) dürfe, du dürfest*; *ich(er) möge, du mögest*; *ich(er) solle, du sollest*; *ich(er) müsse, du müssest*; *ich(er) wolle, du wollest*; *ich(er) lasse, du lassest*. (2) for the preterite or simple conditional: *könnte/n, dürfte/n, möchte/n, sollte/n, müßte/n, wollte/n, ließe/n*.

In the future the modal verb follows its infinitive, e.g. [*ich werde*] *kommen können, kommen dürfen, kommen mögen, kommen müssen*, etc.; *ich werde morgen zu Hause bleiben müssen* 'I shall have to stay at home tomorrow', *wird er rechtzeitig zu Hause sein können?* 'will he be able to get home in time?' The infinitive may be used independently, e.g. *er wird* [*es*] *können* 'he will be able [to]'.

The perfect tenses are formed with *haben*. The unaccompanied perfect tenses may be illustrated by *ich habe* (*es*) *gekonnt* 'I have been able', *ich hatte* (*es*) *gewollt* 'I had wanted to', *ich hätte es gemocht* 'I should have liked to'. The other past participles are *gedurft* 'been allowed to', *gesollt* 'been expected to', *gemußt* 'been obliged to', *gelassen* 'let, caused', etc.

When the modal verb is accompanied by an infinitive and is in one of the perfect tenses the past participles *gekonnt, gedurft*, etc., are replaced by an infinitive. The English order differs from the German in that the modal verb 'could', 'might', 'ought to', etc., is conjugated and precedes a perfect infinitive, e.g. 'he could have come', 'he ought to have done it'. The German equivalent of these phrases are *er hätte kommen können, er hätte es tun sollen*. English is nearer to German when instead of using 'can', 'must', etc., we use the synonymous phrases 'I am able', 'I am obliged', etc.', e.g. *ich habe kommen müssen* 'I have been obliged to come', *ich hatte kommen dürfen* 'I have been allowed to come'. German makes a clear distinction between *er hat es tun können* 'he has been able to do it' (ability) and *er kann es getan haben* 'he may have done it' (possibility), *er hat es tun müssen* 'he has had to do it' (necessity) and *er muß es getan haben* 'he must have done it' (probability), *er hat kommen sollen* 'he was expected to come' (obligation) and *er soll gekommen sein* 'he is said to have come' (report), *er hat mich besuchen wollen* 'he has wanted to visit me' (wish) and *er will mich besucht haben* 'he claims to have visited me' (allegation). This distinction applies occasionally to the past subjunctive tenses, e.g. *Sie hätten das lesen sollen* 'you ought to have read that' and *Sie sollten das gelesen haben* 'you were said to have read that' as the past tense of *sollen* 'to be said to', but usually the past tense would be dependent on *man behauptete wenn das Schiff unterginge* (*sollte das Schiff . . .*) *so müßte jemand ein Verräter gewesen sein*, 'if the ship were to be lost, someone must have been a traitor'.

There is a certain amount of overlap between the modal verbs of capability and possibility *können, mögen* and *dürfen* as also between those of obligation *sollen* and *müssen*. The basic meaning of *ich kann* is 'I know how to', e.g. *ich kann schwimmen* or even with a noun-object *ich kann Deutsch*. However, *ich kann es tun* may imply 'it is physically possible for me to do so' (*es ist mir möglich*), cf. *ich kann heute nicht kommen* 'I cannot come today' and—like *ich darf*—it may sometimes imply that I have permission, e.g. *kann* (*darf*) *ich heute nach Hause gehen?* 'can (may) I go home today?'. The connexion with *mag* is shown more in the third person, e.g. *wer kann* (*mag*) *das sein?* 'who can that be? I wonder who that is' *es mag* (*kann*) *wohl zwölf* (*Uhr*) *sein* 'it may be about 12 o'clock', *wer mag es ihm gesagt haben?* 'I wonder who told him'. As to obligation *ich muß* often implies physical necessity ('I can't help it') like English 'I have to', 'am obliged to' (*ich bin gezwungen, es zu tun*) whereas *ich soll* implies reference to someone else's will ('I am expected to . . .') including the will of Fate ('I am destined to . . .') hence 'I am to . . .', 'I have the duty', 'I ought'.

In the North *ich darf* occasionally impinges upon *ich bedarf* 'I require' or *ich brauche* 'I need', e.g. *Sie dürfen nur klingeln* 'all you need do is ring', the German alternative phrase being *Sie brauchen nur* [*zu*] *klingeln*.

The conditionals corresponding to 'I should be able (or allowed or expected or obliged or willing)' are usually expressed by the preterite subjunctive forms *könnte, dürfte, sollte, müßte, wollte, möchte* ('I should like'), which correspond partly to the English forms, e.g. 'I could (if I would or wanted to)' like *könnte*, 'I should (do it)' like *sollte*, 'I ought (to do it)' like *müßte*. Different degrees of possibility may be expressed by *könnte, dürfte* and *möchte*, but *möchte* sounds bookish and pedantic in North German speech. The German *das könnte der Fall sein* 'that might be the case' carries with it—as a German informant said—a fifty-fifty chance, but if we say *das dürfte der Fall sein* the implication is that the speaker is pretty sure of his ground ('that might well be so'), but is expressing his opinion politely and cautiously. Occasionally *das dürfte allerdings der Fall sein* may carry an

ironical implication of 'well, what do you think?—you might
have known' in reply to a naïve question.

The following is a selection of specific applications of the
modal verbs to illustrate the contexts in which they are used in
ordinary speech. These verbs are important ingredients in
German speech and, in some cases, are neat equivalents of
English idioms.

Dürfen

The sentence *Sie dürfen zu uns kommen* implies—according to the
situation—a permission, a right or a justification. English says
'You may (can) come to us', i.e. we will let you. Hence with a
negative *dürfen* is often translated by 'must', e.g. *Sie dürfen nicht
hingehen* 'you mustn't (may not) go there'.

The verb often has a polite ring. The maid who answers the
door says to the caller *darf ich bitten?* lit. 'may I ask you [to come
this way]?' when inviting him in. A guest when asked to take a
further helping may say *wenn ich bitten darf* [*noch etwas Fleisch*]
'[a little more meat] if I may'. A polite way of expressing con-
gratulations is *darf ich Sie* (*zu Ihrem Erfolg*) *beglückwünschen?*
'may I congratulate you [on your success]?' An example of the
infinitive indicating a polite request is *der Gast bat, sich zurück-
ziehen zu dürfen* 'the guest asked to be allowed to withdraw'.

The use of *dürfen* for 'need' and *dürfte* 'might well be' have
already been discussed.

Mögen

The most prevalent use of *ich mag* is 'I like', *ich mochte* 'I liked'
and *ich möchte* 'I should like'. In this meaning it can be used
either with a simple infinitive or with a noun or pronoun object,
e.g. *ich mag ihn, ich mag diese Suppe nicht, ich möchte es tun, die
beiden mögen sich* 'the two are fond of each other'. In the sense of
'like' it is often reinforced with *gern*, lit. willingly, gladly, i.e. 'very
much'. Sometimes *gern* alone suffices, e.g. *ich täte es gern* for *ich
möchte es gern tun*. From this usage it is but a step to *diese
Pflanzen mögen einen sandigen Boden* 'these plants are partial to a
sandy soil'.

From the other meaning of *mag* a concessive implication has
developed, e.g. *mögen die Leute* (*die Leute mögen*) *sagen was sie
wollen* 'let people say (people can say) what they like', hence its
use in an explicit concessive clause, e.g. *so reich er auch sein mag*

'rich though he may be'. Another development is the use of *mag* (or *soll*) in a warning: *er mag (soll) sich nur in Acht nehmen* 'he had better take care', 'let him take care'. The verb is also used in an unintroduced dependent clause as object to a verb of requesting or wishing, e.g. *ich wünschte, er möge kommen* 'I could wish he might (would) come'; *sagen Sie ihm, er möchte uns abholen* 'tell him please to come and fetch us'—also after a verb of fearing in the past tense, *ich fürchtete, er möchte sich blamieren* 'I was afraid he might make a fool of himself' (as against *ich fürchte, er wird sich blamieren* or *ich fürchte, er blamiert sich*).

Müssen

In the background of *müssen* the constraining agency is less personal than with *sollen*. The obligation is imposed by nature or one's nature and circumstances. If we say *jetzt müssen wir auf das Feld gehen* 'now we must go into the field' we think of time or some other factor governing our actions. The verb can also be used for a necessary deduction or inference, e.g. *nach meiner Berechnung muß er bald hier sein* 'according to my calculations he must (should) soon be here', *er muß unsere Verabredung vergessen haben* 'he must have forgotten our appointment'.

Sometimes the appropriate rendering in English is 'cannot help', e.g. *ich mußte lachen* 'I couldn't help laughing'.

With a negative *muß* comes close to *darf* in such sentences as *ich muß (darf) nicht vergessen* 'I mustn't forget'.

The emotive use of *müssen* comes out in such sentences as e.g. *gerade ihn mußte ich treffen* 'of course I had to meet *him* of all people' with an implication often conveyed by *ausgerechnet* 'would you believe it?'. Examples in the present are *muß dich der Teufel auch gerade jetzt herführen* 'fancy meeting you here at this of all times' or *daß du auch gerade heute kommen mußt!* 'of course you have to come today of all days'. Sometimes *muß* occurs in a sentence indicating a culmination of troubles, e.g. *da muß auch noch das Rad kaputt gehen* 'of course the wheel must go and break down'.

The preterite subjunctive is sometimes used synonymously with that of *sollen* in such sentences as *du müßtest (solltest) vor Scham in den Erdboden sinken* 'you ought to go and hide yourself with shame'.

Somewhat literary is the use of the subjunctive in a negative exceptive clause, e.g. *das werde ich nie von ihm glauben, er müßte es mir denn selbst sagen* 'I'll never believe that of him unless he tells me so himself', for which a synonymous expression is *es sei denn, daß er mir es selbst sagt*. In ordinary speech *wenn er es mir nicht selbst sagt* is sufficient.

Sollen

Like English 'shall' the German *sollen* often expresses a peremptory request or desire, e.g. in the Commandments *du sollst nicht stehlen* 'thou shalt not steal'. According to stress and tone *du sollst* can be stronger or weaker, e.g. *du sollst das tun* with stressed verb expects absolute obedience, but *du sollst fleißig sein* with less stress on *sollst* and uttered in a quieter tone indicates simply 'I want you to work hard'. Similarly with the third person *er soll gleich kommen* 'he is to come at once', 'I want him to come at once' or with mitigating particles *er soll mal eben ans Telephon kommen* 'tell him he is wanted on the phone'. From the sense of enjoining the verb *sollen* is often used in calling for (three) cheers, e.g. *er soll leben—hoch! hoch! hoch!* or in the plural *die Studenten sollen leben!*

Sometimes, by a natural extension, the outside agency or third party is Fate or Destiny just as French can use 'devoir'. Examples are:—*bald danach sollte er den Thron besteigen* 'soon afterwards he was to (was destined to) ascend the throne' or *das soll noch kommen* 'that will come about [all right]!' Nearer the personal are *wie sollte er das wissen?* 'how could he (be expected to) have known?' or *ich soll berufen werden?* 'do you mean to say I am to be invited to the post?' This last use of *sollen* for the purpose of putting something up to one's partner is frequent in such sentences as *soll das ein Scherz sein?* 'is that intended to be a joke?', cf. *was soll das?* 'what's the point of that?'

Like *müssen* the verb *sollen* can also express surprise, once again with a covert hint of the nature of things or destiny, e.g. *wen mußte ich da treffen?! Gerade ihn*—or *wen anders sollte ich treffen als gerade Herrn Müller?!* where English is often content with 'who (on earth) do you think I met but . . . ?' but sometimes inserts 'as ill luck would have it, who should I meet but . . . ?'

In the first person *sollen* sometimes indicates an expectation founded on a previous agreement, e.g. *ich soll zehn tausend Mark dafür bekommen?* 'I am to receive 10,000 m. for it?'

Finally *sollen* followed by the perfect infinitive indicates that a statement is based on report or hearsay. It thus becomes the equivalent of *man sagt, daß*—or *es heißt, daß* or the adverb *angeblich* 'allegedly'. Examples: *er soll die Stadt verlassen haben* 'he is said (reported) to have left the town'; *er soll das Buch gestohlen haben—na, was sagst du dazu?* 'people are saying he stole the book—well, what do you say to that?'; *er soll durchs Examen gefallen sein—ist das nicht toll?* 'I hear he's failed his exam.—isn't it ridiculous?'.

Wollen

This verb normally expresses a wish, plan or intention and is the equivalent of *ich habe den Wunsch (den Plan, die Absicht)* or *ich wünsche (beabsichtige) etwas zu tun*. Occasionally it is translated into English by 'will' (especially in questions) or with the negative 'won't', e.g. *wollen Sie mir das Buch leihen?* 'will you lend me the book?'; *es will nicht gehen* 'it won't go'. The usual equivalent in spoken English is now 'want', e.g. *ich will gehen* 'I want to go'; *Blumen wollen gepflegt sein* 'flowers want (need) tending'; *ich wollte Sie danach fragen* 'I wanted to ask you about it'. Occasionally the idea of intention is brought out in English, e.g. *sie will den Kindern ein Fest geben* 'she is thinking of giving the children a party'; *wie wollen Sie das heute noch fertig machen?* 'how do you expect (propose) to get that finished today?'.

The verb is also used to indicate an imminent act, e.g. *ich will eben weggehen* 'I am about to leave'; *ich wollte es eben tun* (=*ich war gerade im Begriff, es zu tun*) 'I was just about to do it'.

As the obverse of *sollen* when used of reporting by others *wollen* indicates a claim on the part of the subject, e.g. *er will es selbst gesehen haben* 'he says he saw it himself', 'he claims to have seen it'. In speech it is possible to say *ich will's nicht gesehen haben* with the underlying idea 'let's pretend I don't see anything'. The subject's reaction appears also in *das will ich meinen!* 'I should just think so!'.

Lassen

In the full non-auxiliary sense *lassen* means 'to leave' or 'leave off', e.g. *lassen Sie das* 'leave that alone', 'stop it'; *lassen Sie das Spaßen!* 'stop joking!' It can also be used of relinquishing things or handing them over, e.g. *ich lasse ihm die Wahl* 'I leave him to choose'; *lassen Sir mir die Ware billiger!* 'let me have the article cheaper!'.

As an auxiliary with infinitive *lassen* means either (1) 'let', 'allow' or (2) 'make', 'cause'. Examples:

(1) *er läßt mich die ganze Arbeit allein machen* 'he lets me do (leaves me to do) all the work by myself'; *lassen Sie die Kinder einen Augenblick ruhen* 'let the children rest a moment!'.

Sometimes the infinitive dependent upon *lassen* can be translated by an English passive. The object can be a reflexive pronoun either in the accusative, e.g. *ich lasse mich nicht einschüchtern* 'I'll not let myself be browbeaten' (lit. I don't let [people] browbeat me), or in the dative with verbs requiring a dative object, e.g. *ich lasse mir nicht gern befehlen* 'I don't like being ordered about', i.e. letting (having) people order me about. With non-personal subject *es* the reflexive phrase has become the vehicle for the expression of passive possibility, e.g. *es läßt sich denken* (*beweisen*) 'it can be imagined (proved)', *es läßt sich nicht leugnen* 'it cannot be denied', 'there is no denying it', *das läßt sich hören* 'that is possible (can be said)' of a translation.

There are certain stereotyped expressions in which *lassen* in meaning (1) plays a part, e.g. *ich lasse es fahren* 'I let it slip'; *ich lasse es hingehen* 'I let it pass'; *ich lasse es fallen* 'I drop it, let it drop'; *ich lasse das Licht* (*das Feuer*) *brennen* 'I leave the light (fire) on', cf. *laß mal sehen* 'let me see'.

(2) In the sense of 'cause' there are several possible constructions. A person can let (or get) another (to) do something, e.g. *ich lasse ihn kommen* 'I send for him'. Explicit reference may be made by the dative case for the person affected by the action whether one's self or another, e.g. *ich lasse mir ein Haus bauen* 'I have a house built for myself' (lit. 'I get [people] to build a house for me') *ich lasse ihm ein Haus bauen* 'for him'. Hence such prevalent expressions as *ich lasse mir die Haare schneiden* 'I have (get) my hair cut', *ich lasse mir einen Anzug machen* 'I have a suit made,' *ich lasse mir den Mantel schicken* 'I have the coat sent'.

More or less stereotyped are *ich lasse ihn holen* 'I have him fetched, send for him'; *ich lasse den Drachen steigen* 'I fly the kite'; *ich lasse grüßen* 'I send my kind regards'.

The use of *laß* (*lassen Sie, laßt*) *uns* [*gehen*] 'let us go' is discussed in the section on the Imperative.

German has no verb of causation so wide in its scope as English 'make', French 'faire' or Dutch 'doen', e.g. in 'he made me laugh', etc. Though the most prevalent rendering is *lassen*, German occasionally uses *machen*, e.g. *wer macht den Tisch wackeln?* (quoted in the *Sprach-Brockhaus*) 'who is making the table rock?'; *er machte mich glauben, daß er viel Geld hat* 'he made me believe that he had a lot of money'. Sometimes a good substitute is *dazu bringen* (lit. 'bring to the point of'), *dazu veranlassen*, or the stronger *dazu zwingen*, e.g. *wenn ich ihn wiedersehe, werde ich ihn dazu bringen, alles, was er gegen mich gesagt hat, zurückzunehmen* 'when I see him again I shall make him take back everything he has said against me'. Otherwise a change of construction is preferable, e.g. *in einigen Szenen mußte ich weinen* 'some scenes made me cry'; *ich hätte mich fast gebrochen*, (*erbrochen*) 'it nearly made me sick'; *sorgen Sie dafür, daß die Kinder früh zu Bett gehen* 'make the children go to bed early'; *passen Sie auf, daß er die Tür noch mal macht* 'make him do the door again' (of a painter).

Infinitive as noun

The infinitive can be used as a declined neuter noun written with a capital letter and often determined by a definite article. Examples: *Reden ist Silber, Schweigen ist Gold* 'speaking is silver, to be silent is gold'; *ich höre das Öffnen eines Fensters* 'I hear the opening of a window' (the infinitive is often neutral as between active, reflexive and passive)[1]; *im Schießen ausgebildet* 'trained in shooting (marksmanship)'; *ich bin kein grosser Freund vom Reisen* 'I am not very fond of travelling'; *Bottiche zum Aufnehmen des Apfelsafts* 'vats to contain the apple-juice'; *die Arbeiter beginnen sofort mit dem Abladen* 'the workmen will start immediately with the unloading'; *beim Wenden auf einer schmalen Straße* 'when turning in a narrow street'; *ich stelle das Geschirr zum Trocknen* 'I put the dishes to drain', cf. *ich hänge die Wäsche zum Trocknen an die Leine* 'I hang out the washing on the line to dry'; *ich stelle die Flüssigkeit auf den Ofen zum Warmwerden* 'I put the liquid on the stove to warm', *ich war nahe am Einschlafen* 'I was near falling asleep.'

Simple infinitive as object

The infinitive written with a small letter is used as the direct complement of certain verbs especially the modal auxiliaries like 'shall', 'will', 'can', 'must', 'may', e.g. *er wird morgen kommen, ich will warten, er kann schwimmen*, also certain intransitive verbs of which the following are typical examples: *ich bleibe liegen* (*stehen, sitzen*) 'I remain lying (standing, sitting)', *ich gehe schwimmen* (*spazieren*) 'I go swimming (for a walk)' and in the past

[1] Thus the noun of *ich erbarme mich* is *das Erbarmen* 'compassion' and of *ich befinde mich* is *das Befinden* 'state of health'.

tenses with the verb 'to be' as in English *ich war heute morgen schwimmen* or *ich bin heute morgen schwimmen gewesen* 'I have been for a swim this morning'.

The simple infinitive, i.e. without *zu* is also used with the verb *lernen*, e.g. *ich lerne schwimmen* 'I am learning to swim', *ich lerne ihn kennen* 'I am getting to know him'. Like the English 'need' which can be used with or without 'to', e.g. 'he need not write', 'he does not need to write' the German *brauchen* has either the simple infinitive or that with *zu*, e.g. *Sie brauchen nicht (zu) kommen*. With 'dare' in 'I dare not come' German must use *zu*: *ich wage nicht zu kommen*.

The simple infinitive is also used when the main verb is transitive and has an accusative object, e.g. with *lassen*, with verbs of experience like those of seeing, hearing, feeling and finding, and a few others like helping, teaching, causing to act. The verb *lassen* has been discussed with other modal auxiliaries. Examples of the other verbs are: *ich sehe (höre) ihn kommen* 'I see (hear) him coming'; *ich fühle ihn heranschleichen* 'I feel him creeping up'; *ich höre ihn schreien* 'I can hear him screaming'; *ich fand ihn auf dem Boden liegen* 'I found him lying on the ground'. With verbs of experience the infinitive is often replaced by a clause introduced by *wie*, e.g. *ich sah, wie er mit der Hand winkte* 'I saw him beckon with his hand'; *er fühlte, wie ihre Arme zitterten* 'he felt her arms tremble'; *hat irgend jemand beobachtet, wie der Dieb das Haus verließ?* 'did anyone observe the thief leaving the house?' where the subordinate clause could be replaced by . . . *den Dieb beim Verlassen des Hauses beobachtet*.

In short sentences the verb *helfen* is used with the simple infinitive, e.g. *er half mir diese Kiste tragen* 'he helped me carry this crate' (also—*beim Tragen dieser Kiste*), but if there are qualifications of the infinitive the latter often takes *zu*, e.g. *er half mir, über die Krankheit wegzukommen* 'he helped me (to) get over the illness'. The same rule applies to *lehren* 'to teach', e.g. *ich lehre ihn schreiben* 'I am teaching him to write (writing)', but *ich lehre ihn, alle schwierigen Wörter im Wörterbuch nachzuschlagen* 'I teach him to look up all difficult words in the dictionary'.

The simple infinitive is used in an idiomatic way (rather reminiscent of the French *j'ai beau le dire*) in such sentences as *er hat gut murren* 'it's all very well him grumbling'.

It is also used with a verb of implication or meaning like

heißen or *bedeuten*, e.g. *das hieße Sie irreführen* 'that would be (tantamount to) leading you astray'.

The simple infinitive is sometimes used instead of an imperative for short directions, e.g. *Hamburg, alles aussteigen!* 'all alight!'; *einsteigen!* 'take your seats'; *umsteigen nach Lübeck!* 'change for Lübeck!'; *bitte nachschicken* 'please forward', *erst siegen, dann reisen* (a slogan like 'is your journey really necessary?').

Infinitive with zu *as complement*

German makes as frequent a use as English does of an infinitival phrase as complement of the verb 'to be', e.g. 'the only thing is to——'. Some of these subjects have already been exemplified in the section on the independent neuter adjective like *das Dumme* 'the stupid thing', *das Einzige* 'the only thing', etc. Typical German examples are *meine einzige Sorge ist, einen Verleger zu finden* 'my only trouble is to find (finding) a publisher'; *mein Hauptfehler war, zu ehrlich zu sein* 'my chief mistake was to be too honest'; *die erste Pflicht eines Gelehrten ist, seine Belege nachzuprüfen* 'a scholar's first duty is to verify his references'; *was mich betrübt, ist dieses Kind vernachlässigt zu sehen* 'what grieves me is to see that child being neglected'; *würde es nicht Wahnsinn sein, abzulehnen?* 'would it not be madness to refuse?'

A note on 'for (him) to' with infinitive

English often uses an infinitive in connexion with a phrase with a noun or pronoun, e.g. 'for a man (him) to do that'. In German the literal equivalent can be used only to a small extent, e.g. *es ist zwecklos für ihn wütend zu werden* 'it's no use for him to fly into a temper'; *es ist höchste Zeit für ihn, ein geordnetes Leben zu beginnen* 'it's high time for him to settle down'. Very often German has to have recourse to a subordinate clause introduced by *damit* 'in order that', *wenn* 'if' or *daß* 'that', e.g. *damit sein Plan gelingt, muß er alle Kräfte anspannen* (note the change of subject) 'for his plan to succeed he must make a big effort'; *es ist beinahe einzigartig in der Geschichte, daß ein Mann sich solche Gewalt anmaßt* 'for a man to arrogate himself such power is almost unique in history'; *es ist ein guter Gedanke, wenn ein Lehrer schon im voraus seinen Unterrichtsplan überdenkt* 'it's a good idea for a teacher to think out his course well in advance'.

After an expression with 'too' there are sometimes alternatives, e.g. *es ist zu naß, um den Acker zu pflügen* or—*zu naß, als daß der*

Acker gepflügt werden könnte 'it is too wet for the field to be ploughed'; *ich warte gespannt auf das Erscheinen des Buchs* or— *darauf, daß das Buch erscheint* 'I am longing for the book to appear'.

Infinitive determining a noun

In some cases the infinitive phrase is synonymous with the genitive of the verb-noun or the first component of a compound, e.g. *die Kunst zu schreiben = die Kunst des Schreibens = die Schreibkunst*, 'the art of writing'. There are other cases where the synonymous expression would be a subordinate clause. The following are typical examples: *der Vorschlag, das Land zu räumen* 'the proposal to evacuate the country'; *ohne Hoffnung, ihn wiederzusehen* 'without hope of seeing him again'; *der Versuch, ihn umzustimmen* 'the attempt to make him change his mind'; *ich habe keine Zeit, mich zu langweilen* 'I have not time to get bored'; *es hat nicht viel Zweck, über das Vergangene zu reden* 'there's not much point in talking about the past'; *es hat keinen Sinn, Krach zu machen* 'there's no sense in making a row'; *der sicherste Weg, befördert zu werden* 'the surest way to get promotion'.

Infinitive with adjective

The *zu*-infinitive with an adjective is either active or passive in implication. Examples of the former are *bange, alles zu verlieren* 'frightened of losing everything'; *geneigt zu übertreiben* 'inclined to exaggerate'; *bereit, sich zu opfern* 'ready to sacrifice one's self'. The passive use is paralleled in English 'a house to let' or 'fit to keep'. German examples are *leicht zu lernen* 'easy to learn', *billig zu kaufen* 'cheap to buy', *hoch zu bewerten* 'highly to be valued'. When this passive type of phrase is used attributively before a noun the infinitive is replaced by the declined *-end* form, e.g. *eine leicht zu erlernende Sprache* 'a language easy to learn'.

N.B. In English the 'to'-infinitive is used with a superlative or an adjective indicating uniqueness in cases where German would prefer a relative, e.g. *er war der erste, der sich erbot* 'he was the first to volunteer' or *er war der einzige, der kam* 'he was the only one to come'. Only occasionally does one come across sentences like *er war der Mann, so etwas zu unternehmen* 'he was the man to undertake such a thing'. English also often uses an infinitive with 'to be sure or likely', 'to be liable', 'to happen', but German prefers to use an adverb meaning 'certainly', 'probably', 'easily' or 'by chance', e.g. *er kommt sicher* 'he is sure to come', *das geschieht leicht* 'it is apt (liable) to happen', *ich traf ihn zufällig auf der Straße* 'I happened to meet him in the street'.

In English certain verbs like those of knowing, believing, admitting, proving, expecting, liking, wanting, preferring, intending can take an object—'to'-infinitive. German cannot do this in most cases though there is an infinitive construction with words of asking and ordering, e.g. *ich bitte ihn, es zu tun* 'I ask him to do it', *ich befahl ihm zu schweigen* 'I ordered him to be silent'. The other verbs require a *daß*-clause, e.g. *ich weiß, daß das wahr ist* 'I know that to be true'; *ich bin jetzt der Ansicht, daß er falsch gehandelt hat* 'I now believe him to have acted wrongly'; *wir bewiesen, daß er Unrecht hatte* 'we proved him to be wrong'; *ich erwarte, daß Sie fleißig arbeiten* 'I expect you to work hard'; *er möchte, daß ich pünktlich am Bahnhof bin* 'he would like me to be at the station punctually'; *ich will nicht, daß Sie bleiben* 'I don't want you to stay'; *ich möchte lieber, daß Sie nicht zu weit von hier weggehen* 'I prefer you not to go too far away from here'; *ich wollte nicht, daß Sie das hörten* 'I did not mean you to hear that'. A noun with *zum* at times conveys a suggestion of 'enough to make one . . .', e.g. *es ist zum Verrücktwerden* 'it is enough to drive one mad'; *zum Schleißen* 'enough to make a cat laugh', *zum Heulen* 'for crying out loud'; *ich hatte Hunger zum Umfallen* 'I was faint with hunger' (lit. hunger to make me fall down).

Prepositions introducing infinitive phrases

In German the only prepositions introducing infinitives with *zu* are *um* 'in order to', *statt* (or *anstatt*) 'instead of' and *ohne* 'without', e.g. *ich fuhr nach Kiel, um ihn zu besuchen* 'I went to Kiel (in order) to visit him'; *um nur einiges anzuführen* 'to mention but a few things', cf. too *nach ihm zu urteilen* 'judging by him'; *[an]statt mir zu danken* 'instead of thanking me'; *ich tat es, ohne es zu wollen* 'I did it without wanting to'. Other prepositions German combines with *da(r)*, especially when the infinitive phrase refers to the same subject of the main verb, e.g. *ich bestehe darauf, selbst zu bezahlen* 'I insist on paying', i.e. on my paying; *haben Sie daran gedacht, das Fenster zuzumachen?* 'did you remember to close the window?' (your act); *ich war damit beschäftigt, einen Brief zu schreiben* 'I was busy (occupied with) writing a letter'; *ich habe mich daran gewöhnt, mich mit kaltem Wasser zu waschen* 'I've got used to washing in cold water' (also *ich habe*

4

mich an das Waschen mit . . . ̦ewöhnt). If there is a change of
subject the infinitival phrase must be replaced by a *daß*-clause,
e.g. *ich bestehe darauf, daß er bezahlt* 'I insist upon him (his)
paying'; *es endete damit, daß ich nachgab* 'it ended in my giving
way'. When the English phrase with preposition + 'ing' indicates a
relation of time, condition, cause, concession, etc., it is better in
German to use the appropriate dependent clause introduced by
bevor 'before', *nachdem* 'after', *wenn* 'if', *da* 'as', *obgleich* 'although',
etc., e.g. *bevor ich dieses Gedicht bespreche* 'before discussing
this poem'; *nachdem Sie das Formular ausgefüllt haben* 'after
filling up the form'; *da ich mich schwach fühlte* 'feeling faint';
trotzdem er arm ist 'in spite of being poor'; *was meinen Sie dazu,
wenn wir ihm einen Besuch machen?* 'what would you say to our
paying him a visit?'

The present participle

German has a form in *-end* corresponding to the English participle
in '-ing'. After the verb 'to be' it is only used when the form is the
equivalent of an adjective, e.g. *[es ist] reizend* 'charming', *über-
zeugend* 'convincing', *bedeutend* 'significant' and the like. It is
used occasionally for an accompanying circumstance, e.g. *sie
kam lachend ins Zimmer* 'she came into the room laughing', but
often the participle is replaced by a finite verb, e.g. *sie saß und
nähte* 'she sat sewing'. A phrase like 'the gypsies living in a
caravan' is normally replaced by a relative clause: *die Zigeuner,
die in einem Wagen wohnen,* but in the written language it is
possible to use 'living, etc.' as an attributive phrase before the
noun, e.g. *die in einem Wagen wohnenden Zigeuner,* cf. *Dein dich
liebender Vater* 'your affectionate father'.

A note on the German equivalents of English constructions with '-ing'

For the adjectival uses, see the above section on the present
participle in *-end* and note the use of the relative clause, e.g. in
'hills towering over the city' = *die Hügel, die die Stadt überragen.*
There are a number of different ways of rendering the verbal
'-ing' and examples are given in the sections on the infinitive, e.g.
ich sah ihn kommen and the past participle, e.g. *er kam heran-
gesprengt* 'he came galloping up'. Other ways include the following:

(1) Use of noun: 'On receiving the news' = *bei Empfang der
Nachricht;* 'by selling first editions' = *durch den Verkauf von*

Erstausgaben; 'he spends all his time hunting' = *er verbringt seine ganze Zeit auf der Jagd (beim Jagen)*; 'he burst out crying (laughing)' = *er brach in Tränen (in ein Gelächter) aus.* Also a noun infinitive, e.g. *(das Zimmer) hat gründliches Staubwischen nötig* 'needs a good dusting'.

(2) Use of certain adverbs: 'I like reading poems' = *ich lese gern Gedichte*; 'I prefer reading novels' = *ich lese lieber Romane*; 'I go on reading' = *ich lese weiter*.

(3) Use of infinitive with *zu*: 'they started hissing' = *sie fingen an (begannen) zu zischen,* 'it stopped raining' = *es hörte auf zu regnen*; 'I hate having to queue' = *ich hasse es, anstehen zu müssen*; 'we aim at having the flat ready by October' = *es ist unser Ziel, die Wohnung bis Oktober fertig zu haben*; 'I had no difficulty in finding a porter' = *ich hatte keine Schwierigkeit, einen Träger zu finden*.

(4) Use of a *da*-compound with the *zu*-infinitive: 'busy lighting the fire' = *damit beschäftigt, das Feuer anzuzünden;* 'used to washing in cold water' = *daran gewöhnt, sich mit kaltem Wasser zu waschen/ an das Waschen ... gewöhnt.*

(5) Use of a subordinate clause with *daß* 'that', *da* 'as', *wenn* 'if', *bevor* 'before', *nachdem* 'after', *trotzdem* 'although', *die Tatsache, daß* 'the fact that', etc. The conjunctions *daß* and *wenn* may be preceded by *da*-compounds. Subordinate clauses are used especially when there is a change of subject. Examples: 'is there any chance of your being in Hamburg next week?' = *ist eine Möglichkeit vorhanden, daß Sie nächste Woche in Hamburg sind?*; 'we don't like things being left about' = *wir sehen es nicht gern, wenn man Sachen herumstehen läßt*; 'the Highlanders not finding their king' = *da die Hochländer ihren König nicht fanden*; 'before starting' = *bevor wir abreisen*; 'after helping with the washing up' = *nachdem ich beim Abwaschen geholfen hatte*; 'in spite of its being very cloudy' = *obgleich (trotzdem) es sehr bewölkt war*; 'his being a foreigner* = *die Tatsache, daß er ein Ausländer ist*; 'it ended in my giving way' = *es endete damit, daß ich nachgab.*

Past participle

The past participle used in whole phrases as an attribute of a noun precedes the noun, unlike English which says 'the taxes paid by us' when German says *die vons uns bezahlten Steuern.* It can also be used as the predicative attribute of an object, e.g. *ich fand ihn eingeschlafen* 'I found him asleep'. Transposition to the noun-class is brought about by declension, e.g. *der* or *die Angeklagte* 'the accused', *der* or *die Gelehrte* 'the scholar', *ein Vorbestrafter* 'one with previous conviction', etc.

In proverbs the past participle sometimes condenses the meaning of a whole clause, e.g. *frisch gewagt ist halb gewonnen*, lit. freshly dared is half won, i.e. 'faint heart never won fair lady'.

It is frequently used with the verb *kommen* where English would employ a present participle in '-ing', e.g. *er kam gelaufen* (*herangetanzt, gesprengt*) 'he came running (dancing along, galloping)', but if the verb with *kommen* is not a verb of motion the present participle is used, e.g. *er kam singend* 'he came singing'.

German has an idiomatic use of the past participle in short quick commands, e.g. *stillgestanden!* 'attention!' *aufgesessen!* 'mount (your horses)!', *aufgepaßt!* 'look out!', *aufgestanden!* 'up you get!', *nicht lange gefackelt!* 'no dilly-dallying!'. It is more peremptory than the use of the infinitive as imperative, discussed above.

9

VERBAL CONSTRUCTIONS WITH CASES AND PREPOSITIONS – USES OF THE PREPOSITIONS

Verbs with nominative as predicate

The nominative is used as the predicate complement with 'copula' verbs like *sein, werden, bleiben, heißen, scheinen,* e.g. *er ist (wird, scheint) ein fleißiger Arbeiter* 'he is (is becoming, seems) a hard worker', *er blieb einfacher Soldat* 'he remained a private'. The English 'make' in the sense of 'turned out to be' has an equivalent in *abgeben* with accusative, e.g. *er wird einen guten Reiter abgeben* 'he will make a good rider'.

Verbs with dative object

There are a number of verbs, especially those indicating some kind of communication or attitude towards a person and having a person as their subject, which use the dative of the direct object. Examples: *ich klingele ihr* 'I ring for her'; *ich telegraphiere, telephoniere, rufe, winke ihm* 'I telegraph, telephone, call, beckon (to) him'; *ich rate, helfe, danke, drohe, schmeichle, gratuliere ihm* 'I advise, help, thank, threaten, flatter, congratulate him'; *ich diene, gehorche, kündige, huldige ihm* 'I serve, obey, give notice [to], do homage [to] him'; *ich glaube ihm* 'I believe him'; *er gefällt mir* 'I like him'. The above verbs form their perfect tenses with *haben,* e.g. *ich habe ihm geklingelt,* but two verbs take *sein: ich bin ihm gefolgt* 'I have followed him' and *ich bin ihm begegnet* 'I have met him'.

In the case of some verbs there is often a non-personal subject though in principle the first and second persons are possible, e.g. *es gilt uns* 'it is meant for us, applies to us'; *was fehlt Ihnen?* 'what

is the matter with you?'; *es gefällt mir* 'it pleases me, I like it', cf.
es tut mir leid 'I am sorry for it', *es liegt mir* (*es sagt mir zu*) 'it
appeals to me'; *die Jacke steht mir gut* 'suits me', *paßt mir* 'fits
me', *sitzt mir*', 'becomes me'; *es bekommt mir* 'it agrees with me',
es schmeckt mir 'I like the taste of it'; *es ist mir egal,* (*einerlei*) 'it
is all the same to me'; *es geschieht mir* 'it happens to me'.

The dative is often used for the person or object affected by the
action and is sometimes rendered by the English possessive, e.g.
ich wasche ihm die Hände 'I wash his hands', *ich wasche mir die
Hände* (=*meine Hände*) 'I wash my hands', *nimm dir Zeit* 'take
your time'. A dative of advantage or disadvantage is illustrated by
das Pferd lief ihm fort 'the horse ran away from him' (cf. English
use of 'on' in 'the engine died on me'); *das Kleid ist mir zu eng*
'the dress is too tight for me'; *das ist mir ein großer Trost* 'that is
a great consolation for me'. A rather looser use of the dative—
sometimes called the ethic dative—indicates a subjective reference,
e.g. (in talking to children) *daß keiner mir aufs Eis geht* 'now
mind, I don't want any of you to go on the ice'; *seid mir recht
artig!* 'now mind you're good'; *das war dir so 'ne Sache* 'that was
something for you', i.e. something special.

Verbs with preposition for English direct object

In English we 'nod our heads', 'stamp our feet', 'wave our
hands', 'crack a whip', and 'wag our tails' whereas in German it
is necessary to use a phrase with *mit* + dative, e.g. *ich nicke mit
dem Kopf, stampfe mit dem Fuße, winke mit der Hand, knalle
mit der Peitsche, wedle mit dem Schwanze.* For 'I throw stones at
him' German says *ich werfe,* (*bewerfe*) *ihn mit Steinen.*

Verbs with dative and accusative

A large number of verbs have a direct object (thing effected or
affected) in the accusative and an indirect object (usually person
to or for whom something is done) in the dative. As in English
'I give the boy a book' so in German the indirect object precedes
the direct object, e.g. *ich gebe dem Jungen ein Buch,* except when
the direct object is a short pronoun, e.g. *ich gebe es ihm* 'I give
it (to) him, I give him it'.

The types of verbs taking this construction include the
following: (1) verbs of giving, lending, selling, paying, allowing,
e.g. *ich gebe* (*leihe, verkaufe*) *ihm das Buch; ich zahle ihm das Geld*
'I pay him the money'; *ich erlaube* [*es*] *ihm* 'I allow him'; (2) verbs

of communicating some message like those of saying, explaining, ordering, promising, wishing, e.g. *ich sage* (*erkläre, befehle, verspreche, wünsche*) *es ihm*; (3) verbs of taking something from someone, e.g. *ich nehme* (*entziehe*) *es ihm* 'I take (withdraw) it from him'; (4) many verbs formed with (a) such separable prefixes as *ab-, vor-*, etc., e.g. *ich kaufe ihm das Haus ab* 'I buy the house from him'; *ich singe* (*lese, trage, spiele*) *ihm das Lied vor* 'I sing (read, recite, play) the piece to him', and (b) inseparable prefixes especially *ent-*, e.g. *ich entziehe ihm das Recht* 'I withdraw the right from him'.

Verbs with two accusatives

Very few verbs in modern German speech have both direct and indirect object in the accusative. The most typical are *lehren* 'to teach', *fragen* 'to ask' and *kosten* 'to cost', e.g. *er lehrt mich Latein* 'he teaches me Latin' (but with dative *er bringt mir Latein bei*); *er lehrt das Kind kleine Lieder* 'he teaches the child little songs'; *ich frage die Schüler die Jahreszahlen* 'I ask the boys the dates' (but *ich frage ihnen die Jahreszahlen ab*); *ich fragte ihn etwas* 'I asked him something' (but *ich stelle ihm eine Frage* 'I ask him a question', *ich frage ihn nach dem Wege*, etc. 'I ask him the way'); *das Buch kostete mich zehn Mark* 'the book cost me 10 Mk.'. The verb *bitten* can have a double accusative if the direct object is a neuter adjective, e.g. *eins bitte ich Sie* 'one thing I ask you'.

In some cases where English uses a double accusative German has a phrase with *zu*, e.g. *man machte ihn zum König* 'they made him king', *wir wählten ihn zum Vorsitzenden* 'we elected him chairman', *die Fakultät ernannte ihn zum Dozenten* 'the Faculty appointed him lecturer'. The prepositional phrase remains in the passive, e.g. *er wurde zum Lehrer ernannt* 'he was appointed teacher' synonymous with *als Lehrer eingesetzt* 'taken on as teacher'.

Prepositions

Prepositions, which indicate a relation between two items, are in German classified according to the case of the noun with which they are construed. Those with accusative include *durch* 'through' (of place), 'by' (of means); *für* 'for'; *gegen* 'against'; *ohne* 'without'; *um* 'round', 'about'.

Among those with the dative are *aus* 'out of', e.g. *aus dem Hause*; *bei* 'at', 'close to', e.g. *bei Leipzig* (of the battle), *bei ihm* 'at his house'; *mit* 'with' (for both 'in association with' and 'by means of'); *nach* 'to' (of place), 'after' (of time), e.g. *nach Hamburg, nach dem Essen* 'after dinner'; *seit* 'since', e.g. *seit der Zeit* 'since that time'; *von* 'from', 'by' (of agent), 'of' (replacing the genitive case), e.g. *ein Brief von ihm, von ihm geschrieben, der König von England*; *zu* 'to' (especially with personal object).

Some prepositions govern both accusative and dative, the accusative indicating the goal or direction of a movement and the dative the place where something is, cf. the German distinction between *Richtung* 'direction' and *Ruhe* 'rest'. The chief prepositions with this double construction are: *an* (1) to a place near, (up) to (2) at or very near a place; *auf* (1) on to or on top of (2) on, on top of; *hinter* (1) to a place behind (2) at a place behind; *in* (1) into (2) in; *neben* (1) to the side of (2) beside; *über* (1) passing across or over (2) static over or above; *unter* (1) passing under (2) underneath, beneath; *vor* (1) to the front of (2) in front of; *zwischen* (1) to a place between or among (2) at a place between or among.

Prepositions governing the genitive are less common in ordinary speech. Among the chief are *anstatt* 'instead of' (*anstatt meiner*, etc., often replaced by *an meiner Stelle*); *während* [*des Tages*] 'during [the day]'; *wegen* [*des Regens*] 'on account of, because of [the rain]'. There are also the local prepositions with *-halb*, e.g. *innerhalb* [*des Hauses*] 'inside', *außerhalb* 'outside', *oberhalb* [*Kölns*] 'above, upstream of [Cologne]', *unterhalb* 'below'.

Some words follow the noun they govern. The following are a few typical expressions: *Geschäfte halber* 'for business reasons'; *des schlechten Wetters wegen* (*wegen des schlechten Wetters*) 'on account of the bad weather'; *dem Gesetz nach* (more literary: *zufolge*) 'in accordance with the law'; *der Kirche gegenüber* 'opposite the church'; *seinem Stande gemäß, standesgemäß* 'according to status'; (as title) *dem Nordpol zu* 'towards the North Pole'; *das Tal entlang* 'along the valley'; *zehn Uhr durch* 'after ten has struck'; *die ganze Nacht durch* or *hindurch* 'the whole night long' (cf. *die ganze Nacht* [*lang*]); *den ganzen Sommer über* 'throughout the summer'; *den Rhein hinauf* 'up the Rhine', *die Elbe herunter* 'down the Elbe'.

In some cases the relational expression consists of two words bracketing the noun governed, e.g. *um seines Vaterlandes willen* 'for the sake of his country'; *er kam auf mich zu* 'he came towards me', *er ging auf mich los* 'he went for me', *er lief hinter ihm her* or *er lief ihm nach* 'he ran after him', *er ging auf das Ziel hin* 'he made for the objective' (cf. *auf die Gefahr hin* 'at the risk . . .'), *wir mußten durch das Wasser hin* 'we had to go through the water', *nach oben/unten hin wird die Öffnung kleiner* 'the opening is smaller towards the top/bottom'; *der Prozeß zog sich über Jahre hin* 'the case dragged on for years'; *von mir aus kann er tun, was er will* 'as far as I'm concerned he can do as he pleases'; *von Kindheit an* or *auf* 'from childhood'; *von Geburt an* 'from birth (onwards)'; *nach Westen zu* or *hin* 'towards the west' (cf. *gegen Westen*).

The preposition *bis* presents special problems. It is used alone in the sense of 'until' with flexionless forms like *bis Montag, bis zwei Uhr* (also with a place *bis Berlin* 'as far as Berlin') or with an inflected accusative in a date *bis ersten Februar, bis nächsten Monat* for which there is also available the phrase *bis zu* (*bis zum ersten Februar*). The expression *bis Montag*, etc., means, according to the context, either 'until' or 'by'. The word *bis* is often combined with a further preposition and often serves to give emphasis to the latter, e.g. *das Wasser reichte ihm bis ans Knie* 'the water came right up to his knee', *die Bäume wachsen bis auf den Gipfel des Berges* 'the trees grow right to the top of the mountain'; *er ist bis über die Ohren verliebt* 'he is head over heels in love'; *bis in den Herbst hinein* 'right into the autumn'; *bis gegen Abend* 'till towards evening'; *bis vor/nach Ostern* 'till before/after Easter'; *bis zum Betrag von—* 'to the amount of—'. The expression *bis auf* is used as a rule to exclude ('with the exception of, right down to'), but not always, for whereas *bis auf eine Mark hab' ich mein ganzes Geld ausgegeben* means 'I have spent all my money except one mark', the sentence *ich habe alles bis auf den letzten Heller ausgegeben* means 'I have spent everything, even my last farthing'.

It is for the dictionaries to give detailed information on the uses of the prepositions, but a few special cases may be mentioned here. First some local prepositions. For the English 'at', 'near', 'by (the side of)', 'beside' German has *an, bei* and *neben*, e.g. *am Tisch, beim Tisch, neben dem Tisch* 'at the table, at table, close to the table, beside the table' with the characteristic accusative of direction in the case of *an* and *neben*, but not *bei*. The word *an* is used of a ladder against a wall (*die Leiter an der Wand*), a picture on the wall (*das Bild* [*hängt*] *an der Wand/ich hänge es an die Wand,*) an abscess on the finger (*ein Geschwür am Finger*), a ring on the finger (*ein Ring am Finger*, in the North also *auf dem Finger*), telephone (*am Telephon gewünscht* 'wanted on the phone'). There is a difference between *am Himmel* 'in the sky' and *im Himmel* 'in heaven' (cf. *in der Hölle* 'in hell', *im Fegefeuer* 'in purgatory', *im Paradies*). The word *an* is appropriate when something is situated on a line like a river-bank, shore or side of a ship, e.g. *am Ufer* 'on the bank', *am Strand* 'on the beach', *am Wasser*, *am See* 'by the lake-side', *an der See* 'at the sea-side, by the sea' (cf. *ich fahre an die See* 'I go to the seaside'), *am Rhein* (*auf dem Rhein*—of a boat), *an der Riviera*, *am Kai*, *an der Mole* 'alongside the quay or mole', *an Backbord* 'on the port side'. The phrase *am Berg* implies *am* (*Ab*)*hang* 'on the mountain side or slope', whereas *auf dem Berg=auf dem Gipfel* 'on the mountain-top'. There is a similar difference between *am Weg*, *an der Straße* 'by the road side', *auf dem Weg* [*nach*] 'on the way [to]', *auf der Straße* 'on the road [way]', 'in the street' (e.g. of children playing), *im Wege* 'in one's way', *in der Straße* (of where one lives), *an der Kurve* 'on the bend'. N.B. *in halber Höhe* 'half-way up'.

The prepositions *auf* and *in* have some uses differing from those of English 'on' and 'in'. It is easy to see how the word *auf* came to be used of a castle (*auf der Burg*), pulpit (*auf der Kanzel*), the dock in court (*auf der Anklagebank*), the station (platform) *auf dem Bahnhof*, but also *an der Bahn*, but it is extended to rooms (*auf* or *in dem Zimmer*), the post office (*auf der Post*), the stock-exchange (*auf der Börse*), the university *auf der Universität*, *auf der Hochschule* (of a student), but *an der Universität* (of a member of staff), and *in der Universität* (of the actual building). With 'bed' *im Bett* indicates 'under the bedclothes' and *auf dem Bett* 'on the bed', whereas *am Bette* implies 'by the bedside'. To climb up a tree is *auf einen Baum klettern*. There is a difference between *auf dem Felde* 'in the field(s)' and *im Feld* (=*an der Front*) 'in the field', cf. *auf der Wiese* 'in the meadow'. The preposition *in* is used particularly of going to the theatre (*ich gehe ins Theater*), cinema (*ins Kino*, *in einen Film*), concert (*ins Konzert*), opera (*in die Oper*), church (*in die Kirche*, also *zur Kirche*) and school (*in die Schule*, also *zur Schule*, but *aufs Gymnasium* 'to the grammar-school'). Each of these expressions has its corresponding dative of rest, e.g. *ich sitze im Theater*, *im Konzert*, *in der Oper*, etc. Some distinctions are common to both German and English, e.g. *ich schwimme im Fluß*/*das Schiff schwimmt auf dem Wasser*; *in einem Boot*/*auf einem Schiff* (*Dampfer*); *auf* [*hoher*] *See* 'on the high seas, on the open sea'/*im Roten Meer* 'on the Red Sea'; *im Pazifik*, *im Atlantik* (*auf dem Atlantischen*

Ozean); *im Zug* 'in, on the train' (*im Flugzeug* 'in the plane').
The English 'to' used with a place-name is in German *nach*, e.g.
ich fahre nach Deutschland, nach Hamburg, nach der Schweiz,
but with a person its equivalent is *zu*, e.g. *ich kam zu ihm*. With a
personal name the preposition of rest for 'at a person's house' is
bei, e.g. *bei Müllers*.

In the spoken language the following foreign prepositions are
frequently employed:

À 'at the rate of—each', e.g. *fünf Briefmarken à zehn, fünf à fünf*
(*Pfennig*) 'five ten-pfennig, five five-pfennig stamps'.

PER 'by', especially of the means of conveyance or communication, e.g. *per Rad* 'by bike', *per Flugzeug* 'by plane', *per Auto*
'by car', *per Dampfer* 'by steamer', *per Lastauto* 'by lorry, by
road', *per Brief* 'by letter', *per Telegramm, per Telephon.*

PRO 'for (each unit)', e.g. *prozent* 'per cent', *pro mille* 'per thousand',
pro Woche 'per week'.

Prepositional phrases with adjectives and verbs

There are a number of figurative uses of prepositions which can
be roughly classified. They are described here in alphabetical
order.

AN with accusative: the chief adjectives concerned are those
indicating attachment, bordering on, e.g. *anstoßend an* 'adjacent
to'. In the verbs *an* with accusative often indicates the objective
of a thought process, e.g. *ich denke an ihn* 'I think of him', *ich
glaube an ihn* 'I believe in him', *ich erinnere mich an ihn* 'I
remember him', *ich erinnerte ihn an seine Verabredung* 'I reminded him of his engagement'. It can also be used of 'holding
on to' or 'clinging to' or 'linking on to', e.g. *ich halte mich an
ihn* 'I go by him', *ich klammere mich an ihn* [*an*] 'I cling to him',
ich knüpfe an diese Worte an 'I take these words as the starting-
point'.

AN with dative: one set of adjectives has *an* in the sense of 'in
respect of', e.g. *reich/arm an Silber* 'rich/poor in silver', *er ist
mir an Stärke gewachsen* (*überlegen, unterlegen*) 'he is a match
for me (my superior, my inferior) in strength'. Hence *an* can
be used with the verbs of increasing, etc., e.g. *er nimmt an
Stärke zu/ab* 'he is increasing/decreasing in strength'. The verbs
zweifeln 'doubt' and *verzweifeln* 'despair of' also take *an*, e.g.
ich zweifle an ihm.

AUF with accusative, of mental attitude towards some person or thing often has this construction, e.g. *ich bin böse (neidisch, eifersüchtig, stolz) auf ihn* 'I am cross with (envious of, jealous of, proud of) him'; *ich bin neugierig (gespannt, erpicht) auf etwas* 'I am inquisitive about (looking forward to, set upon) something'. With verbs, too, *auf*+accus. indicates the aim, hence *ich ziele (schieße, feuere, zeige) auf ihn* 'I aim (shoot, fire, point) at him'; *ich blicke (sehe) auf ihn* 'I glance (look) at him'; *ich höre auf ihn* 'I listen to what he has to say'; *ich spiele auf ihn an* 'I allude to him'; *ich stichele (schimpfe, trinke) auf ihn* 'I have a dig at him (rail at him, drink to him)'. The construction is also used of basing oneself or relying upon someone or something, e.g. *ich verlasse mich (rechne, schwöre, stütze mich) auf ihn* 'I rely on him (count on him, swear by him, use him as support'). There are many idiomatic uses besides, e.g. *es kommt auf ihn an* 'it depends (rests) upon him'; *ich führe die Sache auf ihren Ursprung zurück* 'I trace the matter to its origin'; *ich übertrage das Eigentum auf ihn* 'I transfer the property to him'; *wie heißt das auf deutsch?* 'what is that in German?'; *er sagte es auf deutsch* 'he said it in German' (but note: *ich übersetze das Wort aus dem Englischen ins Deutsche* 'I translate the word from English into German.'

AUF with dative: less common. It is used with words of bodily deformity to indicate the part affected, e.g. *blind auf einem Auge, taub auf einem Ohr* 'blind in one eye, deaf in one ear'. There are few verbal phrases except those indicating rest, e.g. *es beruht auf einem Fehler* 'it rests upon a mistake'.

AUS with dative, especially with the verbs like 'made of', 'constructed of', 'consisting of', e.g. *es ist aus Holz [gemacht]* 'it is [made] of wood' or *es besteht aus drei Teilen* 'it consists of three parts'.

DURCH indicates the cause of some state, e.g. *durch Mut ausgezeichnet* 'distinguished by courage', *durch Hunger erschöpft* 'exhausted by hunger'.

FÜR like English 'for' often indicates the object for whose benefit something exists or is done, e.g. *das ist wichtig (wesentlich, vorteilhaft) für mich* 'that is important (essential, beneficial) for me'. It also indicates responsiveness in a person's favour, e.g. *ich bin für ihn eingenommen* 'I am taken with him', *er ist sehr empfänglich für Schmeichelei* 'he is very susceptible to flattery'; *er ist blind für (gegen) die Fehler seiner Kinder* 'he is blind to his children's faults'. With verbs *für* sometimes means 'in favour of', e.g. *ich bürge für ihn* 'I go bail for him'; *ich entscheide mich für den Plan* 'I decide in favour of the plan'. Otherwise it is used for the amount of money in a transaction, e.g. *ich kaufte es für zwei Mark* 'I bought it for 2 Mk.'.

GEGEN is very frequent with words of mental attitude directed towards someone and in this sense is usually translated by 'to' or 'towards', e.g. *ich war dankbar (gleichgültig, grausam, gut, höflich, mild, streng) gegen ihn* 'I was grateful (indifferent, cruel, kind, polite, mild, severe) to him'.

IN with the accusative is used with a few verbs like *er hat sich in sie verliebt* 'he has fallen in love with her'; *er mischt sich in meine Angelegenheiten ein* 'he meddles in my affairs'; *das geht ins Geld* 'that will run into a lot of money'.

With the dative it is used of the quality in which one is versed or experienced, e.g. *in der Chemie bewandert (geschickt, erfahren)* 'versed (skilled, experienced) in chemistry'.

MIT is used with verbs (and participial adjectives) of acquaintance, comparison, occupation, e.g. *ich bin mit ihm verwandt* 'related to him'; *er ist mit seinem Vater vergleichbar* 'comparable to his father'; *ich bin mit Lesen beschäftigt* 'occupied with or busy reading'.

NACH is used with a few adjectives to indicate the goal towards which one is striving, e.g. *ehrgeizig nach Ruhm* 'ambitious for fame'. It is more frequent with verbs, e.g. *ich suche (strebe, forsche, fische, grabe, greife, schicke) nach etwas* 'I seek (strive, research, fish, dig, reach, send) for something'; *ich frage nach dem Wege* 'I ask the way'. This preposition is also appropriate with verbs of perception, e.g. *es riecht nach Fisch* 'it smells of fish'; *es sieht nach Regen aus* 'it looks like rain'.

ÜBER normally means 'about, concerning' and is used with the accusative. Adjectives requiring it are *erstaunt* 'astonished', *ärgerlich* 'annoyed', *entrüstet* 'indignant', *traurig* 'sad', *glücklich* 'happy'. It is very frequent with verbs, e.g. *ich spreche (lese, lache, weine, klage, grüble, schreibe, erröte) über etwas* 'I talk (read, laugh, cry, complain, brood, write, blush) about something'; *ich denke über die Sache nach* 'I reflect on the matter'.

UM implies 'on account of' and is often rendered by 'for' to indicate the reason of some action, e.g. *ich bitte ihn um etwas* 'I ask him for something'; *ich beneide ihn um sein Glück* 'I envy him [for] his good fortune'; *ich trauere (weine) um ihn* 'I mourn (weep) for him'; *er hielt um sie an* 'he proposed to her, sued for her hand'. It is also used of the stake or price, e.g. *ich handle um den Preis* 'I bargain about the price', and the degree of difference, e.g. *um drei Meter tiefer* 'deeper by three metres'.

VON means 'from' with the adjective *abhängig* 'dependent on', cf. *es hängt von Ihnen ab* 'it depends upon you'. It can in this sense be used with verbs of separation, like *trennen*, or keeping back, e.g. *ich hielt ihn von dem Verbrechen ab* 'I kept him from the crime'. With verbs *von* comes close to *über* 'about' and is translated by 'of', e.g. *ich spreche (träume) von ihm* 'I speak (dream) of him'; *was wissen (halten) Sie von ihm?* 'what do you know (think) of him?' With a past participle or an adjective of state *von* indicates the cause, e.g. *müde von der Reise* 'tired from the journey'; *schwarz von Menschen* 'black with people'; *von seinen Gefühlen überwältigt* 'overcome by one's feelings'.

VOR with the dative is used of that which is feared or is a threat or causes emotion, e.g. *weiß vor Wut* 'white with rage'; *grün vor Neid* 'green with envy'; *er zittert (bebt) vor Kälte* 'he is trembling (quaking) with cold'; *er wurde vor Hunger ohnmächtig* 'he fainted with hunger'.

WEGEN with the genitive indicates the cause, e.g. *berühmt wegen seiner Tapferkeit* 'famous for his bravery'; *ich schalt ihn wegen seiner Faulheit* 'I went for him on account of his laziness'; *ich komme wegen der Annonce* 'I come in connexion with the advertisement'.

ZU with words indicating readiness, e.g. *ich bin zu allem bereit (entschlossen)* 'ready for all (resolved upon all)'—or fitness for a purpose, e.g. *zum Führer geeignet* 'fitted to be a leader'; *wozu dient es?* 'what is it for?'; *wozu verwendet man es?* 'what is it employed for?'; *ich greife zu einem Mittel* 'I have recourse to an expedient or remedy'. It indicates the resultant product in *zu Pulver zerstoßen* 'to pound into powder', etc. It is also used with 'belong', e.g. *ich gehöre zu dieser Partei (diesem Verein)* 'I belong to this party (society).' With persons it is often used with an adjective of mental attitude, e.g. *er war gut (nett, höflich) zu mir* 'he was kind (nice, polite) to me'.

10

THE ORDER OF WORDS – POSITION OF
NEGATIVES

The order of words

In the phrase with a noun as nucleus the order (article or pronominal + attribute + noun) is in principle similar to that ob-
taining in English, but modern German has largely given up the
pattern *des Königs Sohn* and prefers to place the genitive after
the noun except with a few short personal nouns like *Vaters*, etc.,
without the article. On the other hand German is averse to tacking
on a participial phrase after the noun, e.g. 'a ship bound for Lis-
bon', 'the staircase leading to the back' and prefers *ein nach
Lissabon bestimmtes Schiff* or *die nach hinten führende Treppe*.
However, like English, German places the noun before a short
adverbial or prepositional phrase used attributively with it, e.g.
die Tür hinten 'the door at the back', *der Mann im Monde* 'the man
in the moon'.

In the sentence the basic order in the main clause is in both
languages: subject + finite verb. There are, however, some
differences in the placing of the objects, adverbs, circumstantials
and negatives in relation to the verb. As has already been shown
the infinitive or past participle used in connexion with a finite
auxiliary verb occupies the final position, so that all the objects,
etc., have to be fitted in between the auxiliary and the final verb,
e.g. *ich habe ein Buch gekauft* 'I have bought a book', *ich werde
morgen zurückkehren* 'I shall return tomorrow'. In speech
occasionally a word may follow the infinitive for special emphasis
or as an afterthought, e.g. *ich lasse Ihr Gepäck hinaufschaffen,
sofort* 'I'll have your luggage taken up—at once'. The predicative

adjective is often treated in the same way, e.g. *die Tage sind im Sommer lang* 'the days are long in summer', *das Pferd ist nach der Arbeit müde* 'the horse is tired after working'. If there are two objects, one indirect (in the dative) and one direct (in the accusative) the indirect object normally precedes the direct object, e.g. *ich sagte meinem Freunde die Wahrheit* 'I told my friend the truth'.[1] It is especially the case that the personal object precedes the non-personal, e.g. *man hat ihn (den Mann) des Diebstahls beschuldigt* 'they have accused him (the man) of the theft', *ich lehre den Jungen Deutsch* 'I am teaching the boy German'. An adverbial expression of time may precede the direct object, e.g. *er besuchte gestern seinen Freund*, but not if the direct object is a pronoun, e.g. *er besuchte ihn gestern*. The time-expression comes after the indirect object but before the direct object, if the objects are not pronouns, e.g. *ich habe meinem Freund gestern ein Buch gegeben/ich habe es ihm gestern gegeben*. Time-expressions usually have precedence over expressions of manner and of place, e.g. *wir lasen das Buch gestern ruhig zu Hause* 'we read the book quietly at home yesterday', *wir müssen im Winter schwer arbeiten* 'we have to work hard in winter'.

Inverted order

The verb precedes the subject of the sentence under the following conditions:

(1) in the imperative especially with *Sie*, e.g. *kommen Sie herein!* 'come in!'.

(2) in a question seeking the reply 'yes' or 'no', e.g. *kommen Sie morgen?* 'are you coming tomorrow?'.

(3) in a question beginning with a specific interrogative word ('how?', 'when?', 'why?', etc.) provided that word is not the subject. This order is the same as in English, e.g. *wo wohnt er?* 'where does he live?'; *warum sagen Sie das?* 'why do you say that?'; *wem gaben Sie es?* 'to whom did you give it?'. With a subject interrogative there is no inversion, e.g. *wer hat Sie besucht?* 'who visited you?'; *welches Haus ist zu vermieten?* 'which house is to be let?'.

(4) in exclamatory sentences expressing a wish, when the conditional particle ('if') is omitted, e.g. *wären wir doch zu Hause geblieben!* 'if only we had remained at home!'.

---

[1] With two pronouns the direct object precedes in *ich gab es ihm* (but *gib mir's!*) and *wie die Erfahrung es sie gelehrt hatte* 'as experience had taught her'.

(5) Similarly in an implied conditional clause with the 'if'-particle omitted, e.g. *sollte es regnen* 'should it rain . . .'.

(6) If for the sake of emphasis or to mark the connexion with a previous sentence some word, phrase or clause other than the subject is placed at the head of the whole sentence the subject must come after the verb, e.g. *den Mann kann ich nicht leiden* 'I can't bear that man'; *Fleisch gibt's nicht viel* 'of meat there is not much' *mit Geld kommt man überall hin* 'you can get anywhere with money'; *heute gibt es Schweinekoteletts* 'today there are pork chops'; *zwar war das Haus alt, doch gefiel es uns* 'the house was indeed old, but we liked it'; *wenn Sie nach London kommen, müssen Sie uns besuchen* 'when you come to London, you must visit us'; *da es regnet, bleiben wir zu Hause* 'as it is raining, we are staying at home'.

N.B. The conjunctions *und, aber, sondern* (marking a contrast after a negative) *oder* and *denn* 'for' (a weak motivating particle) do not necessitate inversion of the verb (see co-ordination below).

Straddling or dependent order

In a dependent clause introduced by some specific connexion like a relative pronoun or other pronominal, or an uninflected particle like *daß, ob, wenn, weil, da*, etc., the finite i.e. conjugated, verb normally occupies the end-position. Examples: *der Mann, der hier war; er sagt, daß ich Unrecht habe; ich weiß nicht, ob er morgen kommen will; wenn er in Köln angekommen ist.* The only exception to this rule is the placing of the finite verb ahead of two infinitives, e.g. *wenn ich es hätte vermeiden können* 'if I had been able to avoid it'; *wenn ich ihn werde überzeugen können* 'if I am able to convince him'. The end-position is kept when the auxiliary has a participial phrase in construction with it, e.g. *wenn er ermordet worden ist* 'if he has been murdered'.

N.B. *Denn* 'for' has straight order, e.g. *er konnte nicht kommen, denn er war krank* 'he could not come, for he was ill'.

Position of negatives

The position of the negative *nicht* (and to some extent *nie* 'never', *nirgends* 'nowhere') depends upon several factors, e.g. it cannot follow a past participle or infinitive used with an auxiliary verb or separable verbal particle on the one hand and it stands before the word more specifically negated on the other. Thus German says (1) *ich habe den Mann (ihn) nicht (nie) gesehen*; *wir werden dem Mann nicht helfen*; *ich gehe nicht aus* and (2) *nicht jeder ist zum Millionär geboren* 'not everyone is born to be a millionaire'; cf. *er wagte nicht, das zu tun* 'he didn't dare do that'/*er wagte, das nicht zu tun* 'he dared not to do that' and *ich glaube nicht alles zu verstehen*/*ich bedauere, nicht alles zu verstehen*. With the simple tenses of an uncompounded or inseparable verb *nicht* can go right to the end, e.g. *ich brauche seine Hilfe nicht* 'I don't need his help'; *schlage das Kind nicht!* 'don't hit the child!'; *warum verstecken sie das Geld nicht?* 'why don't you hide the money?'; *Sie stören mich durchaus nicht* 'you don't disturb me at all'. There is, however, a strong tendency to place *nicht* before a word-group, especially one with a preposition, e.g. *klettere nicht auf den Baum!* 'don't climb the tree!'; *wirf nicht mit Steinen!* 'don't throw stones!'; *gewann er nicht den ersten Preis?* 'didn't he win the first prize?'; (*wenn Sie Angst haben, daß man es stiehlt,*) *warum verstecken Sie nicht Ihr Geld?* '(if you are afraid of it being stolen) why don't you hide your money?' In particular *nicht* precedes an adjective complement, e.g. *es ist nicht weit* 'it is not far'; *nicht ganz unbekannt* 'not quite unknown'; *nicht mehr (länger)* 'no more (longer)'.

In the subordinate sentence *nicht* cannot come within or after the final verb group, e.g. *wenn ich ihn nicht erkannt hätte* 'if I had not recognized him'; *wenn ich ihn nicht hätte kommen sehen* 'if I had not seen him coming'.

German uses *kein* very often when English uses 'not' (especially with 'a' or 'any'), e.g. *er spricht kein Deutsch* 'he doesn't speak (any) German', but *er spricht nicht gut (nicht viel) Deutsch* 'he doesn't speak German well (much German)' and *er spricht Deutsch nicht, obgleich er es kann* 'he doesn't speak German, although he is able to'. Cf. further *er stolperte kein einziges Mal* 'he did not stumble a single time'; *Geld hatte ich keines* 'I hadn't any money' or 'money I had none'.

Some positive words have in English negative equivalents, e.g. *rasieren lasse ich mich höchst ungern* 'I don't at all like people shaving me'; *erst heute* 'not until today'; *er zieht nur dann den Mantel aus, wenn er naß ist* 'he doesn't take off his overcoat unless he is wet'; *er arbeitet nur, wenn man ihn dazu zwingt* 'he does not work unless he is forced to', thus avoiding the double *nicht* (*wenn nicht* 'unless').

Occasionally the negative used in a question makes the latter

sound more polite and tentative, e.g. *könnten Sie mir nicht sagen
. . .?*, cf. *könnten Sir mir vielleicht sagen . . .?*.

It is to be noted that German and English have a different
order in the phrases *gar nicht, überhaupt nicht* 'not at all' and *noch
nicht* 'not yet', cf. *das Kind schlief nicht lange* 'the child did not
sleep long' and *das Kind schlief lange nicht* 'the child did not sleep
for quite a long time'.

I I

PARATAXIS – CO-ORDINATION –
VERBLESS SENTENCES – INDIRECT SPEECH

Parataxis of main clauses

A sentence forming a single whole may be formed by the combination of two or more main clauses with or without a specific indication of their connexion. In both languages there are many examples in speech of such sentences as that with an explanatory clause, e.g. *er muß ziemlich krank sein—er kommt einfach nicht hoch* 'he must be pretty ill—he can't get up'; *mache das Licht an, du kannst nicht mehr sehen* 'put on the light, you can't see'; *das gilt nicht, der Ball hat das Netz berührt* 'that doesn't count, the ball touched the net'; *setzen Sie sich hierher, wir wollen ein bißchen plaudern* 'sit down here (and) we'll have a little chat'. If the relation is one of simultaneity as in 'he was working, I was reading' German uses either the conjunction *und* or the introductory particle *während* 'while': *er arbeitete und* (*während*) *ich las*. If the relation is one of cause and consequence the word 'so' is used in the first clause, e.g. *er ist so stark—das kann er leicht heben* 'he is strong, he can easily lift that'. Clauses put together as disjunctive alternatives including an imperative are equivalent to negative conditions (if not, unless), e.g. *komm sofort her, sonst gehe ich ohne dich* 'come here at once or (otherwise) I'll go without you'. A positive condition is also often indicated by an imperative: *gehen Sie bis zur nächsten Ecke, dann werden Sie gleich den Briefkasten sehen* 'go to the next corner and then you'll see the letter-box close by'. A concessive ('although') relation may be indicated by the use of *doch* in the following clause, e.g. *die Kurven sahen so leicht aus und waren doch so schwer* 'the bends looked so easy and yet were so difficult'.

Sometimes German prefers to reverse the order of the clauses and make one dependent on the other, e.g. *ich wäre Ihnen sehr dankbar, wenn Sie mir diesen Brief einstecken würden* 'do post this letter for me, I should be most grateful'.

Parataxis in indirect speech

German, like English, uses close parataxis without any introducing word to indicate the content of a statement or request, e.g. *ich glaube, er ist krank* 'I believe he is ill'; *er sagte, er sei (wäre) krank* 'he said he was ill'; *ich bin überzeugt, er ist nicht böse* 'I am convinced he is not angry'; *ich glaube, es ist Zeit zu gehen* 'I believe it is time to go'; *ich hoffe, die Nachricht erfreut ihn* 'I hope the news will please him'; *ich hoffe, er wird sein Examen bestehen* 'I hope he will pass his examination'; *ich weiß, ich werde ihn nicht erkennen* 'I know I shall not recognize him'; *sagen Sie ihm, er möchte kommen* 'tell him to come, please'; *ich wünsche, er käme* 'I wish he would come'.

Parataxis in conditions

As in English the inversion of the verb as in an interrogative sentence may serve as the indication of a condition, e.g. *hätte ich ihn gesehen, so hätte ich ihn retten können* 'had I seen him, I could have rescued him'; *kommt er morgen, so ist alles gut* 'if he comes tomorrow, all will be well'.

Parataxis in temporal clauses

German often uses parataxis to indicate an event following very rapidly on another, e.g. *kaum saßen wir, da begann die Musik* 'we had hardly sat down when the music began to play'. However, *kaum* is often followed by a dependent 'when' clause, e.g. *kaum hatten wir uns gesetzt, als die Musik begann.*

Co-ordination of words and clauses

Co-ordinating conjunctions may (1) **add** one item to another like 'and', 'both ... and ...'; (2) negate them both 'neither ... nor ...'; (3) indicate an alternative 'or', 'either ... or ...'; (4) indicate a contrast 'but'; (5) indicate a division 'now ... now ...', 'partly ... partly ...'; (6) indicate an explanation 'for'. The German equivalents—except when noted—are followed by straight order.

(1) *und* conjoins both words, e.g. *Vater und Mutter,* and clauses

er las und ich schrieb. For 'both . . . and . . .' German has special
particles, e.g. *er ist sowohl grob wie (auch) faul* 'he is both rude
and lazy'; *Offiziere sowie Mannschaften waren erstaunt, den Feind
so nahe zu sehen* 'both officers and men (men as well as officers)
were surprised to see the enemy so close'. cf. also *nicht nur . . .
sondern auch . . .* under (4).

(2) With *weder . . . noch . . .* There is sometimes straight order
and sometimes inversion in the spoken language, e.g. *ich greife
ihn weder an noch verteidige ich ihn* 'I neither attack nor defend
him', but with *weder* in front there is inversion: *weder greife ich
ihn an, noch . . .* Often the spoken language puts the sentence in a
different way, e.g. *er wußte nicht, was vorging, und kümmerte sich
auch nicht darum* 'he neither knew nor cared what was going on',
cf. *ich weiß nicht, wer er ist, und es ist mir auch völlig gleichgültig.*
In these last examples *weder . . . noch . . .* would be literary and
rather pedantic.

(3) The exclusive alternative ('either . . . or . . .', but not both)
is expressed by *entweder . . . oder . . .*, sometimes with straight and
sometimes with inverted order, e.g. *entweder ist er wirklich sehr
krank (entweder er ist,* more emphatic), *oder er ist ein guter
Schauspieler* 'either he is really very ill or he is a good actor';
entweder bezahlt er die Miete (entweder er bezahlt, more emphatic),
oder ich verklage ihn 'either he will pay the rent or I shall sue him'.
Sometimes a different turn of phrase is appropriate, e.g. *wenn der
nicht krank spielt, dann fresse ich 'n (= den) Besen* 'either he is
malingering or I'll eat my hat'. The non-exclusive 'and . . . or' is
rendered by *beziehungsweise* (abbreviated *bzw.*), or *respektive*
(*resp.*), e.g. *die Länge des Vokals bzw. Diphthongs* 'the length of the
vowel or diphthong (as the case may be)'. When 'or' is equivalent
to 'otherwise' German uses *sonst,* e.g. *geben Sie mir die Hand,
sonst falle ich* 'give me your hand or I shall fall'; *paß auf, sonst
wirst du bestraft* 'pay attention or you will be punished'.

(4) The English 'but' has two main equivalents in German
speech: *aber* and—opposing a negative—*sondern,* the third
allein (cf. 'only') being more literary. Examples: *sie sind arm,
aber ehrlich* 'they are poor, but honest'; *sie sind nicht reich,
sondern arm* 'they are not rich, but (on the contrary) poor', but
sie sind nicht reich, aber freigebig 'they are not rich, but (they are,
anyhow,) generous'. The equivalent of 'not only . . . but also . . .'
is seen in *er ist nicht nur ein Geizhals, sondern auch (= überdies
noch, dazu noch) ein Lügner* 'he is not only a miser, but also a liar'.

(5) The literary equivalent of 'now ... now ...' is *bald ...
bald ...*, e.g. *bald schwankte die Schlacht nach dieser Seite, bald
nach jener Seite* 'now the battle swayed this way and now that'.
The English 'partly' is rendered by *teils*, e.g. *teils hat er die
Schuld, teils ich (habe ich sie)* 'partly he is to blame and partly
I am'. Where the literary language might say *bald kam die Sonne
heraus, bald verbarg sie sich hinter den Wolken* 'now the sun came
out and now it hid behind the clouds' the spoken language might
say *hin und wieder kam die Sonne heraus, dann verbarg ....*

(6) In German the weak particle indicating motive or cause is
denn which keeps straight order, e.g. *ich muß jetzt weg, denn ich
wollte um* 10 *Uhr zu Hause sein* 'I must be off now for I wanted to
be home by ten'; *ziehen Sie Ihren Mantel an, wenn Sie ausgehen,
denn es regnet draußen* 'don't go out without your coat, for it is
raining'. German does not use *denn* as frequently as English uses
'for' and often merely tacks on the explanation without particle,
e.g. *gib mir die Hand—ich kann im Dunkeln nicht sehen* 'give
me your hand [for] I cannot see in the dark'.

Verbless sentences

In the rapid give and take of everyday life the speaker often
contents himself with uttering a single word or short phrase
referring to the chief point to which he is directing attention. Thus
in calling a person it is enough to use the name *Hans!* or a simple
common noun, e.g. *Ober!* 'Waiter!', *Träger!* 'Porter!', cf. also as a
form of address in *Liebling* 'darling', *Schatz* 'sweetheart', *Kind*
'child'. In a state of emergency it is enough to shout *Feuer!* or
Diebe! 'Thieves!' or *Hilfe!* 'Help!' A greeting is usually a noun
or noun-phrase in the accusative which originally came after a
verb of wishing, e.g. *Guten Tag! Guten Morgen!, Guten Abend!
Gute Nacht!*, sometimes shortened to *'n Tag!* or *Tag!*; *Fröhliche
Weihnachten!* 'A Merry Christmas!', *Ein glückliches Neues Jahr*
'A Happy New Year!' *glückliche Reise!* 'pleasant journey!';
Willkommen! 'Welcome!'; *angenehme Ruhe!* cf. 'pleasant dreams!';
Mahlzeit! from *gesegnete Mahlzeit!* said by the hostess to her
guests hoping they have made a good meal; cf. *einen schönen
Gruß an Ludwig!* 'kind regards to Ludwig!' Peremptory commands
or urgent requests may also be highly condensed, e.g. *Vorwärts!*
'Go on!', *Lauter!* 'Speak up!', *Sachte!* 'Easy!', *Feuer!* 'Fire!'
(military command), *Rechts—um!* 'About-turn!' *Achtung!* 'Attention!', *Herein!* 'Come in!', *Vorsicht!* 'Careful!', *Silentium!* or

Ruhe! Sometimes the phrase is extended, e.g. *'raus mit ihm!* 'Out
with him!', *Nieder mit den Verrätern!* 'Down with the traitors!',
cf. slogans from the Second World War such as *Ans Werk!* 'Go
to it' and *Achtung! Feind hört mit.* 'Be like dad, keep mum'
and the nautical *Besanschot an!* (lit. To the mizzen-sheets) 'Splice
the main brace'.

In a request for some object the name of the latter in the
accusative is often sufficient, e.g. *Meinen Mantel!* 'my overcoat!'; *ein Bier!* 'a beer'; *einen Briefblock liniiert!* (in a stationer's
shop) 'a writing-block lined'; *zwei dritter Hamburg hin und
zurück!* 'two third returns Hamburg'; *Ihren Pass!* 'your passport!'.

A reply to a question put up for a simple decision evokes a
short reply, e.g. *Ja* or more politely *Jawohl, Nein, Doch* 'Yes',
'Oh but it is' (to oppose a negative suggestion), *Sicher* 'Certainly',
Natürlich 'Of course', *Selbstverständlich* 'Obviously', *Allerdings*
'Why, certainly', *Keineswegs* 'By no means', *Kaum* (*Schwerlich*)
'Hardly', *Hoffentlich* 'I hope so', *Vermutlich* 'I suppose so'.

Frequently the question itself is much abridged especially
if it is a repeated question or if it has a note of astonishment,
e.g. *Sie?* 'You?'; *Wer?, Weshalb?, Wozu?* 'What for?'; *Wieso?*
'What do you mean?'; *So?* 'Really?'; *Der?* 'He?' Some abridged
questions are clear enough in the given situation, e.g. *Fertig?*
'Ready?'; *Ausgeschlafen?* 'Had a good sleep?'; *Noch da?* 'Still
there?'; *Einverstanden?* 'Agreed?'; *Sicher?* 'Sure?'; *Noch etwas?*
'Anything else?'; *Glas Bier?* 'A glass of beer?'.

Occasionally the speaker sums up his impression of the situation
in a single word, e.g. *Schwindel!* 'A fraud!'; *Unsinn!* 'Nonsense!';
Quatsch! 'Bosh!'; *Kinderspiel!* 'Child's play!'; *Kleinigkeit!* 'A
trifle!'; *Stimmt!* 'You're right!'; *Macht nichts!* 'Doesn't matter!';
Schade! 'Pity!'.

Often the abridged form is exclamatory, singling out a salient
feature either as a noun or adjective, e.g. *Der Lügner!* 'The liar!';
Dieses Elend! 'This misery!'; *Ein Glück!* 'What a good thing!';
Pech! 'Bad luck!'; *Herrlich!* 'Magnificent!'; *Wunderschön!*
'Marvellous!'; *Sonderbar!* 'Queer!'; (in each case of an adjective
being used it is possible to prepose *Wie*, e.g. *Wie herrlich!*).

Street-cries and public notices are often reduced to essen-
tials, e.g. *Warme Würste!* 'Hot dogs!'; *Extrablatt!* 'Special
edition!'; *Kein Eingang!* 'No entrance!'; *Männer* or *Herren*
'Gentlemen', *Frauen* or *Damen* 'Ladies', etc.

Certain expressions were once part of verbs, but have become
stereotyped and often serve as convenient abbreviations, e.g.
bitte! which stands for *ich bitte* 'I ask' and corresponds in many
ways to 'please'. It is used (1) when making a polite request (2)
as the equivalent of 'Don't mention it!' after someone has thanked
one or apologized, and (3) on a rising tone to ask for the repetition
of something not fully heard or understood (4) when offering
something like 'here you are' and (5) *bitte sehr* for an indignant
'I beg your pardon'. The word *danke* from *ich danke* is used in
German not only for 'Yes, thank you!' but also when standing
alone for 'No, thank you!' (cf. French use of *merci!*). Both *bitte*
and *danke* are reinforced by adding *schön* or *sehr*. The form
Bewahre! 'God forbid!' is in origin a third person singular present
subjunctive. The equivalents of English 'I say' are the imperatives
hör mal! (polite *hören Sie mal!*) (to introduce something the
speaker wishes to state, like 'now, listen') and *sag mal!* (to introduce a question put to his partner, like 'now, tell me').

Finally there are the short phrases *Hals- und Beinbruch!* to
encourage someone going in for a test, etc., also *Daumen halten!*
(from *ich halt dir den Daumen*), cf. 'Keep your fingers crossed' and
the superstitious *unberufen!* cf. 'touch wood'.

The single parts of speech and shortened phrases not only
stand alone as in the above examples, but can also in some cases
have a dependent clause in construction with them, e.g. *Unmöglich,
ihn zu überzeugen* 'Impossible to convince him'; *Kein Wunder, daß
er böse war* 'No wonder he was cross'; *Schade, daß er nicht da
war* 'a pity he wasn't there'; *Ein Segen, daß er sich so schnell
erholt hat* 'A blessing he recovered so quickly'; *Schlimm genug,
daß er faul ist* 'Bad enough for him to be idle', etc.

Indirect speech

German, like English, distinguishes by certain procedures three
different types of indirect speech:

(1) reported speech expressed by dependent clauses following
a verb of saying, etc.

(2) reported speech indicated in principal clauses without
explicit verb of saying, etc., to introduce them.

(3) 'hinted speech' (Ger. *erlebte Rede* 'experienced speech' or
verschleierte Rede 'obscured or veiled speech') a device used by a
narrator to indicate what is passing through a person's mind.

The following is an example of (1) and (2) combined.

Mein Freund meinte, wenn ich mich nicht schnell fertig machte, würde ich den Zug nicht erreichen. Es sei schon halb zwei und ich müsse mindestens zehn Minuten gehen, um zum Bahnhof zu gelangen.	My friend expressed the opinion that if I did not get ready quickly, I should not catch the train. It was already half past one (he added) and it would take me at least ten minutes to get to the station.
Er wäre froh, so versicherte er mir, daß ich ihn endlich mal besucht hätte, und er hoffe, daß es nicht das letzte Mal gewesen sei.	He was glad, he assured me, that I had visited him at last and he hoped it was not the last time.
Ich antwortete, ich könnte mir denken, daß er gerne Menschen bei sich sehe. Wäre doch nichts weniger gut zu ertragen als die Einsamkeit. Er möge sich nur in Acht nehmen, daß er nicht ganz melancholisch würde.	I replied that I could imagine him liking to have people to see him, for nothing was harder to bear than loneliness. He had better take care, I said, not to give way to melancholy.

In the above passage the characteristic marks of reported speech are the use of the subjunctive, the substitution of the phrase *er möge* ... for the imperative of direct speech and of the third person *er* for the second person directly addressed.

The following is an example of (2) with the verb of reporting left implicit:

Bevor ich nach Indien abreiste, gab ich meinem Sekretär bestimmte Direktiven. Er solle alle Briefe aufmachen außer denen, die die Bezeichnung 'Vertraulich' trügen, die er nachsenden müsse (solle). Er solle an eine Maklerfirma schreiben, um herauszufinden, welchen Preis mein Haus erzielen würde. Er werde von Zeit zu Zeit durch das Londoner Büro Nachrichten von mir erhalten, aber er dürfe sich keine Sorgen machen, wenn ein paar Wochen vergingen, ohne daß er Nachricht erhielte. Er könne mich in etwa sechs Monaten zurückerwarten.	Before I left for India I gave my secretary certain directions. He was to open all letters except those marked 'Confidential',which he was to forward. He was to write to a firm of house-agents to inquire what sort of price my house would fetch. He would receive news of me from time to time through the London office, but he was not to worry if a few weeks were to pass without him receiving any news. He could expect me back in about six months' time.

In this passage the reported speech consists of principal sentences with the indicatives replaced by subjunctives, the second person of the one addressed by the third person and the imperatives by modal auxiliaries (*sollen, müssen*).

The following is an example of (3) 'hinted' speech or musings:

Nachdem Johanna fortgegangen war, überdachte er die Ereignisse der letzten paar Stunden. Beim Himmel! er hatte doch tatsächlich vergessen, ihr den Brief zu zeigen, den er am Morgen erhalten hatte. Hatte er ihn noch in der Tasche? Nein, da war er nicht—wo zum Teufel konnte er stecken? Er hatte ihn doch nicht etwa auf dem Tische liegen lassen, wo ihn alle lesen konnten. Was für ein Wahnsinn: Augenblick mal: Natürlich, jetzt erinnerte er sich—er hatte einen andern Anzug angehabt, und der Brief war bestimmt noch in der Jackentasche. Er würde gleich einmal nachsehen gehen.

After Joan had gone he went over the events of the last few hours. Good heavens! He had actually forgotten to show her the letter he had received that morning. Had he still got it in his pocket? No, it wasn't there—where on earth could it have got to? Surely he hadn't left it on the table where all could read it. What madness! But wait a minute! Of course, now he remembered—he had been wearing a different suit and the letter must certainly still be in the jacket-pocket. He would go and see at once.

In sharp contrast with the preceding passages the verbs, though in the past tenses, retain the indicative mood, questions are put directly and all the affirmative and negative particles, also asseverations and subjective expressions of emotion are inserted. English and German resemble each other closely in this kind of discourse except in the case cited in Chapter 8. The technique is that of the 'stream of consciousness' (*Bewußtseinsstrom*) as shown in *Sansibar* by S. Andersch.

Indirect statement

When the verb of 'saying', etc., in the main clause is in the present tense, the verb in the dependent clause is normally in the indicative. The dependent clause can either be in immediate contact with the main clause and retain the direct order of words, or it may be introduced by *daß*. Examples with first person of declarative verb: *ich glaube, er wird es machen können/er kann dir helfen/es ist Zeit zu gehen* 'I think he will be able to do it/he can help you/it is time to go'; *ich denke, er kommt bald* 'I think he is coming soon'; *ich weiß, daß er zuverlässig ist/daß er Recht hatte* 'I know that he is reliable/that he was right'; *ich hoffe, die Nachricht erfreut ihn* 'I hope the news will please him'; *ich fürchte,*

er ist krank 'I fear he is ill'; *ich bin überzeugt, er ist nicht böse*
'I am convinced he is not cross' (also *daß er nicht böse ist*); *ich
möchte annehmen (ich neige zu der Ansicht), daß er leicht ange-
heitert war, als er das schrieb* '[I am inclined to think] that he
was slightly intoxicated when he wrote that'. With the third
person of the declarative verb the use of the subjunctive in the
dependent verb indicates that the statement is at least open to
question, e.g. *der Arzt glaubt, daß ich krank bin* 'the doctor thinks
I am ill (and I do not contest his view)' /*der Arzt glaubt, daß ich
krank sei* indicates that I am not so sure; *man sagt mir, es sei
besser zu warten* 'I've been told it is better to wait (but it may not
be so)'.

The subjunctive of the dependent verb is usual after a
declarative verb in the past tense, e.g. *ich dachte, er hätte es
getan/ er wäre hier gewesen* 'I thought he had done it/he had been
here'; *ich fürchtete, er wäre krank* 'I feared he was ill'. In the North
German colloquial the past subjunctive is used more than the
present *habe, sei*, etc., which, however, are often regarded as
more correct. Occasionally an indicative is used with verbs like
dachte, e.g. *ich dachte, er ist (war) hier* 'I thought he was here'.

More complex are English sentences of the type 'a man who I
think is . . .' which is rendered in German by *ein Mann von dem
ich glaube, daß er . . .* or *der—wie ich glaube . . .*

Indirect question

The dependent clause asking the question 'whether' or 'if' is
introduced by *ob*, e.g. *können Sie mir Auskunft geben, ob hier in
der Nähe eine Kirche ist?* 'can you inform me whether there is a
church somewhere about here?'; *ich zweifle, ob er heute kommt*
'I doubt whether he is coming today'/*ich zweifelte, ob er gestern
kommen würde* 'I doubted whether he would come yesterday';
ich wüßte gern, ob er Angst hat 'I should like to know whether he is
afraid'.

When the question is one of specific determination with 'who?',
'what?', 'when?', etc., the specific interrogative word is used as
introducer, e.g. *ich kann mir nicht denken, was er vorhat (was er
eigentlich vorhatte)* 'I can't imagine what he has on (what he was
really intending)'; *wir wollen losen, wer zuerst gibt (geben soll)*
'we'll toss up to see who will (is to) serve first'; *sagen Sie mir,
wann in dieser Kirche die Messe gelesen wird* 'tell me when Mass is
celebrated in this church'; *erklären Sie mir, wie das Gebäude*

beschaffen ist 'tell me what the building is like'; *er gab mir Anweisungen, welchen Zug ich nehmen müßte* 'he gave me directions as to which train I should take'.

Indirect command

The dependent clause corresponding to an imperative sentence often follows up the main clause omitting any introducing particle and the straight order of words is retained. It is also possible to use *daß* with straddling order. In the following examples the use of *sollen* indicates a more peremptory request than the polite *mögen: sagen Sie ihm, er soll (muß, möchte) sofort kommen* 'tell him he is to (he must, please to) come at once'; *bitten Sie ihn (ich bat ihn), er möchte die Papiere mitbringen* (present subjunctive *möge* more literary) 'ask him (I asked him) to be good enough to bring the papers with him'; *ich schlage vor, daß er heute hingeht* 'I suggest he goes there today' or *ich schlage vor, du gehst heute in die Stadt* 'I suggest you should go into town today'; *er befahl, daß die Festung geräumt würde* 'he ordered that the fort be evacuated' (or *er befahl die Festung zu räumen*).

1 2

SUBORDINATE CLAUSES – COMPLEX PERIODS –

EXCLAMATORY SENTENCES

Content clauses with 'what', etc.

A clause introduced by *was* may be the subject of a sentence, e.g. *was er sagt, ist mir genau so schleierhaft wie Ihnen* 'what he says is just as mysterious to me as it is to you', or the direct object of a verb, e.g. *ich habe nie erfahren, was er in Berlin tat* 'I have never heard what he did in Berlin'. After a preposition *was* is usually provided with an antecedent *das*, e.g. *ich erinnere mich sehr gut an das, was er sagte* 'I very well remember what he said'; *ich habe mich sehr geärgert über das, was er geschrieben hat* 'I am very annoyed about what he has written'. In the case of 'who' the spoken language occasionally telescopes the antecedent and the clause-introducer using the preposition with the latter, e.g. *ich korrespondiere mit wem es mir gefällt*, cf. 'I correspond with whom I please'; *ich spreche mit wem es mir paßt* 'I speak to whoever it suits me to'; *alle raten wer welchen Zettel geschrieben hat* 'all try to guess who wrote which note'.

Content clauses with Da-*compounds and* Daß

German has no facility as English has for forming phrases of the type 'through his being . . .', 'in spite of my going . . .', etc., but fulfils the same syntactical function by using as antecedent a compound like *dadurch* or *damit* followed by a *daß*-clause. The following are some typical examples: *ich bestehe darauf, daß Sie selbst hingehen* 'I insist on your going there yourself'; *ich bin dafür, daß er zu uns zieht* 'I am in favour of his moving to our place'; *er hatte einen schlimmen Anfall dadurch, daß er naß wurde* 'he had a bad attack through getting wet'; *kann ich mich darauf verlassen, daß Sie hingehen?* 'can I rely on your going?'.

A looser construction with *daß*, but without antecedent appears in the following examples: *ich wundere mich, daß er so spät kommt* 'I am surprised at his being so late'; *wir standen und warteten, daß der Regen aufhören sollte* 'we stood waiting for the rain to stop'. In these two examples the more explicit expressions would be *ich wundere mich darüber, daß* . . . and *warteten darauf, daß* . . ..

Relative clauses (Relativsätze)

English distinguishes between 'who' for persons, 'which' or 'that' for non-personal antecedents and can omit the relative pronoun altogether when it indicates the object of a verb, including a verb phrase, e.g. 'the man who came/whom I saw/ whose son I taught/whom I gave the book/with whom I spoke' or 'the man I saw/the man I gave the book to', etc.; 'the book which is on the top shelf/the book I read yesterday', etc. German on the other hand has the relative pronouns applying to any antecedents: *welcher/welche/welches//*plural *welche* and—particularly in the spoken language—*der/die/das//die*. Only in the genitive case ('whose', 'of which') are there specific forms *dessen* (masculine and neuter singular), *deren* (feminine singular and plural all genders) and in the dative plural *denen*. Examples: *der Mann, der da drüben sitzt* 'the man (who is) sitting over there'; *der Dampfer, der gerade einläuft* 'the steamer (which is) just coming into port'; *die Frau, die gegenüber wohnt* 'the woman (who is) living opposite'; *das Haus, das zu vermieten ist* 'the house, which is to be let'; *der Freund, den ich besucht habe und an den ich geschrieben habe* 'the friend I have visited and written to'; *der Anzug, für den ich bezahlen möchte* 'the suit I should like to pay for'; *der Mann, dessen Sohn ich kenne* 'the man whose son I know'; *das Kind, dessen Eltern hier sind* 'the child whose parents are here'; *die Vase, deren Blumen Sie so bewundern* 'the vase the flowers of which you so admire'; *der Junge (das Mädchen), dem ich das Buch gegeben habe* 'the boy (girl) I have given the book to'; *die Frau, der ich alles erzählte* 'the woman to whom I told everything'; *das Messer, mit dem ich das Brot schnitt* 'the knife I cut the bread with (with which I cut the bread)'; *die Männer (Frauen, Kinder), die hier wohnen* 'the men (women, children) who are living here'; *die Eltern, deren Kinder Sie drüben sehen* 'the parents whose children you see over there'; *die Häuser, denen man einen neuen Anstrich geben will* 'the houses to which a new coat of paint is to be given'.

When the antecedent is non-personal and especially if it is a neuter noun, the prepositional phrase ('with which', 'by which', etc.) can be replaced by a compound with *wo-*, e.g. *das Messer, womit (mit dem) ich das Brot schnitt*; *das Haus, worauf (auf das) ich hinweise* 'the house I am referring to'. The phrase *mit dem*, etc., is the more prevalent colloquial form in most parts of Germany.

Where there are specific interrogative words, e.g. of place like 'where', time 'when', way 'how', reason 'why', etc. German can, like English, use some of these interrogatives as relatives, e.g. *der Ort, wo* . . . 'the place where . . .'; *die Zeit, wo* . . . 'the time when . . .'; *der Grund, weshalb* . . . 'the reason why . . .'; *die Art und Weise, wie* . . . 'the manner in which . . .'.

The neuter of the adjective when used in a generalizing sense has as its relative *was* instead of *das*, e.g. *das einzige, was wir wissen* 'the only thing [that] we know'; *alles, was er tut* 'everything [that] he does'.

Causal clauses (Kausalsätze)

A causal clause is normally introduced in English by 'because', 'as', 'since', 'for', or 'seeing that'. The German equivalent of 'for' is *denn* which is treated as a co-ordinating conjunction (*und, oder*) and does not entail any divergence from straight word-order. The word *weil* is used much the same as 'because', e.g. *ich gehe den Mantel holen, weil es kalt ist* 'I'm going to fetch my overcoat because (as, since) it is cold'; *der Schiedsrichter pfeift, weil der Boxer einen Tiefschlag gegeben hat* 'the referee is blowing his whistle because the boxer has delivered a foul'. When the main clause contains a negative, the causal clause can either indicate (1) that the state of things posited in the main clause is not the true or exclusive reason for a certain occurrence, or (2) that the occurrence mentioned in the causal clause is the reason for the negative state of things posited in the main clause. The following examples should make this complication clear—in the spoken language the insertion or absence of a pause before 'because' gives the clue: (1) *ich tue's nicht, weil ich es tun soll, sondern weil ich es tun will* 'I don't do it because I am expected to, but because I want to'; (2) *wir können nicht hingehen, weil wir eine andere Einla-*

dung angenommen haben 'we can't go there because (as, since) we have accepted another invitation'.

Examples of the other conjunctions: *da die Nachfrage nach Plätzen sehr groß sein wird* 'as the demand for seats will be very great'; *da er nicht selbst kommen kann, will ich ihn aufsuchen* 'since he cannot come himself I will look him up'; *ist er ein intimer Freund von dir, daß du ihn mit Du anredest?* 'is he a close friend of yours [seeing] that you call him "Du"?'; *sie kann es mir nicht übel nehmen, daß ich nicht pünktlich war* 'she cannot take it ill of me for not being punctual'; *ich kann seine Haltung nicht verstehen angesichts (in Anbetracht) der Tatsache, daß er so viel zu gewinnen hat* 'I cannot understand his attitude seeing that (in view of the fact that) he has so much to gain'; *hast du gar nichts zu tun, daß du da so faul herumsitz[es]t?* 'have you nothing whatever to do, idling about like that?' (called by Erades in *English Studies*, XXXIII, p. 233, a clause of 'motivation'). Of a more literary character is *zumal* in *den kann ich Ihnen empfehlen, zumal er ein williger Junge ist* 'I can recommend him to you especially as he is a willing boy'.

To deny that a particular reason or cause is valid while admitting others, at least implicitly, English uses 'not that' or 'not because' and German *nicht daß* or *nicht (etwa) weil*, e.g. *nicht daß ich keine Lust habe, aber ich muß erst einmal meine Arbeit fertig machen* '(it's) not that I'm not keen on it, but I must get my work finished first'; *nicht daß er mir sympathisch ist, aber ich muß einem Landsmann schon etwas Gastfreundschaft zeigen* 'not that I find him congenial, but I must show some hospitality to a fellow-countryman'. In both examples speakers often use the past subjunctive, e.g. *nicht daß ich keine Lust hätte* and *nicht daß er mir sympathisch wäre*.

Comparative clauses (Vergleichssätze)

Though the zero-construction, i.e. omission of the finite verb whose subject is the comparable item, is the most prevalent in both languages ('he is as tall as I', 'he is taller than I', cf. *er ist so groß wie ich, er ist größer als ich*), occasionally a whole clause is found introduced by German *wie* 'as' or *als* 'than'. Examples: *das ist eine Kleinigkeit für einen so klugen Menschen wie Sie* 'that is a trifle for such a clever man as you are'; *ich bin jetzt schon so alt, wie meine Mutter zu jener Zeit war* 'I am now as old as my

5

mother was at that time'; *er kam früher nach Hause, als man erwartet hatte* 'he came home earlier than expected'.

After an expression of excess with 'too' (*zu*) German uses either an infinitive or full dependent clause with *als daß* 'than that', e.g. *es ist zu spät, um die Verabredung abzusagen* 'it is too late (for us) to cancel the engagement'; *er war zu stolz, um mit ihr zu sprechen* 'he was too proud to speak to her'; *das Haus ist viel zu klein, als daß wir alle darin wohnen könnten* 'the house is much too small for us to live in it'; *er kam zu spät als daß er noch helfen konnte* 'he came too late to be able to help', cf. also *er wußte keinen bessern Rat, als daß er von seinen Erlebnissen erzählte* 'he did not know any better device than to tell of his experiences'.

A fictitious comparison is indicated in English by 'as if' and in German *als ob* or *als wenn* with dependent order, or *als* with the verb inverted, e.g. *ich werde so tun, als ob ich ihn nicht sehe* 'I will act as if I can't see him'; *er sagte es, als ob er es ganz bestimmt wüßte* 'he said it as though he knew it quite definitely'; *das Kind sieht aus, als wäre es krank* 'the child looks as if it were ill'.

Concessive clauses (Konzessiv-, Einräumungssätze)

There are several conjunctions in German corresponding to 'although', e.g. *obgleich, obwohl, obschon*, as in *obgleich der Himmel bewölkt war* 'although the sky was overcast'; *obgleich kein Star in diesem Film beschäftigt ist, ist die Darstellung ausgezeichnet* 'although no star is engaged in this film, the acting is superb'; *obwohl es mir nicht so vorkam* 'though it did not appear like that to me'.

Another way of indicating the concessive relation is the use of 'even if' in English and *selbst wenn* in German, e.g. *selbst wenn der Krieg bald zu Ende ist* 'even if the war will soon be over'; *selbst wenn er hier wäre* 'even if he were here'. Occasionally '(even) supposing' has concessive force, e.g. *setzen wir, Sie hätten den Zug erreicht, so wären Sie doch sehr spät zur Versammlung gekommen* 'even supposing you had caught the train, you would have been very late for the meeting' (N.B. the concession is often shown—in contrast to a mere condition—by the straight order of the main clause without the usual inversion).

The conjunction corresponding to the preposition *trotz* 'in spite of' is *trotzdem* (cf. *nach/nachdem, seit/seitdem*), e.g. *trotzdem*[1]

[1] Germans are sometimes told not to begin a whole sentence with *trotzdem*, but this order is frequent in speech.

er so alt ist, geht er noch jeden Tag zwei Stunden lang spazieren 'in spite of his being (in spite of the fact that he is) so old, he still takes a two-hour walk every day'.

When the concessive clause contains an expression of a quality or characteristic which might normally be expected to have other results, there are several alternatives, e.g. in English 'small as he is (he is very brave)', 'small though he is', 'even if he is small' in addition to the objective 'although he is small'. German also has various possibilities as shown in the following examples: *obgleich er klein ist; wie klein er auch (immer) sein mag; auch wenn er klein ist; so unbedeutend er auch ist* 'insignificant as he is'; *er mag wohl klein sein, er ist aber trotzdem sehr mutig; das Buch ist zwar sehr klein, aber sehr wertvoll* 'granted the work is small, it is very valuable all the same', cf. *der Wind war besser als der Ölqualm, so eisig er war* 'the wind was better than oily smoke, icy though it was'. It is possible to omit the verb in such cases as *obgleich (wenn auch) klein von Gestalt war er doch sehr mutig*, cf. *obwohl noch jung* 'though still young'.

To indicate the maximum disproportion between the fact and the normal expectation, English uses 'ever so' (formerly often 'never so') or 'however' and German *noch so*, e.g. *wenn er noch so reich ist* or *wäre er noch so reich* '(even) if he were ever so rich', 'however rich he is'.

Not all the cases of the use of '(small) as . . .', etc., are concessive, e.g., *so müde wie ich bin, kann ich doch jetzt nicht dahingehen* 'tired as I am I certainly cannot go there' (where the implication is one of cause). If instead of *müde* a past participle like *erschöpft* or *abgehetzt* 'harassed' is used, the *so* can be omitted as in English.

The main clause following a concessive clause is often connected with it by the particle *so* or, more emphatically, by *so . . . doch . . .*, e.g. *obgleich ich zuerst einige Bedenken hatte, so möchte ich ihn doch empfehlen* 'although I had some misgivings at first, I still want to recommend him'.

Consecutive clauses (Konsekutivsätze)

In English these are indicated by 'so that' or 'so . . . that' and this is the normal procedure in German with *so daß* and *so . . . daß*, e.g. *der Krieg ist beendet, so daß wir bald den Frieden haben werden* 'the war is over so (that) we shall soon have peace'; *ich war so überrascht, daß ich sogar vergaß, ihm zu danken* 'I was so surprised that I even forgot to thank him; *so viele Völker sind in unser Land eingefallen, daß alle Stile vertreten sind* 'so many people have invaded our country that all styles are represented'. Occasionally *so* is omitted, e.g. *er arbeitete, daß ihm der Schweiß auf der Stirn stand* 'he worked so that the sweat poured off his brow'.

Conditional clauses (Konditional-, Bedingungssätze)

The most frequent conditional conjunction in English is 'if' and in German *wenn* (which when followed by the present indicative is also equivalent to 'when'). An open condition is shown in both languages by the indicative mood of the verb, e.g. *wenn Sie nach Hamburg kommen, müssen Sie uns besuchen* 'if (and when) you come to Hamburg, you must visit us'. The synonym of *wenn* is *falls* 'in case', e.g. *falls das Museum geschlossen ist* 'in case the museum is closed'. It is also possible to say *für den Fall, daß* and *im Falle, daß* . . .

If the condition is posited as incompatible with reality—a condition called by the Germans the 'Irrealis'—the verb is in the preterite or pluperfect subjunctive, e.g. *wenn er hier wäre* 'if he were here'; *wenn er es getan hätte* 'if he had done it'; *wenn er gekommen wäre* 'if he had come'. (N.B. These are synonymous with the inverted forms *wäre er hier*; *hätte er es getan*; *wäre er gekommen*).

If the condition is a contingency with a slight tinge of doubt the verb can be in the preterite subjunctive or have the auxiliary *sollte*, e.g. *wenn er heute käme* (*wenn er heute kommen sollte*) 'if he were to (should) come today'; *wenn es regnen sollte* 'if it should rain'.

The sole condition is indicated by *nur wenn* or *bloß wenn*, e.g. *nur wenn er sich scheiden läßt, kann er das Vermögen seines Vaters erben* 'only if he gets a divorce, can he inherit his father's fortune'; *bloß wenn die Lichter am Baum brennen* 'only when (if) the tree is lit'.

The main clause on which the condition is dependent is sometimes introduced by *so* or *dann*, e.g. *wenn Sie morgen zu viel zu tun haben, so* (*dann*) *können wir die Sache übermorgen besprechen* 'if you have too much to do tomorrow, we can discuss the matter the day after'.

German has no specific conjunction corresponding to the English 'unless', but renders it by *wenn nicht* 'if not', e.g. *wenn er nicht gern arbeitet* 'unless he likes working'.

Another way of introducing conditions in English is 'on condition that' or 'provided that' for which German equivalents are illustrated by the following examples: *ich werde bei dem Kranken aufsitzen unter der Bedingung, daß er alles tut, was Sie ihm sagen* 'I shall sit up with the patient on condition that he does everything you tell him'; *vorausgesetzt (unter der Voraussetzung) daß alles pünktlich bezahlt wird* 'provided that everything is paid punctually'. A hypothesis or assumption is introduced in English by 'granted' or 'supposing', e.g. *angenommen, er kommt heute (angenommen, daß er heute kommt)* 'granted he will come today'.

A special case of 'unless' is the indication of a condition as an exception, whence the more specific 'except if'. German can render the latter phrase by *außer wenn*, but in a more formal context may use *es sei denn, daß . . .*, e.g. *ich fahre auf keinen Fall vor Juni nach Hamburg, es sei denn, daß (außer wenn) der Vertrag ohne mich nicht abgeschlossen werden kann* 'I shall not in any case be travelling to Hamburg before June, unless (except if) the agreement cannot be concluded without me'.

A clause of 'contingency' (cf. P. A. Erades, *English Studies*, XXXIII, p. 235) is introduced by *falls, im Falle [daß]* or *für den Fall daß*, e.g. *ich nehme meinen Regenmantel mit, falls (im Falle, für den Fall daß) es regnet* 'I'll take my mackintosh in case it rains'.

Final clauses (Final-, Absichtssätze)

These are introduced in English by 'in order that' or 'so that'. The specific final conjunction in German is *damit*, which in the written language is used with the subjunctive, whereas the spoken language prefers the indicative or the use of *können*. Examples: *ich lösche das Geschriebene, damit es nicht schmiert* (literary: *schmiere*) 'I'll blot what I have written so that it does not make a mess'; *er sollte boxen lernen, damit er sich nötigenfalls verteidigen kann* 'he ought to learn boxing so that he can defend himself if necessary'; *ich mache mir eine Notiz, damit ich den Namen nicht vergesse* 'I will make a note so as not to forget the name, cf. *um den Namen nicht zu vergessen*.

Local clauses (Lokalsätze)

These are introduced by 'where' in English and *wo* in German, e.g. *wo mehr Zeit dem Sport gewidmet wird, sieht die Jugend besser aus* 'where more time is devoted to sport the young people look better'; *wo der Wald lichter wurde, begann der Weg anzusteigen* 'where the forest thinned out, the path began to climb'. The word *wo* may also be used with an antecedent designating a place, e.g. *am Herd, wo er gewöhnlich saß* 'at the fireplace where he usually sat'. The English 'wherever' in the sense of 'at all places where . . .' is often rendered by *überall, wo* (lit. everywhere where), e.g. *überall, wo das Eisen vorkommt* 'wherever iron occurs . . .'. A border-line case between the local, temporal and conditional is *es liegt Ihnen gerade gegenüber, wenn Sie über die Brücke kommen* 'it's right in front of you as you cross the bridge'.

Clauses of manner (Modalsätze)

The way in which something is done is indicated in English by a clause introduced by 'as' and in German by *wie*, e.g. *er sah auf Hans, (so) wie man auf ein Pferd blickt* 'he looked at Jack as one looks at a horse'; *er kratzte sich den Kopf, wie es Kinder oft tun, wenn sie verlegen sind* 'he scratched his head as children often do when they are puzzled'. A rather looser use of *wie* is illustrated by *es gefällt mir sehr, wie diese Schauspieler spielen* 'I very much like the way these actors play their parts'.

If the nuance is one of extent rather than purely of manner, English uses 'inasmuch as', 'so far as' or 'in that', and the clause has a tinge of the causal, e.g. *dieser Name ist überraschend, insofern als er nicht im Altenglischen vorkommt* 'this name is surprising in that (in so far as) it does not occur in Old English'. These might be termed restrictive clauses. The negation of a favouring circumstance is indicated by *ohne daß* in *er tanzte gut, ohne daß er Stunden genommen hatte* 'he danced well without having had lessons'.

Another type of clause of manner indicates conformity with a certain norm. English, here, uses 'according [as] . . .' and German *je nachdem*, e.g. *je nachdem wie er behandelt wird* 'according to how (the way) he is treated'. Such clauses may have a shade of the causal about them. There is a slight difference between the types of alternative implied by *je nachdem er kommt, werde ich meine Ferien arrangieren* 'I shall arrange my holidays according to his coming' and *je nachdem ob er kommt, werde ich im Sommer zu Hause bleiben* 'I shall stay at home during the summer on the [off] chance of him coming'.

Under modal sentences may be included the indication of the means or instrument either by *dadurch daß* or *indem*, e.g. *er rettete sich, indem er Wasser trat* 'he saved himself by treading water'.

Proportional clauses (Proportionalsätze)

These clauses indicate 'the more ... the more ...' or 'the less ... the less ...', etc. English uses 'the'+comparative ... 'the'+ comparative and German *je ... desto* (or *um so*) ... Examples: *je mehr wir versuchen, ihm zu helfen, um so unwilliger ist er bei der Arbeit* 'the more we try to help him, the more unwilling he is at his work'; *je länger er im Gefängnis blieb, desto mehr wünschten sie ihn zu befreien* 'the longer he remained in prison, the more they wanted to free him'. Sometimes the correlation of increases or decreases is left implicit, e.g. *im selben Maße wie seine Frau dünner wurde, setzte er Fett an* 'in proportion as his wife got slimmer, he put on weight'.

A clause containing 'all the more' may have a causal implication, e.g. *ich freute mich um so mehr, als er mich gleich erkannte* 'I was all the more pleased that he recognized me at once'. One implying 'still less' is indicated in literary German by *geschweige [denn] daß*, e.g. *er kennt sie kaum, geschweige [denn] daß er in sie verliebt ist* 'he hardly knows her, let alone being in love with her', where the clause is akin to an infinitival phrase, analogous to 'far from' or French 'loin de', e.g. *weit davon entfernt, sie zu lieben* 'far from loving her'.

Temporal clauses (Temporalsätze)

In English time-relations between clauses are indicated by such conjunctions as 'when', 'while', 'before', 'after', 'until'. There are German expressions corresponding to each of these, but it is necessary to distinguish between *wenn* for 'when' with a present (or future) tense and *als* for 'when' for a single event in the past. If *wenn* is used with a past tense the implication is that of 'whenever'. As the interrogative 'when?' is *wann*, that form is used also in the indirect question with whatever tense. The following examples illustrate these various distinctions:

WANN: (*wann kommt er?*). *Ich weiß nicht, wann er kommt* 'I do not know when he is coming'.

WENN: *jeden Morgen gegen acht, wenn ich aufstehe* 'every morning about eight o'clock when I get up'; *wenn ich ihn früher besuchte* 'when(ever) I used to visit him'.

(N.B. Since *wenn* is often used to introduce a conditional clause, the context determines whether it is to be translated by 'when' or 'if'.)

ALS: *als er am Haus vorbeiging, hörte er einen Schuß* 'when (as) he was passing the house, he heard a shot'; *Sie können sich seine Enttäuschung vorstellen, als sie ihm einen Korb gab* 'you can imagine his disappointment when she refused him'; *als der Vater den Brief geschrieben hatte, brachte er ihn zur Post* 'when my father had written the letter, he took it to the post'.

In German there are two words for 'before' as a conjunction, viz. *bevor* and *ehe*. In the spoken language of the North *bevor* is preferred where it is purely a matter of time and *ehe* when there is some idea of preference, as shown by the following:

BEVOR: *bevor ich das Gedicht bespreche* 'before I discuss (before discussing) the poem'; *ich werde nicht wiederkommen, bevor (als bis) die Sache geregelt ist* 'I shall not come again before the matter is settled'.

EHE: *ehe wir uns diesen Bedingungen unterwerfen, werden wir bis zum letzten Mann kämpfen* 'before we submit to (=rather than submit to) these conditions, we shall fight to the last man'.

The conjunction 'till' or 'until' has its equivalent in *bis*, which can be preceded by the negative *nicht eher* 'not before'. Examples of BIS: *es dauerte einige Zeit, bis das Schiff anlegte* 'it took some time till the ship came alongside'; *bis er die Schule verläßt* (=*bis zu seiner Schulentlassung*) 'by the time he leaves school'; *er ruhte nicht* [*eher als*], *bis er den letzten Mann niedergestreckt hatte* 'he did not rest till he had laid the last man low'. For 'not until' or 'not before' a synonymous construction is with the adverb *erst wenn* (*als*), e.g. *erst als er mich sah* '[it was] only when he saw me', '[it was] not until he saw me'; *die großen Ozeandampfer verlassen ihren Hafen erst, wenn die Flut einsetzt* 'the big liners do not leave port till the tide comes in'.

An immediate or very rapid succession is indicated in English by 'hardly ... when ...' for which German has an exact equivalent, e.g. *er war kaum hundert Meter gegangen, als er merkte* 'he had hardly gone a hundred yards, when he noticed ...'; *kaum hatte ich den Mantel angezogen, als der Regen auch schon niederströmte* 'hardly had I put on my overcoat, when the rain started to pour down'. The German *als* happens to cover both 'when' and 'than' (no sooner than).

The word 'after' in English is used as (1) a preposition, e.g. 'after the meal' where German says *nach dem Essen* (2) an adverb, e.g. 'a few years after' where German says *ein paar Jahre nachher*, and (3) a conjunction 'after [he had spoken]' when German says *nachdem [er gesprochen hatte]*. Thus the clause-equivalent of *nach Sonnenuntergang [können wir den Weg nicht mehr finden]* 'after sunset [we can no longer find our way]' is *nachdem die Sonne untergegangen ist.* The time interval may be specified further by adverbs, e.g. *ich machte mich auf, gleich nachdem er mich angerufen hatte* 'I set out immediately after he had rung me up'; *direkt (kurz) nachdem sie vom Tisch aufgestanden war, klagte sie über Schmerzen* 'directly she had got up from the table, she complained of pains'. The limit of 'before' and 'after', i.e. absence of any interval, is indicated in English by 'immediately', 'directly', 'the moment (when)' or 'as soon as', for which the following types of expression are available in German: *wir werden sofort abreisen, wenn die Formalitäten erfüllt sind* 'we shall start immediately the formalities have been completed'; *im Augenblick (in demselben Augenblick), wo er eintrifft* 'the moment he arrives'; *sobald sein Vater gestorben war, gab er das Geschäft auf* 'as soon as his father had died, he disposed of the business'.

For two concurrent periods or for the occurrence of an event within a certain period English uses 'while' and German *während*, e.g. *während er Klavier spielte* 'while he was playing the piano'. To emphasize the completion of a period of time English says 'the whole time' or 'all the time (during which)' and German *die ganze Zeit, wo (während)*, e.g. *die ganze Zeit, wo er sang, unterhielten sich die Leute* 'all the time he was singing, people were talking'; *die ganze Zeit, wo er an der See war* (= *während seines Aufenthalts an der See), arbeitete er* 'he worked the whole time he was at the seaside'; *es wäre besser, ich schriebe meine Erinnerungen auf, während sie mir noch frisch im Gedächtnis sind* 'it would be better for me to write down my reminiscences while they are still fresh in my memory'. Like 'while' the German *während* can in certain contexts acquire an adversative ('but, yet') or concessive ('whereas') character, e.g. *lange Zeit betrachtete man ihn als Schriftsteller, während* (stronger and more literary: *wogegen*) *er in Wirklichkeit nur ein Übersetzer war* 'for long he was regarded as an author, while (whereas) in reality he was a mere translator'; *die Wildente flog weg während sich die Rebhühner nur ein wenig weiter zurückzogen* 'the wild duck flew away, while the partridges merely withdrew a little further'; *ein Neurastheniker klammert sich an seine fixe Idee, während er zu gleicher Zeit darunter leidet* 'a neurasthenic patient clings to his fixed idea while (though) suffering under it'. The synonym *indem* now often indicates 'means' (=*dadurch daß*), e.g. *indem er Wasser trat* . . . 'by treading water'.

For 'as long as' German has the conjunction *solange*, e.g. *solange sie lebte, hatte sie großen Einfluß auf ihre beiden Söhne* 'as long as she lived, she had great influence on both her sons'. Like 'as long as' the German *solange* can acquire a nuance of condition (if, unless), e.g. *ich bin nicht zufrieden, solange meine Mutter dem Plan nicht zustimmt* 'I cannot be satisfied, as long as my mother does not give her assent to the project' (unless my mother gives).

To indicate a starting point of an occurrence English uses 'since' and German *seitdem*, e.g. *seitdem ich hier wohne* 'since I have lived here (since living here)'. As in English *seitdem* can imply cause as well as time, e.g. *seitdem du hier bist, fühle ich mich bedeutend besser* 'since you are here, I have felt considerably better'. The ending point is either *bis* or more specifically the phrases used in the following examples: *ich bin zu denn Punkt gelangt, wo ich am liebsten alle rausschmeißen möchte* 'I've come to the point where I should like to chuck them all out'; *er fuhr fort zu arbeiten bis zu dem Augenblick, wo er sich legen mußte* 'he kept on working to the very moment when he had to take to his bed'. With a sentence like *ich war so weit gekommen, daß ich einen Zorn auf alle und jeden hatte* 'I had got to the pitch of being offended with one and all' the boundary-line between time and consequence has already been passed.

Finally, there are some miscellaneous phrases used in replacement of the single conjunctions. They include those illustrated in the following sentences: *zur Zeit, als ich noch jung war* 'at the time (when) I was still young'; *jedesmal, wo ich versuchte, seine Aufmerksamkeit auf mich zu ziehen* 'every time (whenever) I tried to attract his attention'; *soweit ich mich zurückerinnern kann* (or colloquially *soweit zurück ich mich erinnern kann*) 'as far back as I can remember'.

Complex periods (Satzgefüge)

In a 'period' or complex group of clauses it is advisable to finish off each subordinate clause before proceeding with the next, otherwise there will be an unmanageable series of finite verbs at the end of the whole. The following are some typical examples of multiple subordination of clauses without any impairment of clarity or awkward accumulations:

was möchten Sie, daß ich mit dem Geld tun soll, das wir durch unsere Mithilfe im Garten verdienen? 'what would you like me to do with the money we earn by helping in the garden?'.

er sagte mir, wenn ich einige Minuten Zeit hätte, würde er den Artikel im Reallexikon nachsehen, und mir dann all die gewünschten Informationen geben können 'he told me that if I had a few minutes, he would look up the article in the encyclopedia and then be able to give me all the information I wanted'. (Note how the German sentence is lightened by the omission of *daß* and by the use of the past participle *gewünscht* as an attribute).

es hat keinen Zweck, daß ich den Kindern sage, sie sollen es nicht tun—sie gehorchen doch nicht und ich werde sie bestrafen müssen 'it's no use my telling the children not to do it, for they won't obey and I shall be obliged to punish them'.

es empfiehlt sich, den Absender auf dem Umschlag anzugeben, damit der Brief an Sie zurückkommt, wenn er sich als unbestellbar erweist, weil der Adressat verzogen ist 'you are recommended to write the name of the sender on the envelope so that the letter is returned to you if it turns out that it cannot be delivered because the addressee has moved somewhere else'.

Exclamatory sentences (Ausrufesätze)

The two main types are (1) expressions of strong wish and (2) emotional reactions to a given situation.

The sentence form appropriate to the first is an 'if'-clause, reinforced with one or more particles like the English 'only' and characterized by the finite verb in the conditional mood. The prevalent North German wish-sentence may be exemplified as follows:

Wenn meine Mutter doch Sonntag einen Kuchen backen würde! 'if only my mother would bake a cake on Sunday!'; *wenn er doch bloß (nur) morgen kommen würde!* 'if only he would come to-morrow!'; *wenn ein Klempner doch bloß mal die Regenrinnen heil machte (machen würde)!* 'if only a plumber would repair the gutters'. The past subjunctive of the verb may also express regret that something has not happened, e.g. *wenn ich ihn nur getroffen hätte!* 'if only I had met him!', or with the inverted order *hätte ich es nur gewußt!* 'if only I had known!'; *hätte mein Bruder nur Geld!* 'if only my brother had some money!'. The emotional character of all the above sentences is emphasized by the isolation

of the condition from a main clause or 'apodosis', the implication
of the latter being 'I should be glad', etc.

In the second type of sentence there are ascending grades of
explicitness. Thus in English we can say 'excellent', 'how excellent' and 'how excellent it is' and in German *fein!, wie fein!* and
wie fein es ist! in each case with rising-falling intonation. In German there are two kinds of word order in the full exclamatory
sentence. The 'how' word can be separated from its adjective and
in that case the order is that of an interrogative sentence, though
not with the question intonation. If the word for 'how' immediately precedes the adjective the word-order is that of the
introduced dependent sentence with the verb or verb-phrase at
the end.

Examples of the two kinds of word-order are as follows:
wie zieht sich die Frau immer nett an! 'how nicely that woman
always dresses!' and *wie nett sie sich immer anzieht!*; *wie benimmt
er sich [bloß] unmöglich!* 'how impossibly he is behaving!' (in a
tone of indignation), but *wie unmöglich er sich immer benimmt!*
(in a tone of surprise); *was ist doch diese Gegend herrlich!* 'what a
magnificent district this is!'; *was wurde hier alles erzählt!* 'what a
lot there was to tell!'; *was wurde beim Wandern night alles
gesungen!* 'you'd have marvelled at all the singing we did on our
walk!; *wie gut du heute aussiehst!* 'how well you are looking today!'
or *nein, wie gut siehst du heute aus!*

EXPRESSION OF FEELING – IMITATION OF SOUNDS – IRONY AND EMPHATIC NEGATION – USE OF CERTAIN MODAL PARTICLES

Expression of feeling

Specific forms for the discharge of emotions are the somewhat conventionalized interjections, a type of construction we may call the exclamatory sentence and the use of certain modal or nuancing particles.

Primary interjections: *ach!* expresses interest and wonderment (*ach nein!*), pleasure (*ach, wie schön!* 'oh, how nice'), recollection ('oh, of course'), vexation ('oh, bother it') and sympathy (*ach, wie schade!* 'oh, what a pity'), the mood being shown by the level of the voice and duration of the vowel; *ah!* expresses joy, admiration—or, as in the case of people watching fireworks—tense expectation; *au!* expresses physical pain, other forms of bodily discomfort being shown by *pf!* or *puh!* ('phew', when hot), *uh!* for cold or *brr!* (if shivering); *o* often precedes an exclamation, e.g. *o diese Dummheit!* 'oh, what stupidity!', *o nein!* 'oh, no!'; *och!* in Hamburg of regret or commiseration; *oh!* can register a great variety of feelings as in English; *oho!* indicates a sudden dawning of the truth making one gloat, e.g. *oho, so läuft der Hase* or *aha, aus dem Loch pfeift der Wind* 'oho, so that's the way the wind blows'; *o weh!* expresses sympathy with another's pain or distress, but also self-pity; *ei* is no longer so prevalent, but *ei, ei!* is sometimes used as a jocular threat and *ei* is used when stroking; *ätsch* is often accompanied by the gesture of mockery or defiance called *Rübchen schaben*, the gesture of scraping turnips, equivalent to putting out one's tongue. Enthusiasm is marked

colloquially by *au fein!* or *au backe!* The click that we represent
by 'tut tut' is sometimes given in German as *ttt* or *kkk*—there is an
interjection *igitt igitt!* to indicate disgust or horror, but this is
often replaced by *i!* As in English the mark of hesitation is *hm!*
(a pursing of the lips in pursuit of a solution). To call a person's
attention English uses 'hi!' or 'hey!' and German can use either
he! or *hallo! Hallo!* can also be used when telephoning, but a
German often simply announces his name: *Hier Doktor Müller!*,
adding *wer da?* 'who is there?'. A person taking a telephone
call in Dr Müller's residence might say: *Hier bei Doktor Müller!*

Imitation of sounds

A very full list of these is given by H. Marcus in *Englische Studien*,
vol. 75, p. 175 ff. Here only a selection can be given of onomato-
pœic expressions current in Hamburg. They fall into certain
groups as follows:

(1) Cries of animals: *bäh, mäh* 'baa'; *blöke* 'bleat'; *muh* 'moo';
mrrr 'purr'; *miau* 'mew'; *wau wau* (stressed on second syllable)
'bow-wow'; *y-a* 'hee-haw'; *kikeriki* 'cock-a-doodle-do'.

(2) Calls to animals: *hüh!* 'gee-up'; *brrr!* 'whoa!'; *put put!*
'chick, chick'; *tük tük tük!* (to a hen).

(3) Calls to children: *hops!* 'jump!'; *hoppla!* 'ups-a-daisy!';
kuckuck-ba! 'peep-bo!'.

(4) Sound of inanimate things: *husch* 'sh' (of something flitting
past); *hui* (of the wind); *bums* or *peng* 'bang'; *plumps* 'splash';
bim bam 'ding-dong'; *klinglingling* 'tinkle'; *holterdipolter* 'helter-
skelter'; *hūp* or *tūt tūt* 'honk'; *rattatata* (of a wheel); *paff paff*
'puff-puff'; *tsch tsch tsch-tsch* (of an engine); *tapp tapp tapp* or
pitsch patsch patsch 'pitter-patter' (of raindrops and of children's
feet); *plitsch platsch* 'splish splash' (of splashing through water);
ritsch ratsch (of tearing, e.g. paper); *klopfklopf klopf* 'rat-tat-tat'
(at door); *taritata* or *tati tita* 'tally-ho' or 'yoicks', also the older
term *hallali* (stressed on 'i'); *dadi dada* (of the fire-brigade);
bumbum rum bum (of drumbeats); *tratra* and *schnedderengteng*
(blast on a trumpet); *tralala* (as in English, of singing); *didada* (of
music); *trari trara* (of a brass band).

The nursery names of animals are often formed from the
cries and calls in (1) and (2) above, e.g. *das Hottehüh* 'gee-gee';
die Muhkuh; *das Bähschaf, Mähschaf*; *Mähmäh*, 'baa-lamb';
die Meckmeck 'goat'; *das Wiekwiek* 'piggy-wiggy'; *das Tüktük*

'a hen'; *der Kikeriki*; *die Muschi (Mieze)* 'pussy'; *der Piepsi (Piepmatz)* 'dicky-bird'; *der Wauwau* 'bow-wow'.

Expression of irony and emphatic negation

A negative implication can be given to a positive expression or vice versa in both English and German by the use of the sharp-falling ironic intonation. In German the ironic intention is brought out further by the use of nuancing particles, e.g. *ich bin erschüttert!* 'I'm overwhelmed'; *das kümmert ihn auch grade* or *da wird er sich auch gerade aufregen* 'a fat lot he cares about it'; *das ist mir ein netter Kerl (Kumpan)* 'he's a fine fellow, he is'; *das sind ja nette Sachen* 'nice goings-on'; *da haben wir (das ist ja) eine nette Bescherung* 'a nice little spot of bother'; *fall nur in den Dreck!* or *du willst wohl in den Dreck fallen?* 'that's right, fall in the mud!'; *du hast 'ne Ahnung!* 'a lot you know!'; *das ist auch gerade viel nütze* 'a fat lot of good that is!'.

A very drastic expression for the negative in popular speech is *'n Dreck*, e.g. *er weiß 'n Dreck* or *er versteht 'n Dreck* 'a lot he knows (understands) about it'; *es geht dich 'n Dreck an, was ich getan habe* 'what on earth does it matter to you, what I have done?'. In place of 'no one' English uses 'the devil' or 'deuce' and German: *der Teufel*, e.g. *mag der Teufel wissen, wo* 'the deuce knows where'; *ich kümmere mich den Teufel um die Leute* 'the devil I care about the people'; *ich frage den Teufel danach* 'I don't give a damn for it'.

Other substitutes for negatives are *Essig* (lit. 'vinegar'), e.g. *mit der Sache ist es Essig* 'the thing's no good'; *böhmische Dörfer* (lit. Bohemian villages), e.g. *die Angelegenheit ist mir ein böhmisches Dorf* 'I can't make head or tail of the matter'; *was er mir erzählt, kommt mir spanisch vor* 'what he tells me is double Dutch'; *das war ein Schlag ins Wasser (ein Schlag ins Kontor)* 'that did not get us anywhere'. Jocular expressions are *ja Kuchen!* and *Prosit mahlzeit!* cf. 'What hopes?' 'You may whistle for it'.

Another procedure for indicating a negative is the use of the rhetorical question, e.g. *wer's glaubt!* 'believe it or not'; *der und arbeiten?* 'he work?'; *leih mir fünf Mark!—Erst können (vor Lachen)* 'lend me five marks!—what hopes!'; *und was hat sie nun davon?* 'and what's the good of it to her?'; *wen kümmerts?* or *wer fragt denn danach?* 'who cares?'; *was ist denn weiter groß dabei?* 'what is there remarkable about it?'; *wo werd ich?* or *ich danke bestens!* 'no fear'; *das soll ein Haus sein?* 'do you call that

a house?'; *soll ich dich erst lange bitten?* 'how many more times
am I to ask you?'; *das will ein Mann sein—und läßt sich von dem
Weib kommandieren!* 'is he supposed to be a man—letting that
woman order him about!'; *mit den Leuten soll man etwas fertig
kriegen* 'fancy expecting to get anything done with people like
that'.

Sometimes in a strong asseveration English uses a negative
when German prefers a positive, e.g. *[haben Sie Benzin nach-
gefüllt?]—Nein, das habe ich tatsächlich vergessen. Na, so was!*
'[did you fill up with petrol?]—No, dashed if I haven't forgotten
to. Did you ever!'; *da ist er wahrhaftig über seiner Zeitung
eingenickt* 'dashed if he hasn't gone off to sleep over his paper!'.

A negative is frequent in understatements, e.g. *sie ist gar nicht
häßlich (dumm)* 'she's so ugly (silly)'; *er war nicht gerade der
Klügste* 'he wasn't exactly clever'; *das ist nicht berühmt* 'that is
not up to much'; *der Schnaps ist nicht ohne* 'the schnaps is not too
bad'; *ich tue es nicht ungern* 'I don't mind doing it'.

Use of some modal particles

To indicate the speaker's attitude to what he is saying or to
attempt to evoke an appropriate response in the listener English
often uses a strong stress, e.g. '*I've* no cause for complaint; what's
your trouble?; you *do* want to come, don't you?; you *look* ill.
Well, I *am* ill. These are described and compared with the German
particles which express them in M. Schubiger: *The Intonations of
Spoken English*, p. 32. German is comparable to Greek in the ways
in which it can indicate shades of emotional attitude by its
particles, e.g. *auch, doch, ja, schon, wohl*. They occur both singly
and in a variety of combinations, e.g. *doch auch, doch wohl, ja
wohl, denn auch*.

AUCH in its non-emotive sense is 'too', 'also', e.g. *(Ich gehe
mit)—Ich auch* 'I too', 'so will I'; *(ich gehe nicht mit)—Ich auch
nicht* 'nor shall I'. It can when preceding a word also indicate
'even', e.g. *auch die besten Lehrer* 'even the best teachers', in
which case it is synonymous with *selbst* and *sogar*. In a concessive sentence it is often like '-ever', e.g. *wo er auch sein mag*
'wherever he may be'. Its more emotive connotations include
the following:—(1) emphatic confirmation by the listener of a
tentative statement by the speaker, e.g. *du siehst krank aus.—
Ich bin auch krank* 'You look ill.—Well, I am ill'; (2) resigned

acquiescence by the listener in the speaker's decision, e.g. *wenn Sie nicht mitkommen wollen, kann ich auch allein gehen* 'if you won't come too, I suppose I can go alone'; *ich glaube doch— vielleicht aber auch nicht* 'I believe it all the same, but, of course, I may be wrong'; (3) indicating what might be confidently expected considering all the circumstances, e.g. *er hat das Examen gut bestanden—er hat auch schwer gearbeitet* 'He passed his exam. well—well, he worked hard enough, to be sure' with a nuance 'and so he ought'; (4) reinforcing a request by putting it up to the listener not to forget, e.g. *aber tun Sie es auch* 'make sure you do it'.

DOCH, which primarily means 'however' and is akin to the English 'though', often introduces a note of protest, say in refutation of an assumed premise, e.g. *ich brauche doch keine Angst zu haben* 'I surely need have no fear'; *da hab' ich doch keinen Grund* 'I've no reason'. Like the French 'si' it is used instead of *ja* to contradict a negative suggestion, e.g. *Er ist nicht gekommen?—Doch!* 'He didn't come, did he?—Oh yes, he did!'. Hence it infiltrates into a negative question which the speaker hopes will not be confirmed, e.g. *er ist doch nicht krank?* 'don't tell me he's ill', and into a positive question where there is some doubt to be removed, e.g. *Sie kommen doch?* 'you will be coming, won't you?'. Hence also in a lively expression of wish, e.g. *wenn es doch heller wäre!* 'if only it were lighter', cf. *nur, erst*. It can also be used as a means of pressing a person to do something, e.g. *sagen Sie's ihm doch!* 'well, go and tell him', 'do tell him'. It can be attenuated by the addition of *mal*, e.g. *zeigen Sir mir doch mal die Zeitung* 'show me the paper, will you?'.

JA, when unstressed, draws the listener's attention to some circumstance he may be expected to know, or to agree with, e.g. *Seien Sie nicht so schüchtern—Deutsch ist ja keine Fremdsprache mehr für Sie* 'Don't be so shy—German is certainly no longer a foreign language to you'; *das ist ja fürchterlich* 'why, that's terrible'. Like *auch* it sometimes opposes a positive assurance to an implied scepticism, e.g. *Du solltest gerecht sein—Ich bin ja gerecht* 'You ought to be just.—Well, I *am* just'.

When pronounced with strong emphasis with an imperative *ja* emphasizes the importance of compliance with the request, e.g. *kommen Sie ja rechtzeitig* 'be sure you come in time'; *tun Sie das ja nicht* 'for goodness' sake, don't do that' or 'don't do that on any account'.

MAL or *EINMAL* is often like 'just' with an imperative, e.g. *laß mal sehen!* 'just let me have a look' or is left untranslated, e.g. *erlauben Sie mal, das ist [Roggen]* 'excuse me, that is [rye]' when correcting an error. In a statement it has a slightly different shade, e.g. *wie schön, daß man sich einmal richtig ausruhen kann!* 'how nice to be able to have a proper rest for once in a while!'. Combined with *nun* as *nun [ein]mal* the implication is one of resignation, e.g. *es ist nun mal so* 'well, you see, that's just how things are'.

NUR or—especially in Hamburg—*BLOSS* is used in a lively question, e.g. *was soll ich bloß anfangen?* 'what on earth am I to do?'; *wie kann man nur (bloß) so empfindlich sein?* 'how can one be so touchy?' It occurs in requests, e.g. *seien Sie nur freundlich mit dem Mann* 'now do be nice to the man' or 'mind you are . . .'.

SCHON is literally 'already' and even in a purely temporal sense is used much more frequently in German than 'already' is in English. As a modal particle it emphasizes the adequacy of some item to produce a result, e.g. *schon der Gedanke* 'the very idea (is enough)' or *schon, weil er blind ist* 'for the very reason that he is blind'. Sometimes *schon* implies a somewhat reluctant admission, e.g. *Sie haben schon Recht, aber . . .* 'you may be right, but all the same . . .'. Perhaps its most characteristic use in familiar conversation is to encourage or reassure, e.g. *es wird schon gehen* 'that will go off all right'.

WOHL when unstressed indicates that the speaker feels he has an adequate reason for making his statement, e.g. *er wird wohl kommen* 'I expect he'll come'; *es wird wohl ein ganzes Jahr sein, daß ich ihn nicht gesehen habe* 'I dare say it's a whole year since I saw him'. When pronounced with emphasis it indicates a strong affirmation, e.g. *das kann man sehr wohl sagen.* It is often used in a polite question without stress, e.g. *würden Sie mir wohl sagen . . . ?* 'I wonder whether you would tell me . . . ?' or with similar intention in a statement *Sie kommen wohl vor Tisch noch einen Augenblick bei mir vorbei* 'perhaps you would drop in for a moment before dinner'; *mich entschuldigen Sie wohl* 'you will excuse me, won't you?'

Wohl can be reinforced by *ja*, e.g. *du spielst ja wohl jeden Tag Skat, was?* 'I suppose you play *Skat* every day, don't you?'. When *doch* follows, the implication is that of a grudging assent, e.g. *es gibt wohl doch Leute, die es glauben* 'I suppose there are people who believe it?'.

Forms of address

There are several points to be noted in connexion with the use of forms of address. Foreigners should avoid using for 'Sir!' the phrase *Mein Herr!* which is used by a waiter talking to a client. If the man addressed has a title the polite form is *Herr Doktor, Herr Direktor, Herr Professor,* etc., but the informal mode of address between men on the same level is [*Herr*] *Schmidt.* In speaking of a politician the English sometimes insert and sometimes omit 'Mr', e.g. '(Mr) Attlee'. In German *Adenauer,* etc., is sufficient for (*Herr*) *Doktor Adenauer* whereas *Herr Adenauer* is almost pejorative! As in English an author is referred to by his surname alone, e.g. *Goethe, Kleist,* also a military leader, e.g. *Blücher, Ludendorf.*

In addressing a married woman the most polite and respectful form is *Gnädige Frau,* often used like 'ma'am' by an employee or like 'madam' by a shop assistant. If the woman is unmarried the equivalent form is *Gnädiges Fräulein.* These forms of address are appropriate when speaking to a stranger or when inviting a lady to be one's partner in a dance. If the woman, married or unmarried, has a title the usual form is *Frau Professor, Frau Doktor* for either. A woman is frequently addressed by her husband's title, so *Frau Professor* may imply (1) a married woman having a title in her own right, (2) an unmarried woman having the title in her own right and (3) a married woman whose husband has the title. In ordinary informal conversation *Frau Schmidt* or *Fräulein Schmidt* is sufficient.

In referring to a woman who has become famous in some walk of life, Christian name and surname are given without title, e.g. *Sophie von Laroche, Clara Viebig, Rosa Luxemburg.* A member of the National Socialist party was called a *Parteigenosse* (abbreviated *Pg.*) if a male and *Parteigenossin* if a female, prefixed to the surname, but since the war the equivalent of 'comrade' has been simply *Genosse/Genossin.*

14

GERMAN IN RELATION TO
OTHER LANGUAGES

German like English, Welsh, Latin, Greek, Sanskrit, Persian and
Russian among others, belongs to a family of languages which
we call Indo-European and the Germans call *Indogermanisch*. It
may be that ancestral forms of Indo-European were spoken before
2000 B.C. on the steppes north of the Black Sea between the
Carpathians and Urals whence they have spread into the rest of
Europe and into western Asia. Within Indo-European we note
certain groupings such as Celtic (Welsh, Cornish, Breton; Irish,
Scots Gaelic, Manx), Slavonic (Russian, Polish, Czech, Serbo-
Croat, Bulgarian, etc.) and of more immediate concern to us,
Teutonic or Germanic (*Germanisch*). The special relationship of
German and English arises from the fact that they are members
within Germanic of a branch usually called West Germanic
(German, *Westgermanisch*; French, *Westique*). According to the
archaeological evidence the homeland of Germanic was, in the
second millennium B.C., an area of North Germany between the
rivers Weser and Oder, extending through the Jutland peninsula
and Danish islands to southern Norway and Sweden. It was in the
main from the North Sea coasts and perhaps what is now Den-
mark that the Angles, Saxons and Jutes migrated to Britain
especially in the fifth and sixth centuries, though some Saxons may
have come from colonies they had already established along the
southern shores of the channel, perhaps as far as the mouths of the
Rhine. By 500 the continental West Germanic tribes left behind
were already pushing far into the Low Countries, the Rhineland,
Switzerland and Bavaria into regions formerly occupied by Celts.

Sharply distinguished linguistically from the West Germanic English and German is the branch we call East Germanic (*Ostgermanisch*), all the member-languages of which have long been extinct. Their chief representative was Gothic (*Gotisch*), used by the Arian bishop Ulfilas or Wulfila (311–383) in what is now Bulgaria for his translation of the Bible from Greek. Probably Gothic missionaries brought into West Germanic expressions exemplified by German *Heide, Teufel, Engel, Bischof, fasten, taufen, Kirche* and *Pfaffe*. East Germanic languages were originally an offshoot from Scandinavia, the nuclear area of North Germanic whence the Vikings began to colonize the Atlantic islands in the eighth century some centuries after settlers from southern Sweden had overrun the Danish islands and the Jutland peninsula vacated by the ancestors of the English. From south-west Norway came Icelandic, Faroese and the long extinct Norn dialects once spoken in Caithness and Sutherland, the Hebrides and the Isle of Man (in all of which it was replaced by Gaelic) and in the Orkneys and Shetlands. Amalgamation of Danish with the Anglian dialects of the North-East, the East Midlands and East Anglia appears to have been an easy process in the lands comprising the Danelaw established in the treaty of Wedmore between King Alfred and Guthrum in 879. Even before the Anglo-Saxon settlements here English appears to have been in respect of phonology and vocabulary a link between the West Germanic 'Nordseegermanen' and the Nordic tribes of Scandinavia.

The West Germanic group includes besides German and English the languages of the Low Countries or Netherlands (*Niederlande*), namely Dutch and Frisian. By Wycliff the word Dutch (from the medieval *Dūtsch*—modern *Duits*) was used without differentiation for the peoples and languages we call both Dutch and German, but later they were distinguished in English as Low Dutch (*Nederduits*) and High Dutch (cf. *Hochdeutsch*), respectively, there still being no distinction between Netherlandish and what we now call Low German. We may conveniently apply the term Netherlandish (*Niederländisch*) as the generic title to the Dutch of the Kingdom of the Netherlands and the Flemish (Dutch, *Vlaams* in contradistinction to *Hollands*; German, *Flämisch* or *Flandrisch* as against *Holländisch*) of the northern part of Belgium. The population of Holland in the wider sense is well over 11,000,000 and that of the Flemish-speaking provinces of Flanders (Gent, Bruges, Antwerp), North Brabant and Limburg about 4,000,000 with an outlier extending into the department of Flandre in France between Dunkirk and Lille, totalling some 150,000 speakers. Though in medieval times the language of the Flemish cities and courts had the greatest prestige we find that after the victory of the northern Protestants the centre of gravity was shifted to Holland, where in the seventeenth century Amsterdam and Leiden became the leading cities. Thus modern Dutch has achieved a standard form on a northern basis, called the *Algemeen Beschaafd [Nederlands]*, i.e. general cultured Netherlandish. This is accepted too by Flemish authors except when they use dialect expressions for local colour. The spoken dialects both in Holland and Belgium still show great diversity. In the newspapers there are some relatively unimportant differences due to the divergences of the legal and administrative systems. One offshoot of Dutch is Afrikaans which goes back to the establishment by Van Riebeck of a colony at the Cape of Good Hope in 1652. In this remote position it developed on its own lines and was modified by contacts with nurses and slaves of Malay origin from the Dutch East Indies, Hottentots and Kaffirs in Africa and French, German and British immigrants. Though the language of the Reformed Church was strongly influenced by the Dutch 'Statenbijbel' of 1619–1637, the speech of the Boers became much truncated and its grammar drastically simplified. The official and technical vocabularies are being constantly replenished from Dutch, but are also receptive to English neologisms. An Afrikaans version of the Bible was published in 1925. The use of Afrikaans has been growing especially since the proclamation of the Republic in 1961 and it is now spoken by 85% of the 16,000,000 inhabitants, of whom the majority speak English as well.

Of all the continental Germanic languages the closest akin to English in both phonology and certain features of vocabulary are the Frisian dialects of which the chief survivor today is the West Frisian, i.e. that spoken west of the River Lauwers in the Dutch province of Friesland. In spite of over twelve hundred years of separate development it is easy to illustrate the community of English and Frisian by contrasting with each other the West Frisian and German forms: *brea/Brot, ear/Ohr, dei/Tag, wein/ Wagen, ingels/englisch, skiep/Schaf, sliepe/schlafen, fiele/fühlen, tsiis/Käse, goes/Gans, brocht/gebracht.* Frisians once occupied more of the north-west corner of Europe, originally inhabiting the North Sea lands from the Zeeland islands to the River Ems.

In Friesland itself there are said to be about 460,000 speakers of Frisian, the literary form of which has been standardized since the time of the poet Gysbert Japiex (1603–1666). It is now taught in schools and is used in the church and law-courts. From this nuclear region Frisians moved eastwards into the North German plain, settled the North Sea islands, e.g. Wangeroog, Heligoland, Föhr, Amrum and Sylt and a stretch of the Schleswig coast lands near the Danish border. Germany still has today a small enclave of true East Frisian speakers on the peat-moors of the Saterland between Emden and Oldenburg, a small remnant of those Free Frisians who were great lawgivers and successfully resisted the feudal overlords. While the Germans rightly use the terms 'nordfriesisch' and 'inselfriesisch' for the genuine Frisian dialects spoken north of the Elbe, unfortunately they now use 'ost-friesisch' for the Low Saxon dialect of Oldenburg which replaced Frisian between 1400 and 1700. A term now often used by continental scholars for the English–Frisian group which perhaps once included other North Sea languages is Ingvaeonic (G. Ingväonisch) from the use by Tacitus of Ingvaeones.

THE DEVELOPMENT OF GERMAN IN GERMANY, AUSTRIA AND SWITZERLAND

After Frisian the group of dialects nearest akin to English is Low German (*Niederdeutsch*, popularly *Plattdeutsch*), especially the Low Saxon (*Niedersächsisch*). The titles Low German and High German (*Hochdeutsch*) originally represented the location of the former dialects in the lowlands of Germany and of the latter in the highlands of the centre and south. It was only after the researches of J. Grimm and other philologists that the terms Low and High German acquired linguistic significance when they came to be used to indicate the presence or absence of a shifting of certain consonants. From the following examples it is evident that English and Low German are on the same consonantal level, whereas High German has introduced characteristic modifications. As in Dutch, Norse and Gothic, English and Low German show unshifted *p, t, k* in *Piep* 'pipe', *open* 'open', *Tinn* 'tin', *eten* 'eat', *maken* 'make', *söken* 'seek' in contrast with the High German *Pfeife, offen, Zinn, essen, machen, suchen* respectively. This High German consonantal shifting (*die hochdeutsche Lautverschiebung*) appears to have originated in the extreme south—perhaps northern Italy—in the fifth century, affecting first the Alemannic and Bavarian tribes and then the Franks of the central Rhenish region. It is thought by some to have been due to the infiltration of Germanic tribes among a population of Celts or other non-Germans and it was completed by A.D. 700, before the appearance of the earliest Old High German documents. It did not affect the Saxon tribes of the North or the Franconians of the Lower Rhine. Low Franconian (*Niederfränkisch*) is the nucleus of Dutch and Flemish, which received elements from Low Saxon and Frisian and developed separately from the Low German dialects of Germany owing to its special political and cultural affiliations. There were, however, contacts between them, and in particular Dutch protestants—including Mennonites—migrated to Emden, Bremen and even some of the Baltic towns. In the Carolingian period we prefer to speak of Old Saxon (*Altsächsisch*) rather than Low German. Scholars of the eighth century used the expression 'Veteres Saxoni' to distinguish the continental tribe from the English whom the Venerable Bede calls Angli-Saxones. The English kings had friendly relations with the Saxon emperors—Otto I married Edith, sister of King Athelstan. An Old Saxon alliterative poem on Genesis was translated into Old English. As with Frisian many English words still have their cognates in the Low German dialects. However, in phonology and syntax Low German has undergone increasingly the influence of High German by coming within the Empire. Between 1300 and 1500, after Low German settlers had colonized the Baltic regions east of the Elbe and Oder and the Hanse towns had entered on a period of great commercial prosperity there was a strong tendency, particularly in Lübeck, towards a unified form of a Low German business-language for which we use the term Middle Low German (*Mittelniederdeutsch*). Though one of Luther's followers, Johann Bugenhagen, produced a Low German version of the Bible the spread of Protestantism to the North gave a preponderance to Luther's own writings, which gradually ousted Low German from the Church. Today there is no standard form of Low German, and though each region has tried to regularize its orthography, broadcasts have to be made in the various local dialects.

The recession of Low German since the Reformation was accompanied by the growing preponderance of High German throughout the German-speaking territories. The dividing line is still the Benrath line (*die Benrather Linie*) separating dialects which use the unshifted -*k*- in *maken* and the shifted -*ch*- in *machen*. Starting on the Rhine at Benrath it proceeds north of Düsseldorf, then eastwards leaving Magdeburg and Wittenberg on the Low German side, but interrupted by a High German enclave surrounding Berlin. Till 1945 High German dialects (Silesian and East Prussian) occupied the regions beyond the Vistula. The history of High German language and literature is usually divided into the following periods: (1) Old High German

(*Althochdeutsch*) from the time of the earliest texts about A.D. 750 till towards the end of the eleventh century; (2) Middle High German (*Mittelhochdeutsch*), including the classical age round 1200 with the Court Romance (*Höfischer Roman*) and Love Lyric (*Minnesang*); (3) New High German (*Neuhochdeutsch*) from the rise of the bourgeoisie in the fourteenth century through the Reformation to the modern age, the main developments occurring from about 1700. In the older periods there was no true standard language. The Old High German version of the oaths sworn at Strassburg in 849 in the presence of the armies of Lothair and Charles the German indicates that the language of the Court was a Rhenish Franconian dialect. However, the monastic centres show a great variety of forms. In the Middle High German period no unity was achieved, though poets at the court of the Hohenstaufen emperors or at the Wartburg when coming from different regions tended to avoid the crasser dialect-forms especially in the rimes and borrowed from each other. An effective movement towards a common German language (*Gemeines Deutsch*) is discernible from about 1350, first of all in the documents issued by the chancelleries or secretariats, both imperial and territorial. The official language (*Kanzleisprache*) of the Empire at Prague reflected the blending of Central and Southern High German forms characteristic of that city. The forms used by the Saxon chancellery at Wittenberg were important, for Luther himself tells us 'ich rede nach der sechsischen Cantzley', also that he listened to the talk of the mother in the home, the children in the street and the ordinary man in the market-place. Luther himself was an Upper Saxon (*Obersachse*) speaking an East Central High German dialect, the term Saxon having been extended from the Low Saxon (*Niedersächsisch*) of the North to the electorate created by the union (and subsequent reapportionment) of the electorate of Sachsen-Wittenberg in 1423 with the territories of the margrave of Meissen. The whole of this East Central German region was favourable to unification. It had been colonized from many parts of Germany including the Rhineland, Alsace, Swabia and the northern plain and the speech developed in the mixed settlements tended to be more uniform than elsewhere. German cities too were developing trade with each other and with foreign countries and there was some improvement in communications. The invention of printing with movable type of Johann Gutenberg about 1445 favoured in the end a reduction of the varieties of language used for publishing books—the so-called *Druckersprachen*—in the interests of a wider dissemination than had been possible when books were copied by hand. Luther was the catalytic agent who brought about the crystallization of all these tendencies. His translation of the Bible (1522–1534), his hymns and his polemic writings spread 'Luther-Deutsch' wherever protestantism went. Long after his death East Central German retained its prestige partly through the repute of the grammarian J. G. Schottelius, the Silesian author Martin Opitz and the literary academies (*Sprachgesellschaften*). The language of the educated classes of Meissen came to be regarded as a model. After 1700 the centre was the University of Leipzig especially at the time of J. C. Gottsched, whose *Deutsche Sprachkunst* appeared in 1748. The adhesion to the *Schriftsprache* of the poets Klopstock from Hamburg, Goethe from Frankfurt and Schiller from Swabia assured its final victory. In the eighteenth century Catholic Austria and Reformed Switzerland adopted the standard form, though the language of everyday conversation (*Umgangssprache*) still shows a great variety in phonology, vocabulary and idiom of which some examples are discussed below.

Despite the high degree of unity achieved by German throughout its territory in literary composition and public address the intimate everyday speech of the home and among friends (*Umgangssprache*) offers a bewildering variety of expressions. A more sophisticated form is favoured in the North and Centre especially in regions where the dialect was once Low German. On the basis of a questionnaire sent to all the chief towns in Germany, Austria and Switzerland Paul Kretschmer showed in his *Wortgeographie der hochdeutschen Umgangssprache* (Göttingen, 1918) how diverse were the words in current use locally in such domains as housebuilding (attic, hall, stairs, chimney), furniture (bedstead, cupboard, stool), trades (butcher, grocer, etc.), food, children's activities (marbles, slides, homework, satchel) amid many more. There were relatively well-marked larger regions such as the Rhineland, the Alemannic South-West including Switzerland and the Bavarian South-East extending into Austria. Characteristic differences between the Upper German regions of the south and the rest are seen in the following words where the prevalent North German form is bracketed: *Bub* (*Junge*), *Gasse* (*Straße*), *Stiege* (*Treppe*), *Stube* (*Zimmer*), *Samstag* (*Sonnabend*), *schauen* (*sehen*), *läuten* or *schellen* (*klingeln*), *seiden* (*kochen*). Frequent modal

particles are *freilich* and *halt* in the south, which is unfamiliar
with the northern *man* 'nur'. In grammar we note the southern
predilection for the present subjunctive (*sei, habe*, etc.)—as in the
Standard—in indirect statement where northern speech inclines
to the preterite subjunctive (*wäre, hätte*, etc.); the exclusive use of
the auxiliary *sein* with the past participle of the intransitive verbs
sitzen, liegen, stehen, etc., where other speakers distinguish the
durative aspect by saying *ich habe gesessen*, etc., and employ a
reflexive form for the ingressive, e.g. *ich habe mich gesetzt* and—
again in conformity with the Standard—the sharper distinction
between *her-* and *hin-*, using for the latter colloquially an abbreviated form, e.g. '*naus < hinaus*. In addition to this widespread
regional cleavage there are naturally certain special forms arising
through the political and cultural circumstances of the republic
(*Bundesstaat*) of Austria and the confederation (*Eidgenossenschaft*)
of Switzerland.

Of the seven million inhabitants of Austria 97.4% are German-
speaking with only small minorities of Slovenes in Carinthia and
of Croats and Magyars in the Burgenland. Vienna as the residence
of the Habsburgs and cultural centre of the Austro-Hungarian
empire had contacts with Italy in the south and the Slavonic
peoples (Czechs, Slovaks, Poles, etc.) and Magyars in the east, and
these are reflected in some characteristic words. Thus Italian
influence is seen in *Pomeranze* 'orange' (*pomo* and *arancia*), and
Karfiol (*cavifiore*), though *Erdapfel* is used for *Kartoffel* (Italian
tartuffola 'truffle'). For 'string' Austrian uses *Spagat* (It. *spago*),
which in Germany means the 'splits'! The Tyrolese *Sommer-
frische* 'summer vacation' is perhaps a translation of the Italian
frescura. Slavonic languages have furnished *Jause* 'afternoon
coffee', *Kren* 'horse radish' (also in Bavaria and Silesia), *Schöps*
'wether' (*Hammel*) and Turkish has given *Kukuruz* 'maize'. The
Viennese *Pardeis* 'tomato' is, however, an echo of Genesis III
(*Paradiesapfel*), and *Fisolen* 'scarlet runners' goes back to Latin
phaseoli. French has supplied *Gilet* (*Weste*), *Krawatte* (*Schlips*)
and *Lavor* or *Lavoir* (*Waschbecken*). Of native forms we find even
in the newspapers *Jänner* and *Feber* for *Januar* and *Februar, heuer*
'this year' with its derived adjective *heurig* used of new wine,
schütter 'sparse' 'thinly sown' used of hair or woodland as a useful
opposite of *dicht*. In ordinary speech *vergessen* takes *auf* with the
accusative and the following verbs deviate from the German norm:
plauschen (*plaudern*), *frotzeln* (*uzen*), *raunzen* (*meckern*), *sich*

verkühlen and *Verkühlung* (*sich erkälten und Erkältung*), *aus-kegeln* (*verrenken*), *selchen* (*räuchern*) for drying and smoking meat. Various shopkeepers are the *Greisler* (*Kolonialwaren-händler*), *Fleischhauer* (*Fleischer, Metzger, Schlächter!*), *Kräutler* (*Gemüsehändler*) and—beside *Konditor*—the old term *Zucker-bäcker*. The Viennese Café is still a *Kaffeehaus*, a term current in Germany in the eighteenth century. There the *Kaffee*—with stress on the last syllable—is served in a *Schale* (*Tasse*), often with *Obers* (*Sahne*), especially *Schlagobers* 'whipped cream', abbreviated to *Schlag*. For the astonishing variety of pastries and cakes details may be sought in Rosl Philpot's *Viennese Cookery* (London, 1965). They include *Apfelstrudel, Gugelhupf* (a bun with a hollow for cream, etc.), *Krapfen* 'doughnut', *Fladen* 'French pastry', *Schmarren* 'pancake' and *Kipfel* 'croissant'. Austrians celebrate shrove-tide not like Cologne as *Karneval*, but like Munich as *Fasching*. As in Germany the feast of St Nicholas is celebrated by a procession on 6 December, but *Nikolaus* becomes in Austria *Nikolo* (stress on last syllable) and his companion, Knecht Ruprecht, becomes *Krampus* from the *Krampe*, a hook which he uses to catch naughty children. At Christmas the gifts are known as *das Christkindl*. To show the divergence of Austrian from German usage the following sentence is a good illustration: *ich habe dem Hausherrn den Zins gezahlt* (*ich habe dem Wirt* or *Vermieter die Miete gezahlt*). We greet the Austrians with a *Grüss Gott* or *Küss die Hand* and take leave of them with *Servus*.

Switzerland has four officially recognized languages, namely German 69.3%, French 18.9%, Italian 9.5%, Romansch 0.9%, with a total population just exceeding six million. Among the speakers of German the position is totally different from that of Austria. As Professor R. E. Keller—himself a Swiss—tells us in *German Dialects* (Manchester, 1961), the German Swiss use their own local or regional variety of *Schwyzertütsch* when conversing with their fellow-countrymen, irrespective of social rank, and more rarely on official occasions. They reserve the *Schriftsprache* or *Hochdeutsch*, i.e. Standard German, for use with strangers from outside Switzerland, in formal addresses, in sermons and broadcasts and in all literature other than that of local interest. The term *Eidgenosse* is memorable as the origin of the French Huguenot. In 1520 Geneva, Freiburg and Bern federated in opposition to the Duke of Savoy and the forms *eidgenott* and *aygenot* (1527) penetrated into French, but under the influence of

6

the name of a Genevese leader, Hugues Besançon, were replaced by Huguenot. As a plurilingual nation the Swiss offer less resistance to foreign words than the Germans and particularly in politics and administration admit such forms as *Politisches Departement* (*das Auswärtige Amt*), *Erziehungsdepartement* (*Kultusministerium*), *Kanton* (pl. *Kantone*), *Sektion* (*Abteilung*), *Motion* (*Antrag*), *Initiative* (*Volksbegehren*), *Referendum* (*Volksentscheid*), *Sekundärschule*, *Maturität* (*Reifeprüfung*), *Absolvent* 'school-leaver'. Naturally old Swiss customs are designated by their Alemannic words, e.g. *Kilbi* or *Chilbi* (*Kirchweihe*) for the festival of consecration of a church and the fair, *Kiltgang* for a night-visit by a suitor to his prospective bride and *Hornussen* for a country-sport somewhat like volley-ball or hand-tennis or the Frisian 'kaatsen'. Occasionally rustic words find their way into print, e.g. *Heuet* 'hay-making' and *Zetten* 'to ted [the hay]', but on the whole the two layers of language are kept apart. Like Austria Swiss localities have their culinary specialities such as the *Berner Platte* of Sauerkraut with various ingredients, *Klopfer* (*Zervelatwurst*), *Schaffhauserzunge* 'cream cake', *Kugelpastete* 'vol-au-vent' (Lucerne) and *Leckerli* 'spiced honey-cake' (Basel) in addition to the *Gugelhupf*, *Fladen* and *Krapfen* as in Austria.

In Germany itself some products are associated with particular localities, e.g. *Westfälischer Schinken* (ham) and *Pumpernickel* (dark rye bread), *Königsberger Klops* (meat-ball), *Kieler Sprotten* (sprats), *Lübecker Marzipan*, *Nürnberger Lebkucken* (ginger bread), but *Deutches Beefsteak* 'Hamburger'. Note *Schweizer Käse* 'gruyère' and *Edamer Käse* 'Dutch cheese'.

Outside Europe a German dialect, now designated *Pennsilfaanisch* but formerly Pennsylvania 'Dutch' (from the speakers' appellation *Deitsch*), is spoken in East Pennsylvania, West Maryland and parts of Ohio, Illinois, Indiana and Ontario by the descendants of colonists, who came from the Rhenish Palatinate in the eighteenth century. Its vocabulary and syntax have been much influenced by English (see specimen below). In Canada, too, there are in Manitoba 50,000 Mennonites who speak a Low German dialect, called by them *Plautdietsch*, cf. John Thiessen: *Studien zum Wortschatz der kanadischen Mennoniten* (Marburg, 1963). Elsewhere there are large communities of Germans, e.g. in Brazil, the Argentine and Chile. Of the 73,000 white settlers in the former German South-West Africa, now under South African mandate, there is a high proportion of German speakers.

Yiddish (*Jiddisch*, i.e. *Jüdisch*) or Judaeo-German is a collective term for dialects used by Jews, in which a German substructure is heavily overlaid with Semitic elements (up to 10%) from Rabbinic Hebrew and Talmudic Aramaic, also Romance words stemming in part from the settlements in northern France as early as the ninth century, and many Slavonic ingredients from the Jewish migration to eastern Europe. It has developed a syntax of its own. Eastern Yiddish was widely used from Poland to Rumania and the Ukraine, the Baltic lands, Bohemia, Moravia, Slovakia, Hungary and White Russia. Its literature, written in Hebrew characters, attained an international reputation in the works of Scholem Aleichem (1859–1916), Scholem Asch (1881–1957) and Martin Buber (1878–1965). It is estimated that Yiddish is still spoken by some twelve million people, of whom many live in America, but it is giving ground to Ivrit, the modern Hebrew of the state of Israel.

Of non-German languages spoken on German territory there is only a remnant of the West Slavonic languages once spoken as far west as the Lower Elbe and the Drawehn of Hanover (Polabian from *po Labi* 'on the Elbe'). The Pomorian dialects (*po morze* 'by the sea') such as Slovinzian and Cassubian are now in territory occupied by Poland. South of Berlin there has survived (perhaps from the sixth century), in the country districts of Lusatia (*Lausitz*) including the Spreewald, a community of Sorbs—their own name is *Serbja*, *Serby*—with Bautzen as the chief town. Their language is often known as Wendish (*Wendisch*). Since 1945 the East German government has done much to foster their cultural autonomy by having the language taught in both primary and secondary schools. The East German *Meyer's Encyclopedia* reckons the number of Sorb-speakers as high as 100,000.

16

THE LINGUISTIC INFLUENCE OF
NATIONAL SOCIALISM

Through press reports the public became gradually acquainted with the slogans and peculiar vocabulary of the Nazis from 1925 when Adolf Hitler refounded the Nationalsozialistische Deutsche Arbeiter-Partei (*NSDAP*). Most of the expressions whether constructed deliberately, resuscitated from the German past or given a new semantic slant, were popularized in the nineteen-thirties, but have in turn fallen into disuse since the catastrophe of 1945 and in many cases can claim only a historical interest. The "millennial" Dritte Reich lasted but a few months longer than twelve years, whereas the first Reich—*das Heilige Römische Reich Deutscher Nation*—as heritor of Rome—spanned the centuries from the coronation of Otto the Great in 962 to its final demise in 1806, and the second Reich, founded by Bismarck, lasted from 1871 to 1918 to be followed by the Weimar Republic. New official terms were promulgated soon after the seizure of power (*Machtergreifung, Machtübernahme*) of 30 January 1933 and the party introduced in addition to the National-lied 'Deutschland über alles' the Horst-Wessel-Lied 'Die Fahne hoch . . .' written by a young adherent killed by Communists in 1930. The one-party state soon drastically transformed the system of government and local administration by a co-ordination of functions, called *Gleichschaltung*, a metaphor from directing various sources of electrical energy into a single power-current. Hitler's deputies for the larger regions like Bavaria and Austria were called [*Reichs*]-*statthalter*, an old rendering of 'locum tenens' or lieutenant, paralleled by the Dutch *Stadhouder*. Another ancient word was

Gau 'region or district', administered by a *Gauleiter*, the Reich being divided into 39 *Gaue*. The head of the state was the *Führer*— a title copied from the *Duce* of the Italian Fascists—and the *Führergrundsatz* (or *-prinzip*) was 'Autorität nach unten, Verantwortlichkeit nach oben'. The party itself included the following organizations: (1) the *SA* or *Sturmabteilung*, the Brown Shirts (*Braunhemden*); (2) the *SS* or *Schutzstaffel*, the Black Corps (*das schwarze Korps*) recruited from an alleged racial élite (*Auslese*), using as symbol a couple of zigzags (*Blitzabzeichen*) whereas the national—*schwarzweißrot*—flags mostly carried the swastika (*Hakenkreuz*), an ancient symbol of the sun; (3) the *HJ* or *Hitler-Jugend*, comprising the *HJ* proper of youths from 14 to 18 years old, following the *DJ* or *Deutsche Jungvolk* (10-14 years), and the *BDM* or *Bund deutscher Mädel* (14–21 years), following the *Deutsche Jungmädel* (10–14). Some of the subdivisions employed the old words *Bann* (with *Bannführer*), *Gefolgschaft* 'retinue', *Schar* 'host', *Fähnlein* 'troop' and *Ring*. Members of the party were designated and addressed as *Parteigenossen* (abbreviated *Pg*). Trades Unions (*Gewerkschaften*) were superseded by the *DAF* or *Deutsche Arbeitsfront*. In 1935 began the *RAD* or *Reichsarbeitsdienst*, for which young people of both sexes between 18 and 25 were liable to perform six months' labour-service partly devoted to land-reclamation. Leisure activities and recreation were organized under *Kraft durch Freude*, modelled on the Italian *Dopolavoro* (lit. after work). An organization called *Schönheit der Arbeit* strove to improve factory sites and buildings and provide amenities. Farmers and farm-workers, including *Landhelfer* —school leavers allotted especially to Eastern Germany—came under the *Reichsnährstand*, a body for producing and marketing food-stuffs. From ancient laws the phrase *Blut und Boden* 'blood and soil' (jocularly *Blubo*) was taken to signify the ties of a family to its inherited land. The Hereditary Farm Law (*Erbhofgesetz*) enacted that a farm of a maximum 125 hectares (about 500 acres) should pass undivided to a member of the family, designated as the *Anerbe* by a special court, other members receiving a training grant from the estate and being entitled to accommodation in the event of unmerited indigence. Obsession with the idea of the racial superiority of the Nordics and after them the Falian (*fälisch*), Alpine (*ostisch*), Mediterranean (*westisch*), East Baltic (*ostbaltisch*) and Dinaric (*dinarisch*) strains, fostered by Hans F. K. Günther's *Rassenkunde des deutschen Volkes*, led to the

misuse of the term *Arier* (in *Arierparagraph*), which is properly
applied to the Indo-Europeans of Iran and India. One aim of the
adepts of eugenics (*Rassenhygiene* or *Rassenpflege*) was renordici-
zation (*Aufnordung*, sometimes applied to the peroxiding of hair!)
and the prevention of racial ignominy or *Rassenschande*—an echo
of *Blutschande* 'incest' — in the *Blutschutzgesetz* of 1935. Dis-
crimination against the Jews led to the requirement of an *Ahnen-
paß* 'proof of ancestry'. To ensure a healthy and efficient (*erbge-
sund, erbtüchtig*) posterity the *Gesetz zur Verhütung erbkranken
Nachwuchses* of 1933 sought to prevent the propagation of off-
spring tainted with physical or mental disabilities by providing for
sterilization (*Unfruchtbarmachung*) on a court-order and for full
castration (*Entmannung*) of those found guilty of certain sexual
crimes.

In exercising authority in religious matters the government
concluded a *Reichskonkordat* (last syllable stressed) with Pope
Pius XI in 1933, but met with opposition from a number of
Protestants, who founded a *Bekenntnisfront* (confessional front)
to defend their doctrines against the *Deutsche Christen* and the
non-Christian *Deutsche Glaubensbewegung*. Being anxious to
train a new generation of leaders the party established *Adolf-
Hitler-Schulen*, from which hand-picked pupils were sent on to
a boarding school, called a *Napola* (*Nationalpolitische Er-
ziehungsanstalt*), and then subsequently to an *Ordensburg*. Op-
ponents of the régime and non-Aryans were consigned to Concentration Camps (*Konzentrationslager*) of which the name,
though not the character, was borrowed from that of British
camps for civil internees used in the Boer War. The party was
organized throughout to bring pressure to bear on the individual
citizen. A local group (*Ortsgruppe*) comprised *Zellen* each formed
from several 'blocks' of buildings, each under a warden (*Block-
wart*). A system of winter relief (*Winterhilfswerk*) was organized
and on one Sunday from October to March there was a 'voluntary
obligation' (*freiwillige Verpflichtung*) on citizens to make do with
an *Eintopfgericht* a kind of hotpot of meat, potatoes and vege-
tables—and give the money saved to the relief fund. In addition
to the technical terms mentioned Nazis liked to use emotional or
dynamic words. Among favourite expressions were *fanatisch,
brutal, organisch, völkisch, schlagartig*; *Volkheit* 'nationhood',
Einsatz (cf. military 'operation' 'sortie' 'mission') and *einsatz-
bereit, Durchbruch* 'break-through', *Umbruch* 'upheaval', *Lebens-*

raum (cf. Fr. *espace vital*), *Bestleistung* 'optimum performance', *Endlösung* 'definitive solution'. Certain suffixes like *-lich* and *-haft* formed adjectives, e.g. *blutlich, charakterlich, naturhaft* and prefixes like *ent-* formed verbs, e.g. *entrümpeln* (*Entrümpelung* 'attic clearance'), *entgiften* 'to decontaminate', *entseuchen* 'to disinfect, sterilize', *Entstädterung* 'deurbanization'. It is ironic to reflect that when the *Deutsche Gruß* i.e. '*Heil Hitler!*' with the raising of the right arm soon vanished after the end of the war, one of the best known coinages of the new epoch was *entnazifizieren* 'to denazify'. For further information regarding Nazi influences, cf. the articles by Cornelia Bernig, 'Die Sprache der Nationalsozialisten' in *Zeitschrift für deutsche Wortforschung*, vols. 16 and 17, the *Ergänzungsband* (1935) of *Der Große Brockhaus* and the 1938 edition of *Der Volks-Brockhaus*.

17

LINGUISTIC DEVELOPMENTS IN
EASTERN GERMANY

In 1949 Germany came to be divided between two governments. The western area (including West Berlin) is known as the German Federal Republic (*Bundesrepublik Deutschland* or *BRD*) and the eastern calls itself the German Democratic Republic (*Deutsche Demokratische Republik* or *DDR*). With a view to eventual unification the West refers to the DDR either as the Soviet-Occupied Zone (*Sowjetische Besatzungszone* or *SBZ*) or *Mitteldeutschland*, using the term *Ostdeutschland* for the de facto Polish-occupied zone east of the Oder-Neisse demarcation line. The DDR retaliated by referring to the *Bonner Separatstaat*. The DDR is a so-called *Volksdemokratie* and has a *Volkskammer* in which the overwhelmingly predominant party is the *SED* or *Sozialistische Einheitspartei Deutschlands*, a fusion of communists and socialists. It is one of the *Ostblockstaaten* adhering to the Warsaw Pact (*Warschauer Pakt*) and its economy is geared to that of the USSR. With a totally different form of government and orientation, the DDR has naturally developed linguistic divergences after 1945, especially since the closing of the frontier (*Abriegelung*) and building of the wall in 1961 along the *Sektorengrenze* of West and East Berlin. The aim was to stem the flood of refugees westwards which even the proscribing of *Republikflucht* as a crime could not prevent. Training for life in the DDR begins with pre-school education (*Vorschulerziehung*) in the day nursery or *Kinderkrippe* up to the age of three, run by *Hortnerinnen*, and the *Kindergarten* from three to six, run by *Kindergärtnerinnen*. At the age of six all children must begin attendance in a fully standardized type of school (*Einheitsschule*) as the first rung of a ladder leading in some cases to the Universities and *Hochschulen*. The school prescribed for all (in 1959) is the 10-class [*Allgemeine poly-technische*] *Oberschule* with an *Unterstufe* (6–9), a *Mittelstufe* (10–12) and an *Oberstufe* (13–16), specially gifted pupils being permitted to take two further classes up to the age of 18 in a 12-class *Erweiterte Oberschule*. If mothers go out to work, their children in the ten classes of the *Oberschule* can attend a *Tagesklasse* or *Tagesgruppe* (synonym *Hort*, in contrast with West German use for 'nursery school') where they do their home-work (*Hausaufgaben*), play games, read, debate and practise hobbies. Practically half of the school-children are members of the *Freie Deutsche Jugend* (*FDJ*), founded in 1946, which is recreational as well as educative. The *Pionierorganisation Ernst Thälmann* caters for the political, scientific and technical education of its members. At the age of 14 boys and girls—in the presence of their parents—take part in a ceremony called the *Jugendweihe* at which they take vows to further the happiness of the whole German people, to work for peace and to serve the cause of the socialistic state.

The influence of Soviet terminology is seen particularly in the employment of certain loan-words, including the following: *das Aktiv* (pl. *Aktive, Aktivs*) 'a working group pursuing social economic and cultural aims and the attainment of over-average yields', cf. *Aktivist, Aktivistenbewegung, -feier, -nadel*, etc.; *Kollektiv* 'a working productive community in all branches of labour including literature and art', cf. *Ärzte-, Lehrer-, Forscher-kollektiv*; *Brigade* 'smallest working collective in the socialist economy', cf. *Brigadier, Hausfrauen-, Lehrlings-, Sensen-, Vieh-zuchtbrigade*; *der Kader* (used as early as the Weimar Republic) 'a trained nucleus of the rising generation in all spheres of com-munity life' 'an individual member of such'; *Oblomowerei* 'lackadaisicalness' from the landowner in Goncharov's novel Oblomov (1855), cited by Lenin; *Kombinat* 'a pooling of various branches of industry serving a common purpose and of their stages of production', e.g. *Eisenhütten-, Fischerei-, Lehrkombinat*; *Exponat* 'exhibit at a trade fair'. Corresponding to the Stak-hanovites—from the Russian miner who in 1935 extracted 102 tons of coal in one shift—is the *Henneckebewegung* from a West-falian miner, whose yield in 1948 was nearly four times that of the day's stint (*Tagesnorm*). Apparently there are fewer English loans than in West Germany—apart from the international *Job*, *Hobby*, *Fan*, *Jeep* and the like there is the American *Dispatcher* 'responsible engineer', 'leader of an operation', e.g. *Gemüsedispatcher*. Beside the Russian *Kombinat* is the English *Kombine* (either assimilated or pronounced in the English way), where West German uses *Mähdrescher*. The term *Funktionär* 'trades union leader' is narrower than its ultimate French prototype 'fonctionnaire'. Another French word *Dispensaire* 'public dispensary' is also more eastern. Other divergences appear in the use or frequency of certain affixes, including *-ismus* (often pejorative) *Praktizismus* (implying neglect of ideology), *Reformismus* (somewhat like 'gradualism'), *Revisionismus*, *Inhaltismus* (a type of dialectic materialism); *-heit* with *Interessantheit*, *Westkontaktfreiheit*; *-tum* in *Arzttum*, *Nurgelehrtentum*; *-ling* in *Reifling* 'matriculand' (cf. *Absolvent* 'school-leaver'), *Weihling* 'initiate at the Jugendweihe'; *-ler* in *Abweichler* 'deviationist', *Westler*, *Versöhnler* 'one who is over-conciliatory'; *-ant* in *Kursant* 'member of a course'. Further data are available in the Leipzig edition of Meyer's *Konversationslexikon* (1964); the *Ost-Duden* also of Leipzig (15th edition, 1957 ff); Hugo Moser, *Sprachliche Folgen der politischen Teilung Deutschlands* (Düsseldorf, 1962) with good bibliography; Ernst G. Riemenschneider, *Veränderungen der deutschen Sprache in der sowjetisch besetzten Zone Deutschlands seit 1945* (Düsseldorf, 1963); *DDR 300 Fragen 300 Antworten*, 6th edition (*Verlag die Wirtschaft*; Berlin 1965).

18

ENGLISH INFLUENCE ON

CONTEMPORARY GERMAN

German draws a clear distinction between 'Fremdwörter', i.e. unassimilated foreign words like *Beefsteak* or *Pullover* (though even these are not pronounced as in England) and 'Lehnwörter', i.e. fully integrated adoptions, of which good early examples are *die Mauer* from the Latin masc. *murus* and *das Fenster* from the Latin fem. *fenestra*. Some would use 'Lehnwort' as the generic term for several categories of 'loans'. These would include loan-translations or 'calques' (*Lehnübersetzungen*) such as *Freimaurer* 'free-mason' and *Geistesgegenwart* 'presence of mind', where each element is translated literally. A partial calque (*Lehnüber-tragung*) is exemplified by the ancient *Vaterland* based on patria or the contemporary *Senkrechtstarter* for VTO-plane. Loans include further 'loan-phrases' (*Lehnwendungen*) such as the international adaptation of French locutions in *den Hof machen* and *eine Rolle spielen*. Sometimes a foreign prototype leads to a new application thus producing a semantic loan (*Lehnbedeutung*), e.g. *schneiden* 'to cut (socially)' or *einmotten* 'to mothball (ships, etc.)'. Occasionally German supplies an equivalent of a new concept out of its own resources, thus providing a 'loan-creation' (*Lehnschöpfung*), e.g. *Kraftwagen* for 'automobile', *Autobank* for 'drive-in bank', *Planierraupe* for 'bulldozer'. Loans may deviate considerably from their patterns as in *der Keks* (pl. *Kekse*) for 'biscuit' or *der Koks*—taken from an English plural 'cokes' for 'coke'. There may even be pseudo-loans (*Scheinentlehnungen*) like the German tailors' *Twen* 'man or woman in the twenties' or *Happy End* for 'happy ending'.

The oldest English loans are nautical terms which passed into German through Dutch or the Hanse towns, e.g. *Boot* (Hamburg, 1292), *Dock* (1436 in a Hanse document about London), *Flagge* (sixteenth century), *Lotse* from *Lotsmann* representing 'lodesman'. In 1649 the execution of Charles I and Cromwell's republican government stirred interest in English political institutions, introducing such words as *Debatte*, *Oberhaus*, *Sprecher*, *Hochverrat* followed in the next century by *parlamentarisch*, *Majorität* (also *Mehrheit*), *Opposition*, *Pressfreiheit*, *Jungfernrede*, etc. English scientists and scholars provided *elektrisch* (W. Gilbert), *Kreislauf des Blutes* (Harvey), *Zelle* (N. Grew), *Spektrum* (I. Newton), *Logarithmus* (J. Napier) and *Dampfmaschine* (J. Watt). Before 1800 colonists had added *Rum*, *Punsch*, *Bowle*, (originally *Punschbowle*) to the already known *Pudding*, *Grog* and *Toast* (in both senses). From English writers including Addison, Richardson and Sterne German took over *Blankvers*, *Humor*, *Magazin*, *Spleen* 'moroseness', *Steckenpferd* 'hobby-[horse]' and from English thinkers (from Shaftesbury onwards) *innere Form* 'inward form', *Selbst*, *utopisch*, *Nationalcharakter*, *Deismus*, *Pantheismus* and the like, *Arbeitsteilung* (Adam Smith) and the word *Denker* itself. In 1768 Lessing chose *empfindsam* as the equivalent of 'sentimental' and in 1774 Herder used *Volkslied* to match Percy's 'popular song'. Early loans from English sport include *boxen*, *Rennpferd*, *Jockei* followed in the nineteenth century by many terms from tennis, golf, football, etc., with a strong tendency especially after 1900 to germanize, e.g. *Schläger* 'racket', *Tor* 'goal', *abseits* 'offside'. Contact with business-men helped to spread *Clearing*, *Dumping*, *Manager* and *managen*. To the earlier *Frack* from frock-[coat], *Schal*, *Flanell*, *Düffel* and *Manchester* 'corduroy' (now often *Kord*) were added in the present century *Sweater*, *Jumper*, *Blazer*, *Pullover* and *Bikini*—all masculine. Such words as *Clown*, *Girl*, *Star* came through entertainers and after the war of 1914 America exported words like *Jazz*, *Blues*, *Swing*, *Rock'n Roll*, *Bebop* as well as *Crooner*. The Second War and allied occupation popularized *Pin-up Girl*, *Jeep*, *Blue Jeans*, *Jet* and *Teenager*. Over a century before, the vogue of spiritualism in America brought *Spiritismus*, *Medium*, *Trance* and *Tischrücken* 'table-turning' among others, whereas *das zweite Gesicht* 'second sight' is found much earlier.

As in French and Dutch there has been a great influx of English words since 1945. Among the channels of diffusion are (1) contacts between the NATO forces and German civilians in the regions where they are stationed; (2) the various international mass-media and forms of entertainment such as the cinema, television, variety shows; (3) scientific and technical innovations originating in America and Great Britain; (4) popular magazines of high circulation like *Der Spiegel*. Some pre-war words are thoroughly integrated, e.g. *Film* with plural *Filme*, verb *filmen*, etc. Fission and fusion of the atom left their mark in *Reaktor* 'pile', *Spaltung*, *Verschmelzung*, *Kettenreaktion*, *Kernkraftwerk* 'nuclear power station', *Bremssubstanz* or *Moderator*, *Beschleuniger* 'accelerator', etc. Latterly German has imported *Maser*, *Laser*, *Quasar*, *Brennstoffelement* 'fuel-cell', *Luftkissenfahrzeug* (*Hovercraft*, also *Schwebefahrzeug*) from American 'cushion-craft'. Hundreds of anglicisms are now prevalent in everyday speech including *parken*, *tanken*, *Job*, *Hobby*, *Test*, *testen*, *Trend*, *hitchen* (now replacing *trampen*). Even before the war German supplied some good loan-creations, e.g. *Zeitraffer* 'speeded motion film', *Zeitlupe* 'slow motion', *Engpaß* 'bottle-neck' and since then *Rückkoppelung* 'feed-back', *Klimaanlage* 'air-conditioning', *Kunststoffe* 'plastics'. All these examples are but a tiny selection of items from a vast linguistic transaction, which has led to the formation of what the French call *franglais* and which in some ways parallels the 'à la modism' of seventeenth century German. For further information on English loans, cf. Agnes B. Stiven, *Englands Einfluß auf den deutschen Wortschatz* (Marburg, 1936); Philip Motley Parker, *The Influence of English on the German Vocabulary to 1700* (Berkeley, 1950); F. P. Ganz, *Der Einfluß des Englischen auf den deutschen Wortschatz 1640–1815* (Berlin, 1957) and for the latest period the well-documented authoritative work of Broder Carstensen, *Englische Einflüsse auf die deutsche Sprache nach 1945* (Heidelberg, 1965). For German words in English, cf. C. T. Carr, *German Influence on the English Vocabulary* (Society for Pure English Tract 42, Oxford, 1934).

19

WORD-FORMATION IN
CONTEMPORARY GERMAN

The two chief ways of extending the vocabulary are still 'composition' (*Zusammensetzung*) resulting in 'compounds' and 'derivation' (*Ableitung*) by means of prefixes and suffixes resulting in 'derivatives', cf. W. Henzen, *Deutsche Wortbildung*, second edition, Tübingen, 1957.

Compounds

Most compounds belong to the part of speech of their last component. To form new nouns it is possible to compound two nouns as in *Vaterland* or an adjective with a noun or a verb-stem with a noun. The last two are more prevalent in recent German than formerly and constitute vogue-words as well as technical terms. Examples of adjective+noun are: *Großaufnahme* 'close-up', *Kleinsiedlung* 'small-holding', *Vollmilch* 'full-cream milk', *Vollkornbrot* 'wholemeal bread', *Volltreffer* 'direct hit', *Süßstoff* 'saccharin', *Fertighaus* 'pre-fab.', *Blaupause* 'blue-print', *Engpass* 'bottle-neck', *Dünndruckpapier* 'India paper', *Schwarzfahrt* 'joy-ride', *Schwarzmarkt* 'black market', *Schnellboot* 'speed boat', *Hochhaus* 'sky-scraper', *Kurzarbeiter* 'short-time worker', *Schwerarbeiter* 'worker in heavy industry'. Examples of verb-stem+noun are: *Bückwaren* 'under the counter goods', *Sprengkommando* 'demolition squad', *Wohnküche* 'kitchen living-room', *Rollsitz* 'sliding seat', *Rollfeld* 'tarmac', *Rollschuh* 'roller skate', *Rolltreppe* 'escalator', *Drehtür* 'revolving door', *Reißverschluß* 'zip-fastener', *Heizsonne* 'bowl-fire', *Fahrdraht* 'trolley wire', *Abtropfbrett* 'draining board', *Faltboot* 'collapsible boat', *Leih-*

haus 'pawnbroker's shop', *Stehlampe* 'standard lamp', *Stehspiegel* 'pier-glass', *Fallobst* 'windfall', *Fallschirm* 'parachute'. Words in -*d*, -*t* and -*b* have the vowel -*e* in the joint between the components, e.g. *Badeanstalt* 'public baths', *Wartegeld* 'retaining fee', *Klebepasta* 'sticking paste'.

Many compound adjectives are now formed from noun + adjective and in some cases the adjective component forms whole series and is practically equivalent to a suffix. Examples: *wasserdicht* 'water-proof', *schalldicht* 'sound-proof', *feuerfest* 'fire-proof', *maschenfest* 'non-laddering', *krisenfest* 'hard' (of currency), *kußfest* 'kiss-proof' of (*Lippenstift* 'lipstick'), *splitterfrei* 'non-splintering', *alkoholfrei* 'non-alcoholic', *sturmfrei* 'not liable to interference' (of a students' 'digs' or *Bude*), *lebensfähig* 'viable', *salonfähig* 'fit to appear in a drawing-room', etc. Adjectives like *grasgrün* have been discussed in the section on adjectives.

The use of separable verbal particles is still productive of compound verbs. Thus the Nazis introduced *aufnorden* for 're-nordicize' and modern slang has *aufpulvern* 'ginger up'. The primary meaning of separable verbs is concrete with *ab*-, 'off'; *an*- 'on'; *auf*- 'up', 'open'; *aus*- 'out'; *bei*- 'at'; *herein*-, *hinein*- 'in'; *heraus*-, *hinaus*- 'out'; *herunter*-, *hinunter*- 'down', etc.; *mit*- 'with', 'together'; *nach*- 'after'; *zu*- 'to'; *zurück*- 'back'; *zusammen*- 'together', etc. A number of compounds copy Latin verbs, e.g. *anspielen* 'allude', *beistehen* 'assist', *mitarbeiten* 'collaborate', etc.

Derivation by Affix

Noun-suffixes still productive in non-literary speech as well as in writing are the following:

-*ER* not only for the personal agent, e.g. *Sänger* 'singer', *Schauspieler* 'actor', *Hörer* 'listener', *Schwimmer* 'swimmer', but also for the instrument or means, e.g. *Aufhänger* 'hanger', *Schwimmer* 'float', *Roller* 'scooter', *Stecker* 'plug', *Sender* 'transmitter', *Wecker* 'alarm-clock', *Lutscher* 'baby's comforter'.

-*UNG* still much used for actional nouns, e.g. *Staffelung* 'staggering', *Entfettung* 'slimming', *Tarnung* 'camouflage', *Eignungsprüfung* 'aptitude test', *Vermahlung* 'flour-milling', *Ziehung* 'draw' (of a lottery), etc.

-*SCHAFT* is not only a suffix of relationship, e.g. *Mutterschaft* 'maternity', *Vaterschaft* 'paternity', *Kindschaft* 'filiation', *Witwenschaft* 'widowhood', but also especially a collective suffix, e.g.

die allgemeine Studentenschaft 'guild of undergraduates',
Dozentenschaft 'University teaching staff', *Genossenschaft* 'a
co-operative', *Ärzteschaft* 'medical profession', *die (juristische)
Fachschaft* '(legal) professional group', *Knappschaft* 'miners'
lodge'.

-(ER)EI frequent in colloquial German for something long drawn
out or repeated and troublesome, e.g. *die Schererei* 'trouble,
fuss', *Drückebergerei* 'scrimshanking', *Kletterei* 'clambering
about', *Parteigängerei* 'political factions', *Gängelei* 'keeping on
leading strings', cf. 'spoon-feeding'. A competing formation is
shown by *das Gesinge*, etc.

Among the adjective-suffixes the following have attained
considerable vogue:

-IG like English '-y' to form adjectives indicating the possession
of like qualities (colour, etc.) or with a verbal base indicating
propensity. To the first belong *kalkig* 'limy', *kreidig* 'chalky',
zuckerig, milchig, blutig, wässerig, grasig, schlickig, 'oozy',
tintig 'inky', *morastig* 'boggy', *sumpfig* 'marshy', etc. The second
type, too, is continually being expanded, e.g. *glitschig* 'slippery',
wendig 'manœuvrable', *schlaksig* 'rangy', *knurrig (brummig)*
'grumpy', *quietschig (quäkig)* 'squeaky', *kratzig* 'scratchy',
patzig 'pert', *schneidig (schmissig, schnittig)* 'smart', etc.

-LICH more in literature, e.g. *sportlich* 'sporting', *kontraktlich*
'contractual', *gesanglich* 'choral', *tonlich* 'tonal'.

-ERISCH corresponding to nouns in *-EREI*, e.g. *halsbrecherisch*
'break-neck', *großsprecherisch* 'swaggering', *geheimtuerisch*
'mysterious, cagey', *schauspielerisch* 'actory, histrionic'.

-BAR is still very prolific for forming adjectives of passive possibility, e.g. *unübersetzbar* 'untranslatable', *befliegbar* 'negotiable
by aircraft', *begehbar* 'practicable', etc.

The inseparable verbal prefixes like *be-, er-, ver-, zer-,*
occasionally form new words especially the privative prefix *ent-*
used like English 'de-', e.g. *entwerten* 'de-value', *enteisen* 'de-ice',
entgasen 'de-gas', *entgiften* 'de-contaminate', *entnazifizieren*
'de-Nazify', *entmilitarisieren* 'de-militarize', *entkeimen* 'sterilize',
entrahmen 'skim (the cream)', *entrümpeln* 'clear (the attics)', 'clear
(the rubble)'.

Especially between the wars and during the Second World
War a number of 'letter-words' have come into use, e.g. *Schupo*
(= *Schutzpolizei, -polizist*) 'police(man)', *Sipo (Sicherheits-
polizei)* 'security police', *Gestapo* (= *geheime Staatspolizei*)

'secret police', *Kripo* (=*Kriminalpolizei*) 'C.I.D.', *Vopo* (=*Volkspolizist* of Eastern Zone), *Agfa* (=*Aktiengesellschaft für Anilinfabrikation*), *I.G. Farben* (*industrie*), from *Interessengemeinschaft* 'pool', cf. in England the I.C.I., *Ufa* (=*Universum-Film-Aktiengesellschaft*), *Flak* (=*Fliegerabwehrkanone*) 'A.A. gun', *Pak* (=*Panzerabwehrkanone*) 'anti-tank gun', *Krad* (=*Kraftrad*/plural *Kräder*) 'motor-bike' (cf. *Kradfahrer*). Other initial words are *U-Bahn* (=*Untergrundbahn*) 'the Tube', *D-zug* (=*Durchgangszug*) 'express train', *FD-zug* (*F*=*Fern-*) 'long-distance express', *DGB* (=*Deutscher Gewerkschaftsbund*), cf. TUC; *DEG* or *GdED* (=*Gewerkschaft der Eisenbahner Deutschlands*, cf. NUR; *I.G. Bergbau*, cf. NUM[1]; *A.A.* (=*Auswärtiges Amt*) cf. F.O.; *Abg.* (=*Abgeordnete*) cf. M.P., *CDU* (=*Christlich-Demokratische Union*), *SPD* (=*Sozialdemokratische Partei Deutschland*); *BGB* (=*Bürgerliches Gesetzbuch*) 'Civil Code'; *PS* (=*Pferdestärke*) cf. H.P.; *FS* (=*Fernsehen*) cf. T.V., *NWDR* (=*Nordwestdeutscher Rundfunk*); *A.G.m.b.H.* (=*Aktiengesellschaft mit beschränkter Haftung*), cf. Co Ltd.; *DIN* (=*Deutsche Industrie-Normung*) 'standardization' sometimes interpreted as *das ist Norm*; *DM* (=*Deutsche Mark*); *DB* (=*Deutsche Bundesbahn*), cf. B.R. University titles include *Dr phil.* (=*doctor philosophiae*); *Dr med[icinae]* cf. M.D.; *Dr J.U.* (*juris utriusque*) cf. LL.D.; *Dr Ing.* (=*Doktor-Ingenieur*); *Dipl.* (=*Diplom*) with *Ingenieur* or *Kaufmann*; *cand. phil.*, etc., for a candidate before finals. There are also euphemisms such as *GK* (=*Geschlechtskrankheit*) cf. V.D. and *Tbc* (=*Tuberkulose*) cf. T.B. Colloquial abbreviations are *f.k.* (=*feiner Kerl*) and *K.O.* (=*knockout*).

---

[1] J. I. Steenberger distinguishes 'letterwords' like *Nato*, *Benelux* from 'initial words' (*De Nieuwe Taalgids* LX, p. 42).

20

GERMAN REGIONAL DIALECTS

The larger dialect-regions of Germany are named after the tribes as they emerged during the Merovingian period. Thus we still speak of [Low] Saxon ([*nieder*]*sächsisch*), Franconian (*fränkisch*) —divided between Low and High Franconian, each with sub-divisions—Alemannic (*alemannisch*) and Bavarian (*bairisch*). The line of demarcation between Low and High German which passes north of Aachen crosses the Rhine at Benrath (whence the name 'Benrath line') north of Düsseldorf, proceeds north of Kassel, but leaves Magdeburg in the Low German region. It has receded since medieval times in the eastern sector so that Berlin is now in a High German enclave.

The present geographical location of the chief dialects is shown by the following table:

| | LOW FRANCONIAN (Wuppertal, Cleve) | LOW GERMAN | | COLONIAL DIALECTS |
		LOW SAXON		
CENTRAL GERMAN	CENTRAL FRANCONIAN (RIPUARIAN—Cologne. MOSEL FRANC.—Trier.) RHENISH FRANCONIAN (Mainz, Frankfurt.)	THURINGIAN	UPPER SAXON	SILESIAN BOHEMIAN

SOUTH AND EAST FRANCONIAN

UPPER GERMAN	ALEMANNIC: (SWABIAN) Württemberg (ALSATIAN) (LOW ALEMANNIC) Strasbourg Baden (HIGH ALEMANNIC) Swiss German	BAVARIAN incl. AUSTRIAN

Notes

(1) Low Saxon is characterized by *-et* (*wi helpet*) in the plural of present indicative, whereas Low Franconian and the dialects of the colonists of the Slavic territories east of the Elbe have *-en* (*wi helpen*). Characteristic Low German and Low Franconian forms are the unshifted *slāpen, tō, wāter, māken* and—except in a few dialects—the coalescence of accusative and dative in *mī, dī*.

(2) West Central German (*westmitteldeutsch*) and East Central German (*ostmitteldeutsch*) are divided by the watershed of the Fulda and Werra. The Franconian dialects retain *p-* initially (*Pund*), and when doubled (*Appel*), whereas Thuringian, Upper Saxon, Silesian, etc., shift to *pf* or, in the case of Silesian, to *f*. The Central German diminutive suffix is *-chen*, e.g. *Mädchen*.

(3) Middle Franconian has the unshifted *t* in *dat, wat, et, dit* and Ripuarian keeps *p* in *helpen* and *werpen* (Moselfränk.: *helfen* and *werfen*) and *v* in *leven, sterven*.

(4) High Alemannic affricates *k-* in *Chind, Chilch* (*Kirche*) and keeps the vowels *ī, ū, ȳ* undiphthongized. Alsatian has *hüs* for *hūs*, but Swabian diphthongizes *ū* in *Haus* and *ī* in *Zeit*, etc. The Alemannic diminutive suffix is *-li, -le* or *-la*, e.g. *Mädli*.

(5) Bavarian [and Austrian] have a diminutive in *-rl*, e.g. *Maderl*. Bavarian retains the old duals *ös* and *enk* for 'you two', but uses them for *ihr* and *euch*, e.g. *schaut's* (*=schaut ihr*).

Outside of Germany the dialect known as Pennsylvania German (Pennsylvania Dutch) is a Rhenish Franconian dialect brought by immigrants from the Rhenish Palatinate, especially in the eighteenth century (see below).

Dialect literature

Low German: Klaus Groth, *Quickborn*, Fehrs' novels, Blunck's lyrics (Holstein); Fritz Reuter (Mecklenburg).

Mosel Franconian: quoted in works of Klara Viebig.

Silesian: Andreas Gryphius, *Die geliebte Dornrose* (1660); K. von Holtei, *Schlesische Gedichte* (1830); G. Hauptmann, *De Waber* (1892).

High Alemannic (Swiss): J. Gotthelf (Bitzius), *Uli der Knecht*, etc.

Low Alemannic (South Baden): J. P. Hebel, *Alemannische Gedichte* (1803).

Alsatian: G. D. Arnold, *Pfingstmontag*.

Bavarian-Austrian: L. Anzengruber, P. Rosegger, K. Schönherr.

21

SPECIMENS OF LOW GERMAN, SWISS GERMAN, PENNSYLVANIA GERMAN, YIDDISH

Modern German translation from St Luke xv, 11–19

Es war einmal ein Mann, der hatte zwei Söhne. Und der Jüngste der beiden sagte zu seinem Vater: 'Vater, gib mir doch das Erbteil, das mir zukommt!' Und das tat er. Er verteilte das Vermögen unter sie auf.

Und es dauerte gar nicht lange, da packte der jüngste Sohn alles, was er hatte, zusammen und ging auf die Reise, weit weg in ein fremdes Land. Und da? Da lebte er in Saus und Braus und brachte bald sein Geld hindurch. Und als seine Taschen leer waren, da kam eine schwere Hungersnot über das Land. Da hatte er mit einem Mal nichts mehr zu beißen und zu brechen. So ging er denn hin und bettelte bei einem Bürger des Landes um Arbeit. Der schickte ihn hinaus auf das Feld: er solle die Schweine hüten. Und er hätte sich gern satt gegessen an den Trebern, die die Schweine kriegten. Aber auch die bot ihm niemand an. Da kam er zu sich und sagte: 'Wie viele von meines Vaters Tagelöhnern haben nun Brot in Hülle und Fülle! Und ich? Ich kann mich vor Hunger nicht bergen. Bevor ich ganz versinke, mache ich mich auf den Weg und gehe zu meinem Vater und sage: 'Vater, ich habe mich versündigt gegen den Himmel und gegen dich. Ich habe es nicht verdient, daß ich noch dein Sohn heiße. Aber laß mich dein Tagelöhner werden!'

The following is a Low German (East Holstein) version of the above taken from *Dat nie Testament in unse plattdütsche Modersprak* by Johannes Jessen, Brunswick, 1933 (by kind permission of Vandenhoeck & Ruprecht Verlagsbuchhandlung Göttingen).

Dor wär mal en Mann, de harr twee Söhns.
Un wat de Jüngste vun de beiden wär, de sä to sin Vader: 'Vader, giff
mi doch dat Arwdeel, dat mi tokamen deit!' Un he dä dat. He deel dat
Vermögen ünner ehr.
Un dat duer gornich lang, do pack de jüngste Söhn allns, wat he harr,
tosamen un güng up de Reis', wiet weg in en frömdes Land. Un dor?
Dor lew he in Suus un Bruus un bröch bald sin Geld hendör. Un as sin
Taschen lerri wärn, do käm en swore Hungersnot öwer düt Land. Do
harr he mit eenmal niks mehr to bieten un to breken. So güng he denn
hen und beddel bi en Börger vun düt Land üm Arbeid. De schick em
rut up dat Feld: he schull de Swien höden. Un he harr sick gern satt
eten von de Sluw, de de Swien kreegen. Awer ock de bod em nüms an.
Do käm he to sick sülbn un sä: 'Woveel vun min Vader sin Daglöhners
hebbt nu Brod in Hüll un Füll! Un ick? Ick kann mi vör Hunger nich
bargen un mutt to Grunn gahn! Awer nä! Ehr ick gans versacken do,
mak ick mi up'n Weg un gah to min Vader un segg: 'Vader, ick heff
me versünnigt gegen den Himmel un gegen di. Ick heff dat nich
verdeent, dat ick noch din Söhn heeten do. Awer lat mi din Daglöhner
warn!'

Some features of Low German

Unshifted consonants are exemplified as follows: -p in up/H.G.
auf; t- in to kamen/zu kommen, -t- eten/essen, bieten/beißen,
heeten/heißen, -t in dat/das, rut/raus, mutt/muß, lat/laß; -ki- in
breken/brechen, -k in och/auch, ick/ich, sick/sich.
Flexionless datives in to sin Vader/zu seinem Vater, bi en Borger/
bei einem Bürger, vun düt Land/von diesem Land.
Pronominal forms: mi/mich, mir; di/dich, dir; he/er; em/ihn,
ihm; ehr/sie, ihr, ihnen.
Preterite forms: duer/dauerte, pack/packte, lew/lebte, broch/
brachte, beddel/bettelte, schick/schickte; käm/kam.
Auxiliaries: heff/habe, harr/hatte, warn/werden.

Swiss German (Bernese)

From *D's Evangelium Lukas bärndütsch* von Johann Howald,
Bern, 1939 (by kind permission of the Buchhandlung der Evg.
Gesellschaft. Berchtold Halles Verlag, Berne).

Es isch a Ma gsi, dä het zwe Sühn gha. Du het dr jünger vo dene
beide zum Vatter gseit: Vatter, gi mer dä Teil vom Vermöge, wo mir
ghört! Und dr Vatter het ne Hab und Guet verteilt. Und nach ere
churze Zyt het dr jünger Suhn alles zäme gramisiert, was ihm ghört het,
und isch wyt ewägg zogen i nes anders Land, und dert het er afah

liederlech läben und het sys ganze Vermöge vergüdet. Und won er nüt
meh gha het, isch i däm Land e gwaltigi Hungersnot usbroche, und
är het afah Mangel lyde, da het er Schritte ta und het sech ane Bürger
vo däm Land häre gmacht, und dä het nen uf syni Fälder geschickt, dass
er dert tüi d'Säu hüete. Da wär er zfriede gsi, wenn er sy Mage hätti mit
däm Glyche chönne fülle, wo d'Säu gfrässe hei (mit de Hültsche vom
Johannisbrotboum). Aber niemer het ihm's ggäh. Da isch er zue sech
sälber cho und het gseit: Wie vieli Taglöhner het my Vatter, die hei
Brot i Hülli und Fülli, und i chume hie vor Hunger um! I will ufstah
und zu mym Vatter gah und zuen ihm säge: Vatter, i ha gsündiget gäge
Himmel und gäge di. I bis nümme wärt, dass i dy Suhn heisse! Halt mi
für eine vo dyne Taglöhner!

Some features of Swiss German

Shifting of *k-* to *ch-* in *churze, chönne, chume*; *s* replaced by *sch*
in *isch*; loss of nasal in prepositions *vo* and *i*. Short vowel retained
in *Vatter* and *ewägg*; diphthong retained in *liederlech, guet, zue*;
undiphthongized *ī* in *mym, syni, ū* in *usbroche, ufstah, ü* in *vergüdet*
(= *vergeudet*). Syncope of vowel in *gsi, gmacht, zfrieden* and
apocope of final vowel in [*der*] *jünger*.

Final -*i* for -*e* in inflexions, e.g. *gwaltegi, syni*. Characteristic
verb forms: *isch, gsi*; [*i*] *ha, het, hei, gha*; *ta* (= *getan*).

Pennsylvania German

> Heit is 's xäctly zwansig Johr,
> Dass ich bin owwe naus.
> Nau bin ich widder lewig z'rick
> Und steh am Schulhaus an d'r Krick
> Juscht neekscht an's Dady's Haus.
>
> Oh horcht, ihr Leit, wu nooch mir lebt,
> Ich schreib eich noch das Schtick:
> Ich warn eich, droh eich, gebt doch Ach,
> Un nemmt uf immer gut enacht,
> Das Schulhaus an der Krick.
>
>   PASTOR H. HARBAUGH

owwe = oben; Krick 'creek'; enacht = in Acht.

Pennsylvania Dutch, i.e. Deitsch or German, is the language
of settlers from the end of the seventeenth century till 1775
coming from south-west Germany and especially the Palatinate.
In the above extract the most striking features are the unrounding
of *ü* to *i* (*z'rick, Schtick*) and of *eu* to *ei* (*eich*), the retention of the
short vowel in *widder* and *nemmt* and the medial palatalization

of *st* in *juscht* and *neckscht*. Though German is still prevalent in Lehigh, Berks. and Lebanon counties, it incorporates a large number of English words. cf. H. L. Mencken, *The American Language*, I, pp. 616–21, with references to literature.

Yiddish

Rabbi Dr Kokotek (of Liverpool) kindly supplied the following passage transliterated from *A kaas fun a jidine*, by Jizchak Leib Perez (born near Warsaw, 1851).

Dos schtibl is ibergefilt mit kelim; es schtajt a himelbet, farhangen mit zerissene forhenglich—durch di lecher kukt aross dos betgewand, on zichloch, mit roite farfederte ojgen. Es schtajt a wigel, von welchen es schajnt aross a grojss gelblech kepele fon a schlofendig kind—es schtajt a kasten, beschlogen mit blech, mit a offenem hengelschloss. Es miss dort schojn kajn groiss aschiros—. Rechent noch zu a schaff, a fass wasser, a lopate, wet ir farschtajn, as men ken schojn in schtibl kajn schpilke nischt arajnwarfen.

Translation of the Yiddish passage

A Jewish woman's excitement

The little room is over-filled with objects. There stands a four-poster, hung with torn curtains. Through its holes peep torn beddings, without covers, with red feather-like eyes.

There stands a cradle, out of which appears a big yellowish head of a sleeping child.

There stands a chest, covered with hammered tin, with an open-hanging lock. It hardly contains any great wealth. Add to this also a water-basin, a barrel of water, a spade; and you will understand that you could not drop (even) a pin into this little room.

Note: Hebrew words are *ka-as*, *kelim* (plural of *keli*) and *aschiros*; Polish *lopate* and *shpilke*.

SELECT BIBLIOGRAPHY

PRONUNCIATION

BITHELL, Jethro. *German Pronunciation and Phonology* (with full bibliography). London, 1952.

BARKER, M. L. *A Handbook of German Intonation.* Heffer, Cambridge, 1925.

MOULTON, W. G. *The Sounds of English German.* Chicago, 1962.

WARDALE, W. L. *German Pronunciation.* Edinburgh, 1955.

GRAMMAR

CURME, G. O. *A Grammar of the German Language* (2nd ed.). New York, 1952.

STOPP, Frederick J. *A Manual of Modern German.* London, 1957.

GREBE, P. Ed. *Grammatik der deutschen Gegenwartssprache* (Der große Duden IV). Mannheim, 1959.

JORGENSEN, P. (tr. G. Kolisko), *German Grammar*, 2 vols. In progress, London, 1959.

EGGELING, H. F. *A Dictionary of Modern German Prose Usage.* Oxford, 1961.

KUFNER, H. L. *The Grammatical Structures of English and German.* Chicago, 1962.

HISTORY OF GERMAN

BACH, A. *Geschichte der deutschen Sprache* (7th ed.). Heidelberg, 1961.

JUNGANDREAS, W. *Geschichte der deutschen und der englischen Sprache.* 3 vols. Göttingen, 1946.

LOCKWOOD, W. B. *An Informal History of the German Language.* Heffer, Cambridge, 1967.

PRIEBSCH, R. and COLLINSON, W. E. *The German Language* (5th ed.). 1962.

DICTIONARIES

BREUL, K. revised by BETTERIDGE, H. T. *Cassell's German and English Dictionary.* London, 1957.

JONES, Trevor. *Harrap's Standard German and English Dictionary* (in progress). London, 1963.

SPRINGER, Otto, Ed. *Langenscheidts Enzyklopädisches Wörterbuch der englischen und deutschen Sprache*, 2 vols. (English-German). Berlin, 1962.

Der Sprachbrockhaus—ein Bildwörterbuch der deutschen Sprache (6th ed.). Wiesbaden, 1951,

APPENDIX: THE ALPHABET

PRINTED FRAKTUR		WRITTEN FRAKTUR		ROMAN LETTERS	
𝔄	a	*(script)*	*(script)*	A	a
𝔅	b	*(script)*	*(script)*	B	b
ℭ	c	*(script)*	*(script)*	C	c
𝔇	d	*(script)*	*(script)*	D	d
𝔈	e	*(script)*	*(script)*	E	e
𝔉	f	*(script)*	*(script)*	F	f
𝔊	g	*(script)*	*(script)*	G	g
ℌ	h	*(script)*	*(script)*	H	h
ℑ	i	*(script)*	*(script)*	I	i
𝔍	j	*(script)*	*(script)*	J	j
𝔎	k	*(script)*	*(script)*	K	k
𝔏	l	*(script)*	*(script)*	L	l
𝔐	m	*(script)*	*(script)*	M	m
𝔑	n	*(script)*	*(script)*	N	n
𝔒	o	*(script)*	*(script)*	O	o
𝔓	p	*(script)*	*(script)*	P	p
𝔔	q	*(script)*	*(script)*	Q	q
ℜ	r	*(script)*	*(script)*	R	r
𝔖	ſs	*(script)*	*(script)*	S	s
			(script)		ß
𝔗	t	*(script)*	*(script)*	T	t
𝔘	u	*(script)*	*(script)*	U	u
𝔙	v	*(script)*	*(script)*	V	v
𝔚	w	*(script)*	*(script)*	W	w
𝔛	x	*(script)*	*(script)*	X	x
𝔜	y	*(script)*	*(script)*	Y	y
ℨ	z	*(script)*	*(script)*	Z	z

INDEX